"Here we stand in misbelief at the collapsing of the institutions that have formed our lives. Gladly, Al Roxburgh and Roy Searle offer us hope. Their book *Forming Communities of Hope in the Great Unraveling* reminds us that God is still present and acting, that God has given us practices to join with him in the forming of his people anew. *Forming Communities* is a riveting masterpiece written to churches seeking a path forward in our times of disillusion and decline."

—**David Fitch**, Lindner Chair of Evangelical Theology, Northern Seminary, Chicago

"Elvis Costello sang, 'wake me up with a slap or a kiss.' Roxburgh and Searle do both. The 'wake up slap' is the uncomfortable account of the unraveling of Western culture leading toward dark times. The 'wake up kiss' is the light they shed on a hopeful path rooted in daily life, oriented toward discerning what God is already doing and exploring how to participate in that work. Read this if you wish to be roused to a new day."

—**Rick Lewis**, Professional Mentor, Anamcara Consulting

"After a seventy-five-year story of a (somewhat) cohesive social and church life in the West, current disruptions cascade into every facet of life. We major in the habits that are consistently failing. Roxburgh and Searle explore our circumstances, name the roots, and draw us into hopeful stories and practices. With significant attention to Jeremiah, Luke, Benedict, and the Celts, they envision communities that dwell, discern, and explore, with the conviction that God initiates among and around us."

—**Mark Lau Branson**, Senior Professor of Practical Theology, Fuller Theological Seminary

"This book is for pastors and other church leaders who are seeing the changes affecting the church and society and know there are no quick fixes. Roy and Al invite readers on a journey of discovering the possibilities and opportunities of finding God at work in the midst of the everyday moments of our lives, inviting us to open ourselves to what God is doing during the unraveling. They invite the church to cultivate the communities of hope needed for a hopeless world."

—**Nathan Luitjens**, Executive Conference Minister, Central Plains Mennonite Conference

"Reader beware. This book is one that will take you first to a place of unsettledness, as it exposes the complex cultural and ecclesial tumult now being experienced across the West. But thank God, it doesn't leave us hopeless in that place of disorientation. Rather, its authors invite readers to join a journey, toward a destination still hidden, but on a path of trust, and with steps which can be faithfully found together."

—**Judith Paulsen**, Professor Emerita of Evangelism, Wycliffe College, University of Toronto

"When church leaders with a lifetime of experience ask awkward questions about how we do things, you probably need to pay attention. Al Roxburgh and Roy Searle have seen the church go from a dominant cultural force to marginal curiosity and ask how we might now be an effective spiritual presence in today's world. Instead of trying to fix things by clever techniques they take us back to some key Bible narratives and the insights of Christians of earlier generations. It's a book that may challenge you at a deep existential level, while offering accessible examples of attitudes and practices that can be lifegiving for both leaders and communities."

—**John Drane**, author *The McDonaldization of the Church*

"Along the way, the most important journey you make for yourself (and perhaps even attempt to lead others along) you realize you are completely off grid—no map, unfamiliar territory and the Sat Nav dial is spinning. What to do? Jesus-followers in the West might be tempted to turn tail. This book offers an alternative. It suggests ways to walk on in the company of calm, reasoned, well-seasoned, and hopeful travelling companions. Yes, the way ahead is still unknown. But the wisdom of this book can transform the journey from exile to pilgrimage. I hope others will take it up."

—**Sally Mann**, Co-Director, Red Letter Christians, United Kingdom

"Roxburgh and Searle issue a sobering and unapologetically provocative call for Euro-tribal churches and their leaders to rediscover their place in God's alternative story. Drawing deeply from Scripture and the wells of Celtic and monastic Christianity, their vision is daringly simple, yet profoundly compelling. I found myself resonating on so many levels—and if you're hungry for pathways to renewal rooted in the way of Jesus, you will too. A vital and timely read!"

—**Kate Coleman**, Co-director, Next Leadership

"This is not just a book but a map of the heart, helping a generation navigate the complexity, paradoxes and challenges in the borderlands places of faith. It's not just a book of ideas, these are hard won words, born out of a lifetime of pilgrimage. There is a spirituality alive in these words allowing us to move beyond the familiar to pursuing the one who as Heschel said 'rings our hearts like a bell.'"

—**Jonny Clark**, Program Manager for Public Theology, The Corrymeela Community, Northern Ireland

Forming Communities of Hope in the Great Unraveling

Forming Communities of Hope in the Great Unraveling

Leadership in a Changing World

Alan J. Roxburgh
and Roy Searle

CASCADE *Books* • Eugene, Oregon

FORMING COMMUNITIES OF HOPE IN THE GREAT UNRAVELING
Leadership in a Changing World

Cascade Books
An Imprint of Wipf and Stock Publishers
199 W. 8th Ave., Suite 3
Eugene, OR 97401

www.wipfandstock.com

PAPERBACK ISBN: 979-8-3852-2089-2
HARDCOVER ISBN: 979-8-3852-2090-8
EBOOK ISBN: 979-8-3852-2091-5

Cataloguing-in-Publication data:

Names: Roxburgh, Alan J., author. | Searle, Roy, author.

Title: Forming communities of hope in the great unraveling : leadership in a changing world / by Alan J. Roxburgh and Roy Searle.

Description: Eugene, OR: Cascade Books, 2025.

Identifiers: ISBN 979-8-3852-2089-2 (paperback) | ISBN 979-8-3852-2090-8 (hardcover) | ISBN 979-8-3852-2091-5 (ebook)

Subjects: LCSH: Christianity and culture. | Christianity—21st century. | Missions—Theory.

Classification: BR115.C8 F61 2025 (paperback) | BR115 (ebook)

VERSION NUMBER 05/06/25

This is one of numerous books I've written over the years. All through the processes of writing there has been one still center—Jane. Over our more than fifty-five years together she has been and is the love, stability, and joy that gives me the ability to write. This book is for Jane with deep love, thanks, and joy.

—Alan Roxburgh (Vancouver, April 2025)

I dedicate this book to my dear friend, Trevor Miller, with whom I shared leadership of the Northumbria Community for many years. His support and companionship—"guarding my heart and watching my back" for over thirty years—have helped me to grow and thrive as a leader in a rapidly changing world. I acknowledge and honor all those who have modelled godly leadership—both women and men—from whom I have learned so much. My gratitude extends to the teams, groups, churches, charities, communities, and organizations that I have had the privilege to lead.

—Roy Searle (Newcastle-upon-Tyne, April 2025)

Contents

Introduction

How lonely sits the city
that was full of people!
How like a widow she has become,
she who was great among the nations!
She who was a princess among the provinces
has become a slave.

. . .

The roads to Zion mourn,
for none come to the festivals;
all her gates are desolate
her priests groan,
her virgins have been afflicted,
and she herself suffers bitterly.

Book of Lamentations, chapter 1

"Lord, I will trust You, help me to journey beyond
the familiar and into the unknown.

Give me the faith to leave old ways and
break fresh ground with You.

. . .

I will trust in the darkness and know that my times
are still in Your hand.

I will believe You for my future"

**From the Brendan liturgy, Celtic Daily Prayer, Book One
Northumbria Community**

What This Book Is About

This book is written in the context of our world being shaken. The tectonic plates of our social, environmental, political, and economic lives are coming apart, melting into the air of an unknown future. A great unraveling is underway. The institutions we've come to take as normative now fail to address the multiple cascading crises of our time. A Facebook post sparsely states: *Trying to explain to my parents that basically nobody under forty right now expects good things to happen to them ever again.* Books with titles like *When the Church Stops Working*[1] immediately draw the attention of leaders desperately trying to make sense of such disruptive change.

Churches and their leaders have awakened to this shaking of their foundations, but most don't know what to do about it. We wonder why the techniques and methods that brought success are no longer working. Some are becoming aware of how implicated they are in this unraveling of all things, but have little to offer in terms of alternatives. In a Zoom meeting with some New Zealand church leaders, several mentioned that for the Gen Zers they know, the idea of church no longer made sense to them. Someone else responded: "It's not just Gen Z, it's all of us across the generations!" Leaders are being shaken by these realities. The changes and disruptions they're experiencing leave them disoriented, confused, and exhausted. Like those who set out with Paul on what we call the second missionary journey, we are experiencing increasing confusion and disorientation as it becomes clear that our well planned methods no longer match the situation (Acts 16:6–15). The struggles of these leaders to make sense of the unraveling are a small expression of what so many are experiencing. Throughout this book we will repeatedly state that we're in a place we've never been before. It is a place that makes less and less sense to us.[2] We will propose that this place is not amenable to quick fixes or easy solutions. It represents the beginning of a time that will be very different from the times in which all the generations now alive have experienced. We will argue that what lies before us is a dark night. The

1. Root, *When the Church Stops Working.*

2. Obviously, God's people have been in such a place before and this book looks at some of those places in Scripture and in the overarching story of the church. But as will be argued in chapter 1, this is a place where current generations of leaders in the modern West have never been before.

hope that things will soon be made right is delusional. What is happening to us and our societies is akin to the fear expressed in Lamentations:

> How lonely sits the city that was full of people! How like a widow she has become, she who was great among the nations! . . . The roads to Zion mourn, for none come to the festival; all her gates are desolate; her priests groan . . .[3]

This unraveling cannot be addressed simply by adjusting current forms of church life or clergy training. Initiating new strategies or developing better vision statements and strategic plans won't help us. Instead, these strategies will misguide by giving us a false sense of our ability to fix things. We are witnessing the end of a world, a way of life that has shaped how we live and move in the world. We confront the end of an era with little sense of what lies ahead (*the roads to Zion mourn . . . her priests groan)*. We're entering a liminal space; there is no returning to the norms of the past several generations. Most of the skills and practices of our professional training as clergy won't help us engage this space. The challenges before us are daunting. Like the poet expressing the despair of the captives in Babylon ("How do we sing the Lord's song in a strange land?"—Ps 137) leaders feel overwhelmed by the sense that the roles and practices that have given them identity and vocation no longer address this new space.

Our churches are as implicated in this great unraveling of our world as any other institution. What lies before us is a dark night, not a new dawn. But we are not doomsayers. We write with the conviction that God's purposes for the world are undiminished. In this descending darkness, God continues to call into being communities of hope that will be patiently formed in this coming night. It is Christian communities that know how to live in the emerging night that will participate with Jesus in the reweaving of this broken world.

The unraveling isn't the primary story we want to tell. We want to turn our attention from the lament and the analysis of where we've all gone wrong (which we need to do) to see that another story is running through the veins of this world, a story that is present in each of our own neighborhoods. This story runs like a subterranean river that flows beneath this present, apocalyptic unraveling with an intentional direction. It's this story that the Euro-tribal churches have lost as they became absorbed in this dying modern story over the past seventy-five

3. Lam 1:1–4.

years. We have fallen asleep to this story; we are out of relationship with the Christian story of God's hope. We don't, therefore, know how to form communities of hope. We have been dwelling in a false story, asleep to our situation,finding it hard to awaken to a radically different place and know what to do.

Martin Luther King Jr. talked about building "a tunnel of hope from a mountain of despair."[4] Beyond all the current analysis of this unraveling, the churches are being called to join the Spirit in discerning again the story that will reweave the desiccated life of this world. This awakening journey that lies before us involves a movement from our defaults of control and management to a renewed confidence in the One who is making all things new. This involves a movement from reliance on technique and data to discovering a wisdom that comes out of dwelling in a place with others, practicing discernment, and exploring how to be God's people in unknown spaces. It is a call from a place of helping and meeting needs to a place of becoming guests with the other in order to listen to the ways the Spirit is remaking the world.

As we will point out through many sections of this book, a guiding text for our work is found in Acts 16:6–15. As Paul and his companions set off on what we call the second missionary journey, they go with the confidence that the methods of the first journey would be right for this one. On two different occasions, Luke makes it clear that "the Spirit prevented them from carrying out their plans." They regrouped in Troas to figure out what was happening. There, Paul had his vision of a man of Macedonia. This man was pleading with them to come over and *help* them. The young Christians concluded that the Spirit had finally given them a vision—they were going over to Europe to help. Things didn't turn out as this little band of leaders imagined. At the end of the text, in all their disorientation around the unraveling of their plans, they met the woman, Lydia. The Spirit's word to them through Lydia was the invitation for them to come and *dwell* (not help) in Lydia's house, as guests rather than hosts. As we will see, this is the fundamental shift of imagination and practice into which the Spirit is now calling the Euro-tribal churches.

Other voices are telling a similar story about our moment of unraveling. Pope Francis is often quoted as saying: "We're not living in an era

4. King Jr., *Letter from a Birmingham Jail.*

of change but a change of era."[5] The commentator N. S. Lyons initiated his Substack blog *The Upheaval* in this way:

> We are living through an era of epochal change. At few times in history have so many currents of civilizational transformation coalesced and crashed into us at once, and at such speed. To say that we are being unmoored by massive technological, economic, environmental, geopolitical, and socio-cultural shifts would be to insufficiently limit our description of what is occurring. Vast new ideational, epistemological, and arguably even theological frameworks for how to understand and interact with reality have emerged and are now spreading across the world . . . But in our bones many of us can feel the rumbling of the earthquake, and intuit the terrible truth: we are experiencing a tectonic upheaval, a rending, uprooting, cataclysmic shift.[6]

These are the realities confronting the Euro-tribal churches. Roy heard among clergy that everyone was expressing that *it's not working* any longer. These pastors anxiously said that the ways they'd been trained and the methods they'd been given weren't going to work again. They were sensing that something deep and profound had shifted, but still couldn't find the words to name what it was. All that they knew was that they no longer had the energy for one more program or new method.

Something is happening that can't be addressed by trying to adjust our systems or develop programs for fixing church life. Our tools, the conviction that we have the agency to make things happen, our capacities to plan and manage the outcomes we want, are no longer addressing the unraveling. This realization has made leaders tired and anxious. They're longing for a place to stop, breathe, rest, escape. A colleague of Al's in Glasgow described how clergy training courses were feeling more like therapy for emotionally shattered people. Roy shared similar observations, noting the fatigue and fragility that comes from being confronted by hastening decline. The challenges are real and existential. Fanciful and fictitious claims about revival only deny the experienced reality of leaders. Such claims close down the possibility of discerning what the Spirit might be saying to us in this disruptive unraveling. Likewise, searching for solutions in conservatism or fundamentalism is both fruitless and

5. Pope Francis addressing the decennial national conference of the Italian church, 2015.

6. N. S. Lyons, "The Upheaval," Substack, April 7, 2021.

quenches the essential task of asking questions and discovering new and living ways of being God's people in the unraveling.

This book addresses leaders experiencing this unraveling. Its aim is to direct us toward the practices we'll need to form communities of hope in a dark time. This is not a book of lamentation, as important as it is to recognize we confront a woeful situation. Rather, it is a book about hope in the working of Christ's Spirit in the midst of the unraveling. We are not offering a formula or program. Our conviction is that as we learn to walk together as communities of companions we'll discern the shape of the road ahead. This book is for leaders who feel the unraveling, who know there is no going back. You know things are precarious. You sense the call of the Spirit to form communities of hope but aren't sure how to do this. Might the Spirit be calling you to join with others, with companions, in forming communities of hope where you dwell? The Spirit of Christ is at work in this dark time. Join a journey to discern how we attend to the Spirit in our communities and so discover how to lead. We begin by summarizing some of the underlying convictions animating us in the writing of this book.

Confessions and Convictions

Forming communities of hope amongst God's people requires several things. First, the capacity to step back from our anxious drive to fix this unraveling (even though it's impossible, there is still within us a deep-down default that convinces us we can and ought to fix it). Stepping back means discovering how to change our attention from the drive to fix things in order to stop, be still, and listen. A simple, but utterly difficult, countercultural, thing to do. Our need right now is to push pause on strategy, planning, innovating, and so forth. Until we do this we can't know how to dwell, be present, long enough to see the story that is shaping the Euro-tribal churches or discern God's story. Practically all of our leadership forms have come from the modern story, a story that has distorted our sense of being God's people. Only in pushing pause can we begin this work of discernment.

By itself, however, this crucial work of examination and analyzing what has been happening to our societies and the churches becomes discouraging. Something else is required. It involves learning how to ask different questions than how to develop strategies to fix or reform our situation, or how to be innovative or engage the data more creatively. The more basic and transformative question we have to ask is what the Spirit is calling God's people to do, at this moment. The discernment question redirects our attention from technique or our own agency in making something happen toward the agency of God in this unraveling. This alternative imagination for leadership is rooted in a series of convictions that inform this book's response to our emerging dark times. These convictions undergird the proposals we make about forming communities of hope in this time of unraveling.

This Is God's World!

> In the beginning God created the heavens and the earth . . . And God saw that it was good . . . And God saw everything that he had made, and behold, it was very good. (Gen 1, RSV)

This is God's world. God is the Creator, Sustainer, and Agent of the creation. It is God's acting that brought creation into being and God's acting that sustains all creation. This basic conviction is the decisive factor in everything. It means we begin from the conviction that God is not absent,[7] like some deistic clockmaker who got the whole thing going and then stands aside in silence. Creation's hope is rooted in this conviction that God has acted in creation, not just back then at the beginning but throughout all of time and history and most clearly in the death and resurrection of Jesus Christ. God's agency is experienced in the giving of the Holy Spirit, and is to be expressed in the new community among the nations. This "stress on God's action is an important corrective to the often decidedly sociohistorical focus . . . with its emphasis on human agents."[8]

Our starting point, therefore, in understanding and assessing this unraveling is that God is acting in the disruptions confronting us. Our primary work, therefore, involves worship and discernment. Our analysis in the early chapters of this book is not offered as those without hope. Our vocation as the church and, especially, as leaders, is directed toward forming communities that are continually asking what the Spirit is doing ahead of them in their communities and neighborhoods, in order to join

7. This is the clockmaker God of the Enlightenment who made an elegant machine, started it going and now lets it function on its own internal laws with no need for and no demands from its Maker.

8. Harink, *Paul among the Postliberals*, 17.

with God there. This is the question we address in this book, a question about the way we lead. All other questions are relativized by this one question. As Euro-tribal Christians, we have dwelt deeply in a story that denies any need for this question, a story about our own agency. This is why we default so easily to methods of visioning, futuring, innovation, and data analysis.

Lesslie Newbigin stated, "At the heart of the Christian message was a new fact: God had acted . . . in a way that, if believed, must henceforth determine all our ways of thinking."[9]

The point we are making is that this fact has ceased to determine how we think and act as Christians. Our leadership methods are drawn from systems shaped by the conviction that human agency is at the base of everything. As Newbigin proposed, that new fact "provided the starting point for a whole new chapter in human thought and action, a new beginning which was destined to shape what we now call Europe."[10] However, at least since the Enlightenment, God's agency has been discarded by the culture and its churches. This is the fundamental crisis at the heart of the unraveling. Current forms of the Western story are failing. As these dependencies on our own agency and our own techniques fail, leaders are feeling adrift on a cold sea still looking for lifeboats in the methods given to them in the modern era. What drives the writing of this book is the conviction that the unraveling is not the primary nor true story of our time. God is at work reweaving a broken creation and inviting us to join in this work of salvation. Our unraveling and all its anxieties, is the place from which we learn to discern the ways God is acting. To join God in this other place will require what the apostle Paul described as a conversion or transformation: "Do not be conformed to this world but be transformed by the renewal of your mind . . ."(Rom 12:2, RSV).

Creation is good. God sustains it in a space of grace, redemption, and reconciliation irrespective of the ways we have taken it into our hands and bent it to our own making. Everything we write is written in the frame of this conviction and hope. We are not filled with fear or a dire sense of events but with confidence that this redeeming, reweaving Creator is still reweaving all things in these disruptive times.

9. Newbigin, *Proper Confidence*, 4.

10. Newbigin, *Proper Confidence*, 7.

God in Jesus Christ and by the Spirit Is Remaking Creation

God is acting, in Christ, by the Spirit, and through the church for the healing of all creation. This acting is directed toward both the reweaving of creation and the unfolding of its life with God. Creation is being called toward a doxological future. Therefore, the unraveling isn't the true story of our present or our future. This is not a claim that history is the narrative of human progress through the means of human agency. This understanding of what is happening defaults us back into a post-Enlightenment modernity that has no need for God's agency. The disruptive nature of the current unraveling across all systems of the modern story carries in it the possibility of awakening churches to the ways they've been absorbed by a crumbling story of power and success, of human agency, but also to this other narrative that is running beneath all other stories, namely, that it is God in Christ who is remaking the world. It is this story of the triune God's remaking of creation to which the churches are being called. In the midst of a dark time, an eschatological hope informs our ways of being in the darkness as God's people.

This is the underlying import of the doxological introduction to the book of Ephesians. It was written in a time when people were confronted with the futility of life. There seemed to be no hopeful answer to the question of why we exist and where the world is going. Of course, there were a myriad of stories proposing ways of answering these questions, especially from the gnostics who claimed to have the secret methods, the technologies, for controlling the fearful and overwhelming "powers of the air" (Eph 2:2 RSV). The gnostics represented a broader search, seeking to make clear the secret meaning of the creation and our place in it. This is why, in Ephesians 1:8, the writer makes it clear that this *mystery*[11] is found in God's intentions and those intentions have been revealed to us all in Jesus Christ. The answer to the questions of why we exist and where the world is going are no longer a secret or a mystery. They have been made clear in the incarnation, life, death, and resurrection of Jesus. The writer then goes on to make it unambiguous what it is that God has revealed in Jesus Christ, namely, that before the creation itself, it was God's intention that in and through Christ, there was "a plan for the

11. As Markus Barth points out, the word *secret* is to be preferred over that of *mystery* because the writer of Ephesians is pointing to something quite different from that of the gnostics or the mystery religions of the day with their narratives of technique and control. See Barth, *Ephesians 1–3*, 85.

fullness of time, to unite all things in him, things in heaven and things on earth" (Eph 1:10 RSV). It is in the context of this proclamation that what has been hidden since the beginning of the world (that the whole of creation will be healed and brought together in Jesus Christ) is now revealed, that the rest of Ephesians goes on to describe the purpose of the church—to be the living manifestation of this purpose in Christ. The church has a vocation in Christ. It is not to save itself but to be the sign, witness, and foretaste of what God is already doing through Christ and the Spirit. Everything else is incidental.

The Incarnation Makes Manifest Where the Reweaving Takes Place

The incarnation of Jesus makes manifest where God's reweaving takes place. God acts offstage, away from presumed centers of power and recognized drivers of the social, political, and economic agendas. The ways in which God's Spirit is reweaving all things is to be discerned beyond the realm of professional elites, outside the dominant methods and techniques shaping our era. God acts outside institutions of control and power that look as if they are the only ways of working. Modern organizations with their professionalized, *ordained* experts and bureaucratic elites aren't able to recognize the ways of God. The magi came to Herod, the head of state who controlled the mechanisms of social order. Furthermore, they came to Jerusalem, the center of political and religious power, but all Herod could do was threaten because something was out of his control and therefore menacing.

The incarnation exemplifies the way God acts. The coming of Jesus was a completely offstage event that fit no one's calculus. It wasn't to the Holy City, that perceived center of all things of God, that Jesus came. It was to an unpretentious, backwater town. As Nathaniel would say later about the young teacher, Jesus, "could any good thing come out of Nazareth?" (John 1:46). This offstage coming of God is made clear in the kinds of people with whom the birth announcements are shared. These announcements come to ordinary people with no stake or place among the powerful, important, or famous. In this way the incarnation is a statement about the seeming unproductiveness and mystery of God's working. There was no conception among the elites and leaders of Israel that the Messiah would come in this way. Furthermore, the notion that God (YHWH) would enter human life through a virgin as a vulnerable baby was beyond the conceivable. It was like asking someone to describe to you the taste of the sun. These things don't add up; these are not the ways God works. And yet here was where God became flesh—by coming all the way down and dwelling amongst us as a vulnerable child.

To all of us who live beyond the Enlightenment, with its relentless embrace of the abstract and universal, this child born in the utter flesh and ordinariness of a local place is foolishness at best and ignorant stupidity at its worst. It seems an ignorant myth of uneducated people to be dismissed. The incarnation points us toward the ordinariness of the places where we dwell, to the everydayness of our lives as where God is working out this new creation. In the everyday, among the despised and unrecognized of globalization, this is where God is remaking all things.

The modern narrative, with its stories of heroes, strong leaders, and powerful visionaries, cannot see or make sense of this story. However, the churches, with their strategies for renewal, innovation, adaptation, or visioning futures have also forgotten this incarnation story at the heart of their identity. There can be no resistance to the determinations and commodifications of the market without this story, this incarnational commitment to coming all the way down to dwell in a place as one who needs to receive the care and hospitality of those who live there with us. This is a movement beyond tactics, programs, or strategies into a completely different practice of leadership. The conviction that God's purposes are made clear in the incarnation points to a radical choice to dwell in the place where we are, and with the people of that place because this is how the Spirit of Jesus is present in our own unraveling of a globalized, market-driven, commodifying, contemporary West.

We are not, therefore, discouraged or despairing because taken-for-granted systems and institutions that have formed our lives and shaped our experiences are collapsing. We are not discouraged or disoriented when global elites with their stories of power and success come apart. In this dark unraveling, the Spirit will call back into life communities of hope among ordinary people who are off the radar of our normative expectations.

But there is also a caution. At the heart of the incarnation of Jesus is mystery. We have no calculus that enables us to make sense of what God has done in Christ. In the incarnation, God continues to stand across all our efforts to turn our confessions into programs, to take the movements of the Spirit and turn them into tactics. This is where we need to resist turning the incarnation of Jesus into a series of principles for making churches work again. The incarnation irrevocably calls us to our local place but, just as critically, in those places it calls us to dwell in the mystery of God, not the tactics we produce. This is the hard task for the modern church calling for a renewing of the mind (Rom 12:2).

God's Workings as Mystery

Those raised in a Christian narrative world carry within them these words from Scripture: "'For my thoughts are not your thoughts, neither are your ways my ways,' declares the Lord."[12] This involves Christian life in a great tension, namely, the conviction that God is present and acting in the world in ways that we can know and discern but, also, at the same time, we recognize that we see through a glass darkly.[13] This means we can never make certain or legible the actions of God. In every part of life, there exists this space of mystery around God's working in the world and our own understanding of that working. We can never turn this mystery into certainty. We can never turn the workings of God amongst us into strategies that give us certainty, clarity, power and control. The actions of God always call us into a relationship that requires trust and risk because we can never know how this participation with God is going to turn out. We cannot define the outcomes and, at the same time, be in relationship with the One who is remaking this world.

We might remember the confrontation in Exodus 3 between Moses and God. Moses had been living in the backside of the desert for many years after fleeing Egypt where he had been raised a Jew in the courts of Pharaoh. As he was herding his father-in-law's sheep, wrestling with questions of Egypt and his own identity, he turned aside to see a bush that burned but was not consumed. He was made aware that this was a holy place where God was present (what we sometimes call a *thin place,* where the transcendent breaks into our world) and needed to take off his shoes. In the burning of the bush, Moses was confronted with the mystery of God, with one who is Holy and cannot be controlled. In the ensuing engagement between God and Moses, Moses was given a new vocation by God. He was to return to Egypt, confront Pharaoh, and lead his people out of captivity. We might remember what followed.

12. Isa 55:8 NIV.

13. 1 Cor 13:12 NIV.

Moses offered reasons why he could not turn up in Egypt and confront Pharaoh: he wasn't a good speaker and he didn't have the powers of the Egyptian magicians. At each turn God countered: Aaron would speak for him, he was given a rod that was more powerful than anything the Egyptian magicians may have had.

These responses weren't sufficient for Moses. He wanted something more before he was willing to act. The tension in the conversation between Moses and God came to the fore when Moses claimed that his own people, the Israelites, wouldn't believe he had been sent by God unless he could know the name of the One who was sending him. This may seem like an innocuous request to the modern imagination. It was anything but. In Moses' world to have someone's name was to have control over that person; it was to have the power to make them do as one needed or wanted to do. Moses was asking for control of God. In response to Moses' question of "Who shall I say that sent me?" God gave a profoundly enigmatic response: "Tell them YHWH has sent you." There are numerous ways of interpreting this term, known as the tetragrammaton. At a straightforward level, it expresses the otherness of God, God's infinite, qualitative difference. In the context of our framing, God gave this enigmatic name to tell Moses he could not have God's name in the way he wanted it. In this irruptive vocation to which Moses was being called, he could not have control of God's name: he was not allowed to have control of either God or the situation into which God was sending him. Moses could not manage the outcomes of this calling or control its results. He could only choose to act by trusting the One who is "I am who I am" (Exod 3:14). The future into which Moses was called could not be mapped.

This question of control and management, of naming and managing outcomes, is a critical issue of Christian imagination in our time. The leadership defaults of the past seventy-five years make it appear normal that being in control of one's outcomes and managing directions are simply normative elements of good leadership. Here we encounter something radically different. In our unraveling, the anxiety and disruptions of this moment make this default response even more acute. The need to make everything legible so that we can manage forward is high. But this is not the way of God's kingdom. We are not permitted to know in this way. Mystery can never be made legible. Leaders with a modicum of biblical or theological training know this conviction about the freedom and mystery of God to be true. That God is working in the world in ways that are often not legible to us, that are at best opaque, is something we acknowledge conceptually. However, we are the generations shaped by a story that keeps telling us we have the power and ability to render the opaque and mysterious legible. This is one of the founding myths of the modern era. We have all become like modern magicians who see themselves as able to turn the hieroglyphs of our world into legible and, therefore, controllable formats. That is the formula—to make legible is to render us control. We, as human beings, have the agency to write the maps so that all mysteries are resolved. We can decipher YHWH and make God work for our own ends. In the words of Hartmut Rosa, "Our encounter with the uncontrollable and our desire or struggle to bring it under control form a red thread that runs through all areas of our lives."[14] One of our convictions in writing this book is that this red thread runs right through the imagination of church leaders and the expectations of congregations. Without a change of our minds and practices we will never be able to hear what the Spirit is saying to us in these dark times.

We shall encounter throughout this book this tension of controllability and mystery. Over and over again we shall confront this red thread, this desire to manage and control, to find formulas that will make sense of our world and give us, therefore, the strategies to prevail. All of this is now present across the Euro-tribal churches. The tension of our life with God has been resolved, and like the Sorcerer's Apprentice, we think we can assume God-like agency. The tension is in this confession we make of God's mystery and in the irresistible desire for control over our environments and the journeys we undertake. It is present in our thirst for data with its siren-like promise to make all things legible. This tension will be present throughout as we come to see the ways the modern story continually distorts Christian practices (just as Egypt distorted Israel's life). We will find ourselves looking for ways to take God's name and turn it into some method of controllability that will make our world legible so we can manage the outcomes. When confronted with the unraveling of a story that has shaped us for so long, this tension becomes overwhelming.

14. Rosa, *Uncontrollability of the World*.

To Discern the Spirit's Reweaving, God's People Must Be Rooted in Place

Communities of hope discern alternative ways of living in a desiccated world. This hope will not come from current systems of church life nor from the clergy guilds they've formed. Just as Jesus came all the way down to pitch his tent right beside ours, so the Spirit's reweaving can only be discerned as we risk dwelling in the local and being with the other who is the neighbor. The Spirit reweaves the world from within the particularity of the places where we dwell. This hope is discerned in the neighborhoods where we live and, especially, amongst those outside places of power. This is the meaning of the incarnation that the Euro-tribal churches have failed to see.

As local communities of Christ we are called to dwell in our neighborhoods with an anticipatory posture. It is one that believes that the purposes of God are being unfolded not just in the doxological community, but in and with the people among whom we dwell. Therefore, we can only know what the Spirit is forming (which is profoundly different from future planning or future proofing our churches) as we take the risk of dwelling in relationships in the local among unchosen and unexpected people. For Paul this involved an unplanned, disorienting encounter with Lydia. The meeting bent his categories, changed his perceptions, and redirected his convictions about how the Spirit was working (Acts 16:13–15). Dwelling in the place where we live in this way will mean laying down our needs to control relationships or manage their outcomes. Such laying down, however, is the only way we might make things legible, which means attending to where God is at work among people, where it is that God turns us from despair, anxiety, and exhaustion toward a trust in the One who does not fit our expectations.

Communities of Hope See What God Is Doing Through Discernment

Rooted in place, communities of hope practice discernment. Discernment is about a certain kind of trust. It is a trust that God is working in the world. This trust invites us to risk being in a relationship with the other, the stranger. It is these kinds of relationships with others that open the space for us to hear God. Furthermore, such discernment is the work of the people, not experts or professionals.

Discernment of the people is a lost practice of the churches at this moment. Discernment must be reclaimed from the professionalization of the ordained guilds. It is not about professionals directing a community in visioning, strategies, and outcomes. It involves God's ordinary people listening to the Spirit through their encounters in their communities. The initiatives of leaders, in terms of mission and vision statements, close off the possibility of discernment. To the extent God's people dwell in practices of discernment, they will join with the One who is making all things new.

This discernment is the work of the people as they risk the relational work of joining with Jesus in their neighborhoods. It involves relationships rather than strategies. It is more about attending to their stories and praying out of engagements with people. It is about sitting with the other, as Paul and his companions did with Lydia in Philippi, rather than the strategic planning of a leadership team.

To see what these convictions mean for being God's people in a place we've never been before, we need to take a step back and name where we are at this moment. We want to say something about the current story the churches have dwelt in for much of the past century. Chapter 1 presents a brief account of a story that has shaped modern societies for a long time, but particularly since the end of World War II. This seventy-five-year period has shaped how all the living generations now read the world and shape leadership. Chapter 1 offers a mapping of this period and an accounting of what it has meant for the church's own identity and the ways our notions of leadership have been deformed by this story.

The Organization of the Book

The book is written around five sections, each building on the other.

Section One addresses the question we hear every time we gather with church leaders, lay and ordained. In one form or another these leaders are asking in a post-COVID context where nothing is going back to normal: What happened? Where are we? How did we get to this place for which little has prepared us? This first section seeks to describe what has been happening and the unraveling that now confronts us.

Section Two responds to the next question leaders are asking after they engage with Section One: What do we do? This section proposes that this is the wrong question. We need to be asking a fundamentally different question: In Scripture and our traditions, how has God turned up with God's people when they have found themselves in disruption and unraveling? To do this we turn to Scripture and illustrations from the early centuries of the church.

Section Three proposes that our listening to the question posed in Section Two reveals a series of practices for sustaining communities of hope in the midst of dark times. These practices are identified as *Dwelling, Discerning,* and *Exploring.*

Section Four offers a series of pathways for forming communities of hope within these practices.

Section Five provides a conclusion.

SECTION ONE

Where Are We? What Happened?

SECTION ONE TURNS TO the question of where we find ourselves at this moment. When church leaders were confronted by the pandemic and had to deal with the closing of regular church life, they developed all kinds of work-arounds to continue some sense of normalcy. For many, developing online services to keep people connected became a major part of their work. All of these difficult, demanding adjustments were done with the anticipation that, somewhere in the near future, things would go back to normal. That is not what has happened. With the ending of lockdown and the gradual return to some kind of regular life, it has become clear that the church is not returning to life before COVID. This is not just about the church but also many other ways of life we've taken for granted. Something has shifted, or come undone. We can feel this unraveling of our ways of life but it's difficult to find the language that makes sense of what has been happening. The common questions we hear are: What's happened? Where are we?

This section paints a picture of what it is that has happened. It's not the complete picture but it's a big part of what has happened. It describes a particular story that shapes our modern context. This story, though part of a much larger story, took its present form right after World War II. It is one of the dominant stories shaping the West. It has colonized not only the life of our societies but also that of the churches and the formation of their leaders over the past seventy-five years. It is this story that is now coming apart; it is unraveling. Without understanding the nature of this story, it is difficult to address the question of what has happened with the ending of the pandemic.

CHAPTER ONE

Where Are We?

> It feels like I've had the ladder up against the wrong wall all this time.
>
> —A pastor's experience of being in this unraveling

> Our era has already lived through or is preparing to live through the collapse of three most powerful attempts to replace religion. The collapse of Nazi Germany is the failure of a neo-paganism whose master thinkers are Nietzsche and Heidegger. The collapse of Communism is the failure of Marxism. The third collapse looms . . . the collapse of capitalist democracies, which would be the failure of scientism, of our attempts to reduce the problems of human kind to a false objectivity, to a sort of mental and physical hygiene, in the manner of "unbridled capitalism" and psychoanalysis.
>
> —René Girard, *When These Things Begin*

The Unraveling

THE TWO OF US (Roy and Alan) are Christian writers and leaders from each side of the Atlantic. Roy lives in northern England, Alan on the west coast of Canada. We are each witnessing a prolonged, painful questioning amongst Christian leaders around what is happening to church communities and our societies after the pandemic of 2020–2022. These years brought lockdown, apocalyptic predictions, heroic actions, heightening anxieties, and the wish that somehow, in some way, everything would go back to some wished-for normal. Instead, we confront an unraveling of pre-COVID life on both sides of the Atlantic.

At the beginning of the pandemic, saying we were confronted by a fundamental unraveling of the modern story and of our church systems drew skepticism and rebuke. Today, the opposite is the case. Church organizations hold online conferences about the disruptions besetting once-stable institutions and a sense of liminality[1] seems everywhere. Pastors are offered seminars on how to deal with burnout. Ever more books are being written offering prescriptions and tactics for being a successful post-pandemic church, courses are popping up offering ways of developing personal spirituality in difficult times, methods are being offered to rekindle church life out of the embers of the pandemic.[2] Overall, such books focus on immediate tactics but provide little theological attention to the question of God's agency—of what it is the Spirit might be doing in this new liminal situation. As Andrew Root stated in a webinar conversation, the crisis of the Protestant churches is that they have the wrong diagnosis of what is going on and, therefore, their tactics are misdirected. That is exactly right. The diagnoses being offered in most of these books, webinars, and consultations revolve around the conviction that we have to fix the church and we do that through our own agency and smarts.

The erosion of trust in almost all of our institutions (political, social, educational, judicial, media) has been a profound and disruptive experience for us. This erosion of trust in the systems and institutions of the churches, as well as in its forms and practices of leadership, is accelerating. What is happening? How do we account for this dissolution of so much that we have taken for granted? How do the churches address this situation? What will it mean for them to form communities of hope in the midst of these unprecedented disruptions, the multiple cascading crises confronting not just the churches but all of society? As British political and social theorist Maurice Glasman, asks: "What's Going On?" and "How did we get here?"[3]

1. We will say more about *liminality* in the chapters that follow. In liminality people find themselves in a place they've never been before, where their taken-for-granted ways of life have stopped working as they did. It is an experience of broad disruption across systems accompanied by a disorienting experience of not knowing what to do. An example of this in Canada is seen in the health care systems. Going to an emergency room used to mean entering a space of safety and confidence but, today, it is anything but these things.

2. See, for example, Kotan, *Being the Church in a Post-Pandemic World.*

3. Glasman, *Blue Labour,* 11–31.

COVID was never the cause of this pervasive sense that something has gone terribly wrong. The anxious moment that confronts us is the result of the unraveling of a story we have lived in for a long time. It is a story that is about a new faith in our own capacities to shape the kind of world we need and be the agents of our own destiny. This is a story that told us that life can be lived well without God. At so many levels we have drunk deeply of that story since the end of World War II. It is a story that has inevitably turned our attention to our agency as, for example, leaders in the churches, and our capacities to come up with tactics and techniques to right the ship and set a new direction. As it comes apart we're increasingly unsure about where we are as societies and churches, or what we need to do. This is because we no longer know how to shift our attention off our own sense of agency to see what God is doing in the midst of us. In the simplest of terms—the churches have lost their capacity to pay attention to God. This is why we see a constant stream of requests from leaders for how to develop disciples. This chapter frames an account of this story and its devastating effects upon us as societies and God's people.

A Story Isn't Working

We're awakening to the reality that the story we have lived and for which we were trained has stopped working. This disorienting realization affects not just our leadership, but our personal lives. Whether it's climate change, a visit to an emergency ward, or dealing with a parent in need of long-term care, few of our taken-for-granted systems are working the way they should. We see our children or grandchildren unable to buy their own homes or being displaced from their rental homes because they can no longer afford the rent hikes. There's an underlying fear that the ground under our feet has been shifting as what feels like a never-ending list of crises keeps coming at us. In this situation, we have to ask what has happened. How did a world that used to make sense and seem manageable suddenly come apart?

It was a summer BBQ and friends regathered after lengthy times abroad. As the conversation moved back and forth, David asked: "What's going on in Paris? Why all the riots?" Suddenly, we were plunged into the question of what's going on in our societies. Once the group felt permission to talk about what was concerning them, the flood gates opened. Why has global warming come so fast and so hard? Is the war in the Ukraine really about good guys and bad guys? We thought these old battles among empires and ideologies had been relegated to the dustbins of history since the 1990s.[4] They're all back. What happened to our liberal confidence in a world that is always getting better?[5] The list of conversation moments could go on. Running just under the surface of our lives lurk these questions of what's gone wrong with the story that was once so filled with the promise of ever better lives. Who can make sense of it all?

This story that shapes us is based on the conviction that we have the power to make our world and societies into what we want and our capacities to make all things legible in order to manage and control them to our own ends. It is coming undone right in front of us. We are coming undone with it because we have no alternative story. This is a story whose feedback loops keep us believing our professionalization, management, control, and techniques can all be placed at our service (human agency) to make a world of our own choosing and imagining. This overarching story has birthed smaller stories, like globalization, and produced cadres of elites guided by the mantra that we can form and reform as we desire. This story has long antecedents but took its current form after World War II. It has shaped the Western imagination since then.

This is the story that is failing us. It is the unraveling of this story that is raising the anxious question: What happened? People sense we're in a place we've never been before. We're less and less confident about how to deal with this situation even while armed with more and more data that makes clear the extent of our crises. Most of the tools and models of success shaped over the last seventy-five years no longer address the challenges before us. The problem is that our formation and mentoring has all been within this dominant story. We're confronted with the end of an era in which all we have are the tools that made it successful. Our confusion and anxiety come from the fact that we're ill prepared to lead in this unraveling; we keep using the tools we have and finding them unable to address the time.

The Zoom conversation with the church executive was all too familiar. Richard is a veteran denominational leader. He's seen all the proposals and programs for solving the challenges confronting his pastors and congregations. His question was straightforward: "Alan, what's

4. See Fukuyama, *End of History and the Last Man.*

5. See Gray, *New Leviathans.*

going on? Why are the institutions in which we've invested our lives and identities no longer working? We're watching loss, burnout, and decline across the board. Nothing we're trying is working. We have more data than any group can absorb but we've no sense of what to do about the loss, blame, lament, and decline."

So began another conversation on the question: What's happening? It's a question taking up the concerns of many leaders as they try to navigate in a place they've never been before. They feel stuck with nowhere to turn for answers.[6] We are in a place we've never been before.

The list of crises confronting us is long and getting longer. In such a disorienting space, it's hard to see where we are. There is so much disruption all at once. Following two years of lockdown, little has returned to the normal we hoped for. A lot of faithful people didn't return to church. Increasing percentages of people no longer consider the churches as offering a hopeful narrative in the midst of the crises before us. A heating climate scorches cities with unheard-of temperatures. Vast swaths of land catch fire, and unprecedented winter storms and upper atmospheric rivers bring unheard-of flooding and disasters. Economies aren't working. Fewer and fewer people can afford housing. In all of this, it's not just that our anxieties grow, but that Christian life, and the churches that are supposed to embody that life, seem irrelevant.

Even those stunning pictures from the multibillion-dollar James Webb telescope can't deflect our fears of war, loss of income, or the nagging questions of whether we'll be able to support our families. These aren't small problems. They're huge, complex challenges to our capabilities and identities. Some leaders have poured themselves into institutions that are now failing them. Those who can are getting out. Others are trying to fix things knowing deep inside there is no way of fixing any of it. Our default instincts tell us we ought to have a strategy for fixing the situation, but, at the same time, there's this gnawing sense something has gone terribly wrong with the story in which we're living. Like the writer of Lamentations, we're awakening to a place we've never been before, where the skills, capacities, and strategies in which we were so well trained can't help us make sense of our crises.

6. The attendant question of what to do is right behind but we'll deal with this a little later, because as critical as this question might seem, it is the wrong question to start with.

What to Say About This in Terms of Where We Are as Leaders?

First, we need to recognize that we're in a place we've never been before. The place we're now in isn't addressable with most of the skills and habits that have formed us. This is what makes the present moment disorienting for leaders across all systems. Leaders deal with lots of change in our churches. Change is a constant. Until recently, we've been confident we could address change through the processes of visioning and strategizing we'd learned. It always seemed that with the right tool we could set a new direction and manage change. But these are precisely the kinds of actions that are no longer working for most of us. What's disorienting is that we don't know what to do about it.

Not everyone is convinced of this accounting. Resistance to hearing these words about unraveling and disorientation has been high, as leaders continue to believe that better interpretation of data and the right application of techniques will put us back on a manageable track. Some believe that with clearer outcomes and harder work, it is still possible to recreate thriving congregations. Some propose that renewed congregational life is possible with better innovation or some kind of commitment to gospel purity or radical discipleship. What lurks in the midst of these promises is a conviction that, done properly, we have the agency to fix the unraveling of our churches. At the same time, increasing numbers of leaders are aware that current methods aren't addressing our situation, but they don't know why.

It is particularly the churches of the European migrations and colonizations (the Euro-tribal churches)[7] that have lost their way in the modern story. In this unraveling, they've lost their place of privilege and status, their identity near the center of their societies, and their sense of who they are. They are lamenting their situation even as everyone else passes by, no longer recognizing them for who they once were as churches in our societies.

What is happening to these churches is far more than a series of sociocultural changes. It is also God's merciful compassion on a people who have fundamentally lost touch with their story as God's people. Because of this, we do not have an imagination that can carry us forward.

7. We have called these churches Euro-tribal to identify them as the churches that emerged from the various European and English reformations. In describing these churches we are distinguishing them from the many immigrant churches that have come to the West, as well as recognizing that churches from the reformations are as tribal as any other group in the world.

We do not understand that this unraveling is not about some personal, disruptive experiences; it's not about me and my feelings. This unraveling involves the *severe compassion* of Christ toward this part of the church. It is about God's severe judgement on the Euro-tribal churches. In our colonization by the modern story, we have lost the language that can make sense of all this. As Lamentations makes clear, the teachers, priests, managers, futurists, innovators, and prognosticators have become irrelevant in this situation. Lamentations tells us that these sorts of leaders have become unrecognizable in the streets.

The French writer Bruno Latour argues we've been searching, these past several years, for a way out of the crisis formed by COVID, only to realize that beneath that crisis lie other crises which we're at an impasse to address (global climate change, the massive diasporas of refugees around the world, the atrophy of trust and belonging, and so on). In the midst of these complex, daunting realities, war has returned as ideologies we thought long dead are reappearing with a vengeance. Western nations confront the failure of democratic institutions as they reveal themselves incapable of addressing these crises. The faith of citizens that the state will provide direction in the midst of it all is at an all-time low. As people lose trust in the institutions that have shaped Western democratic, social, economic and religious life over the past century, they are tribalizing into reactive groups of fear and blame that are, increasingly, unable to hear one another. As we will argue, sociocultural, political-economic explanations for our unraveling are woefully insufficient as a reading of what is happening.

Second, the primary story that has shaped our societies over the last seventy-five years is failing us. There may not be agreement on why this is the case, but enough of us are now aware that we're living in the wrong story. In North America we grew up in a story called "the American Dream."[8] It has numerous forms including that of a Christian nationalism that now informs the understanding of a significant percentage of American evangelicals. This story came into full bloom after World War II when a "Golden Era" emerged (what the French had already called

8. The "American Dream" is the belief that every citizen has an equal opportunity to be successful and economically prosperous if they work hard and show initiative. It is presented in the F. Scott Fitzgerald novel *The Great Gatsby* (1925), but also see Putnam's *Our Kids*.

Trente Glorieuses),[9] promising a future of growth and progress for everyone. Those terrible ideologies from the early part of the twentieth century that optimistically prophesied their progressive version of the end of history[10] had been displaced by the bright sunlight of technological progress, democratic institutions, a successful managerial class, and cheap goods. For those of us inaugurated into the middle class through post-World War II educational systems, this story came to be the one, true story. We became convinced that the world was ours for the taking and, if we worked hard enough and got the education required, we would climb the ladder of prosperity with a good, secure job, our own home, and God's blessing. This story fueled the expansion of congregations and shaped the formation of leaders right up to the present moment. In the post-COVID world, it is coming to be seen as a tragically failed story creating generations who are angry and anxious about their future.

Third, habits and the strategies of success we've taken for granted are no longer working. Across all sectors of society, people's experience is that of falling behind, of losing our place on the escalator of progress. Class is no longer a protection from precarity. The systems that formed our societies over the past century are broken and with them the methods of management that made us successful. Those institutions of optimism and progress we built in the postwar era can no longer address the unraveling confronting us. We're now asking unimagined questions about ways of life we've taken for granted: Why has so much stopped working at this moment in time?

Until quite recently, we thought the ship would right itself. We assumed that if we could work a bit harder and smarter, prayed more, and invested a bit more faith in our institutions, things would return to some kind of normalcy. If we did the right analysis, honed our skills in innovation and adaptation, then we'd produce thriving congregations. Undergirding our actions remained the conviction that the societal story we've lived in all this time would turn out to be true after all. But none of that has turned out as we hoped. The crisis before us is more unsettling than we'd imagined. This story about our capacities to create the outcomes we want through our own agency, our abilities to use technology and our capacities to manage outcomes, has failed us. We've entered a

9. Technically, a thirty-year period of unparalleled economic growth across the West between 1945 and 1975.

10. Fukuyama, *End of History and the Last Man*.

very different world from that story. We've entered a dark wood without maps. The story that's shaped us for generations can't engage this new place. In a *New York Times* article, David Brooks reflected on what columnists had got wrong in this analysis of the times:

> As a newspaper columnist, I'm paid for one skill above others: careful observation. But sometimes I'm just slow. I suffer an intellectual lag . . . Reality has changed, but my mental frameworks just sit there. Worse, they prevent me from even seeing the change that is already underway—what the experts call "conceptual blindness." I'm trying to address one period's problems through the last period's frameworks . . . It's not until I dismantle and reconstruct those preconceptions that everything becomes obvious—until the next historical change.[11]

Searching for Explanations

The story that has characterized our societies for the past seventy-five years is a competing theological worldview to Christianity. Yet, it has become the dominant story of the West and its churches. An extremely seductive worldview[12] has become the dominant mode of thinking and acting for the churches. As Lyons states in Substack, it is a worldview that has "successfully seized and merged itself with the state's power across the Western world, and is rapidly going global." Inside this story lie specific understandings of leadership and of how the churches are to function. As a result, training schools (seminaries) and institutional systems (denominations)[13] produced a new bourgeois professional class of leaders for the churches who are, in reality, shaped around the modern narrative of method and control. We have formed middle-class, white-collar (no pun intended) elites,[14] leaders[15] who, alongside acting

11. Brooks, "I Was Wrong about Capitalism," https://www.nytimes.com/2022/07/21/opinion/david-brooks-capitalism.html.

12. See the Substack interview with N. S. Lyons, https://substack.com/profile/33861109-ns-lyons/note/c-15206207.

13. We're not saying schools and denominations were formed after the end of World War II but that the narrative world of these preexisting systems came into a new shape in the postwar era.

14. See, for example, Guilluy and DeBevoise, *Twilight of the Elites*.

15. A term to describe this group that is borrowed from church language is *clerisy*, coined by Samuel Coleridge in the 1830s to refer to a class of people charged, like the medieval clergy, with instructing and directing the masses.

as caregivers (pastors as therapists) and teachers, are trained to be the managers and strategists for this modern story within the churches and denominations. These were the values that would direct the denominations and their congregations in the post-World War II rocket ride to success. One outcome of this narrative's power is how the churches lost their identity in a liquid, globalized world. Their leaders lost their vocations as agents of God's future in Christ, becoming little more than therapists and purveyors of middle-class values for a narcissistic culture or strategists of progress.

That post-World War II ride went deep into our collective imaginations, colonizing our understanding of the world, reshaping the practices of newly educated, postwar middle-class elites. They became our leaders. This story still reigns in our processes of training and credentialing. It continues to determine how congregations and denominations are addressing the unraveling. All of us born after the end of World War II (which means all those now in leadership) are the products and priests of this leadership story. In the language of Scripture, this is the kingdom we've constructed, inherited, and lived in through this era. As this story unravels, its seductive power remains colonized in our imaginations and responses. Christian identity confronts an existential struggle around what story will shape it in this unraveling. This is a road we've not traveled before. If we are to form communities of hope in this dark time, we'll need to be clear about this story and the precarity of identity it has produced in the Euro-tribal churches.

Lamentations hovers over our questions of "Where are we?" and "What happened?" Its opening lines are a theological reading of what is happening to our churches. It express the fear and anxiety leaders struggle to express:

> How lonely sits the city
> that was full of people!
> How like a widow she has become,
> she who was great among the nations!
> She who was a princess among the provinces
> has become a slave. (1:1–2)

A variety of sociocultural, political-economic explanatory frames are being offered to account for this unraveling of modern societies and the churches in them:

- Some go back to the birth of the modern (somewhere in the fourteenth and fifteenth centuries or even further back into the twelfth).
- Others argue it was the unintended consequences of either the reformations or Enlightenments (their preoccupation with method in terms of Cartesian rationalism/idealism, notions of the free individual and the Leviathan-like state [Hobbes], the natural savage [Rousseau], and the social contract [Locke], that have produced the current malaise).
- We might go back even further to the emergence of nominalism in the late Middle Ages.[16] The cumulative result was the flight of faith into the private and personal[17] and the creation of a binary world between faith and fact, truth, and belief.[18]
- Others point to the birth of historiography (a theory of history) that limited knowledge to human making and, thereby, evacuated any transcendent meaning from an emerging modernity.
- Still others place our current unraveling in a far broader frame, proposing that just as Christianity triumphed over paganism in the third century, bringing its own forms of socialization within a monotheist and transcendent understanding of the world, so we are now experiencing another revolution in which a new paganism is being birthed that is ending any vestiges of Christendom in the West.[19]

Taken together, these multiple explanations present a complex story of how Western societies and their churches came to this current malaise. They paint a broad canvas of tectonic shifts that are remaking the West and Christian life. Chapter 2 offers a more limited explanation of what's happened.

16. A renewal movement that contributed to the separation of God from Creation with the unintended consequence of a modern, immanentist understanding of the world (witnessed in the turn to technique, management, and outcomes) where God is no longer required as an explanatory framework—we became our own agents with little need for reference to any kind of heteronomous order. See Robinson and Roxburgh, *Practices for the Refounding of God's People.*

17. We see this in the ways clergy training became fixated on the therapeutic so that a major part of the modern story became the therapeutic self. See Lasch, *Culture of Narcissism*, and Rieff, *Triumph of the Therapeutic.*

18. See Newbigin, *Foolishness to the Greeks.*

19. See, for example, Frederick Christian Bauerschmidt, "After Christendom," https://www.commonwealmagazine.org/after-christendom.

CHAPTER TWO

A Seventy-Five-Year Story

Introduction

OFFERING HELPFUL WAYS TO explain the unraveling disrupting Western societies is neither simple nor straightforward. As leaders we've been trained to look for certain kinds of explanations to the question "What's happened?" The explanations we develop are usually from within:

- Functionalist frameworks (What's stopped working, why, and what do we do to get it working again or replace it),
- Therapeutic frameworks (What's happening to me/us in all of this? What am I/we experiencing in this unraveling? How do I/we take care of myself/ourselves?),
- Ideal-type frameworks (We need to be again an Acts 4 church; we need to develop holistic discipleship; we need to get back to biblical truths),
- Tactical frameworks embracing the latest discoveries from cognitive science or the business world (new forms of innovation or adaptation methods).

These frames can contribute to what Brooks calls a conceptual blindness. Embracing these frameworks will not only be an insufficient response to the unraveling, but in fact, will miss the fundamental point of being God's people.

Stories are the narrative tools we use to make sense of where we are and how to engage this moment. Our stories in our leadership tool box are no longer adequate for making sense of what's happening to the churches or society. Our stories about the nature of leadership have been developed since the end of World War II. Their purpose has been to turn leaders into effective managers, strategists, or therapists. A leader's sense of competency, therefore, comes from his/her ability to use these skills in a society that accepts them as normative. But such competencies and the story they embody are no longer able to address the disruptions confronting congregations and the systems that resource them. Currently, the best efforts of leaders are being poured into finding ways to fix a church-world created since the end of World War II. Distress, anxiety, burnout, and exhaustion characterize the experiences of countless clergy as they continue to operate inside this story. There is little ability to see the unraveling with theological eyes that ask about God's presence and judgement in it all.

This chapter examines the story that has shaped churches and leaders over this seventy-five-year period. When describing this as a seventy-five-year story, we are not meaning to say that it suddenly appeared and took shape immediately after World War II. It is a story that was gestating for several hundred years and was the shaping of the modern experiment. We have hinted at the contours of this story above. The American philosopher Matthew B. Crawford sums it up when he states that we continue to be informed "by the agenda of the Enlightenment . . . This agenda shaped a very partial view of the human person, one that we have been operating with for centuries but has become in various ways poorly suited to our circumstances."[1] This story, therefore, has antecedents in the period from the seventeenth and eighteenth centuries. These antecedents form the modern West, becoming the normative *big* story of the West right after WWII. This book pays attention to what we're calling the seventy-five-year story while recognizing that this story came out of and represented this prior history. A gradually developing story quite quickly came to dominance in the first part of the last century and, we would argue, is unraveling in the first third of the twenty-first century.

At the end of World War II, the West sought to create a world order that would rebuild the one devastated by two world wars. Instead, what they created, intentionally or not, was a profoundly different world from

1. Crawford, *World Beyond Your Head*, 8.

the one that people had known prior to this twentieth-century Thirty Years' War. Those constructing this new world wanted to forge a political, economic, and social order that would prevent such wars from ever happening again. It involved the creation of a global monetary system, a form of world governance to assist nation-states to keep the peace and provide the means to distribute monies for development.

The ending of World War II coincided with the ending of what could be called the industrial era and the emergence of a new technological era that would transform not just the West, but also global economies and class structures. Extensive new systems of education were created to resource this global technological revolution. Following the war, a new kind of educated class was required to fill the needs of this new era. These transformations coalesced around populations that were rapidly being emancipated from traditional societies where identities were locked into places and roles. This massive concentration on education amidst an emerging technological society created a whole new class system, a so-called middle class, with a new kind of white-collar elites and knowledge worker that would come to reshape the nature of society at the midpoint of the last century. Despite a Cold War and the nuclear threat, these postwar developments produced what came to be called a golden era of growth, sustained economic expansion, and the broadening of freedoms across race, class, and sex. It would, so the promise declared, usher in an era when all boats would rise and progress would run on an endless curve upward. It was clear to almost everyone that a unique period of social and economic growth had arrived.

An optimistic, confident story emerged from the ashes of bombed cities, gas chambers, and death camps. Victorious liberal democracies, driven by their technological prowess, offered an optimistic road to a new future. The nation-state, liberalism, capitalism, and technology combined to promise a future of expansive growth and the freedom for individuals to become whomever they chose. This bright, new world would be serviced by a new class of technocratic elites, who, through the centralized planning of the bureaucratic state and scientific management, would create an expanding middle class of educated professionals. These new middle-class leaders would solve and fix just about any challenge that confronted people, from disease to exploring outer space. What was birthed was a generation of elites, professionals, and experts who could go where no *man* had ever gone before. The promise was that everyone who worked hard and sacrificed would be lifted into the beneficent future by the power of technology, the bureaucratic state, and a liberal economy.

This postwar settlement, by the late 1950s, was producing a new story about itself. It involved society characterized by a new kind of person—the self-actualizing individual. Unlike the mothers and fathers who had gone to war and sacrificed so much for "God and country," this generation was being educated to move in very different directions within what the American economist John Galbriath described as the "Affluent Society."[2] What was emerging were highly individualized societies shaped by the dual notions of self-actualization and consumption.[3]

From the end of World War II to the present, the Euro-tribal churches functionally recreated themselves around this story. Undergirding and strengthening this massive social shift and its new story were the waves of suburbanization following World War II, shaped in the US by the construction of the great interstate highways. These suburban populations were, initially, largely composed of white (and white-collar) professionals. The Euro-tribal churches mostly abandoned the cities to become the religious center of the new suburbs. These demographic and societal shifts remade Protestant congregations, reoriented clergy training, and redirected the strategies of denominations. The members of these congregations were newly minted members of this emerging, professional middle class and their leaders (the clergy) were trained to be their servants and acolytes. To become a leader in these churches, one had to apprentice in a professionalizing educational system. This system required a degree to be properly ordained and it formed trainees in a story that emphasized rational method, programs, and technique, along with the therapeutic skills needed to care for expressive individuals. The identity of a leader was that of an educated elite. Almost all of society was taken up with this story of production, technology, growth, and managerial success. It promised an ever-expanding future for the individual who could succeed in the brave new world of a deindustrialized, globalized society, and success to the church leader who knew how to nurture this new kind of individual.

The blue-collar worker, characterized by loyalty to work, family, and place, began to disappear. In the once powerful, working-class industrial

2. Galbraith, *Affluent Society.*

3. Among the many, many references to these themes see, for example, Rieff, *Triumph of the Therapeutic*; Sennett, *Fall of Public Man*; Lasch, *Culture of Narcissism*; and Bauman, *In Search of Politics* and *Individualized Society.*

belt of America, voices were silenced as they increasingly felt like unwanted aliens in the Euro-tribal churches. Those filling the pews of Sunday services had become highly individualized professionalized, technocratic elites. This became the normative story for Euro-tribal churches.

What is fascinating is that just like blue-collar workers of mid-America fifty years ago, this replacement story of middle-class professionalized elites is, itself, coming apart. The precarity of the working classes is becoming the precarity of the white-collar classes. This is why church leaders are feeling anxious, distressed, and disoriented. Their formation has been built around this story of largely white-collar congregations. How are these experts (the ordained with masters and doctoral degrees) responding as they become aware that their skills and methods are no longer working in this new place? It's putting their identity as persons and leaders under threat. As church systems fail, leaders grow more and more aware that somehow, somewhere along the way, they became curators of institutions more than co-creators with God. They're exhausted because they have few places to talk about what's happening to themselves. The weight of expectation, obligation, and the pressure to come up with answers and arrest decline with diminishing resources, weighs heavily.

Disruption is hard. It upends assumptions, disturbs routines, makes life feel chaotic. It's hard to give voice to these feelings in ourselves. It seems easier to keep doing what has always been done, hoping somehow for better results. Attempts at revision, reimagining, renewing, or finding another pure gospel keep taking us into cul-de-sacs. Accepting the reality of such disruptions takes huge courage.

From the town where Roy used to live, for him to go for a walk in the countryside he had to cross the main East Coast railway line. At the gates to the rail crossing stood a large sign warning him to "Stop, Look, and Listen." Failure to pay attention could lead to loss of life. Pandemic lockdown measures provided us with a chance to stop, look, and listen. Normal church activities were forced to stop. This was a gift, inviting us to ask fundamental questions of the why, what, and how of what we have become as churches. Most congregations and their leaders have not taken the time to do this stopping and asking. What the pandemic did was lay bare long-festering fissures across society. They'd been covered up with Band-Aid strategies from within the regnant story, but such deflection is no longer possible. What is being laid bare in the multiple, cascading crises of our moment are the cracks in the seventy-five-year story, which has been shaping the Euro-tribal churches since World War II.

The Ending of the Story

This seventy-five-year story is coming undone. This tectonic shift is resulting in a traumatic remaking of our culture, institutions, and churches. An existing clergy class has been trained for this golden era, excelling in methods of management, counseling, innovation, and strategic planning. They were formed to be professionals skilled in the arts of futuring, fixing, managing, and maintaining. The tools in their tool kit are those of this seventy-five-year story. This is why, as congregations awaken to the unraveling, they still seek methods to create thriving congregations with missional strategies. We are going to need something more than thriving congregations or innovation or church planting. As chapter 3 will argue, these are the "Jerusalem stories" that could not account for the disruptions that overtook Israel around 587 BC.

The unraveling of an era is difficult to comprehend. Much of what we've taken for granted is dissolving in front of us. Out of nowhere, it seems, we're confronted with the raw power of autocratic military might after talking about the "end of history"[4] and world leaders had uttered the words "never again" after the Holocaust. Across the West, protests abound across class lines we believed had disappeared in a globalized world that promised to lift all boats. Truckers' protests in Canada or the re-emergence of yellow vest-like protests in France and Holland are about the re-emergence of class when we thought we were all equal. We accepted the story that we were living in a world where a globalized economy produced a broadening middle class and conferred the good life on all. We're realizing that the reality is very different as we witness the re-emergence of a Downton Abbey-like world in which a small number of *upstairs* billionaires hire middle-class professional elites to run their economic and political hegemonies alongside the emergence of a huge underclass. Few anticipated the re-emergence of the cultural, economic, social, racial, and sexual divides we now confront. There are hardly any left who remember the euphoria of the post-World War II golden age when, it seemed, everything was possible and we were all to thrive in the technological "age of Aquarius." Seventy-five years on, festering grievances and forgotten wounds have come back with a vengeance. A growing frustration at being ignored and discounted among the "downstairs classes," provides the context for burgeoning populist and nationalist movements that the

4. See Fukuyama, *End of History and the Last Man.*

ruling classes neither understand nor want to engage. There are various interpretations for these disruptions:

- Some see this unraveling resulting from a resurgence of xenophobic, white, racist populisms.
- For others, it is the result of the huge distortions created by a neoliberal order that diminishes the middle classes and relocates political power in small elites of economic oligarchs.
- For yet others, the causes lie in the inability of the political, media, intellectual, and economic thought leaders to hear the grievances of working people whose anger isn't primarily because globalization has left them behind (an economic interpretation) but that their values around place, family, belonging, and how we make decisions for one another have been mocked and dismissed as archaic and nonprogressive by social media, political gnostics, and elites who supposedly know what's best for everyone.

The Euro-tribal churches are lost in the fog of it all. They are turned in on themselves, preoccupied with their own needs. They've lost the plot to their own story as God's people. The best they seem able to do is choose sides in the right–left, progressive–conservative divide or choose some "woke" issue around which they'll take their "virtue-signalling" stand. Their identities as God's people hardly turn up in conversation. Woke progressivism or nativist nationalism seem to be the options left to churches that lost the plot to God's story.

Answers to how we address this unraveling won't come from reorganizing denominations or new strategies for reaching generational cohorts; they will not come from fresh methods of innovation, tactics of change, or skills for thriving congregations. Answers won't be found in methods borrowed from all the usual places, conferences, and gurus. These roads are finished. As in the story shaping the book of Ezekiel, the Spirit is somewhere else, weaving a radically different story. We can't pretend any longer. It was a great ride, but it's over. We're at a turning point. The socioeconomic story about who we are and how we get the good things in life no longer works. An era that began right after the end of World War II and has defined whole generations since then, is coming apart.

The ending of this seventy-five-year story offers a turning point to the Euro-tribal churches. It can redirect them to God's story. But, as we shall argue, this is no easy road. It is a journey that must encounter God's hard compassion. Hope does not spring out of technique or method. Confronting the unraveling of our churches requires us to confront the narrative world of Lamentations. Hope begins in the recognition of what we have become, rather than its continued denial in proposals for renewal or revitalization or some new kind of missional endeavor.

Dark Times

If we interpret what's happening to the Euro-tribal churches only in terms of an unraveling, or the ending of an era, the result will be discouragement and more anxious flourishes of fixing techniques. As Paul Kingsnorth has expressed so well, the ground is shifting everywhere—it is indeed the case that we are in dark times, a dissolution of things is underway.[5] Apart from the false claims from certain segments of the priestly class that all is well and all things will be well, much as the prophet Jeremiah encountered, there is a general sense of things coming apart. This is producing a season of lament. There is a fear that dark times are ahead. It would be wrong to pretend otherwise. There is every reason for us to feel lament. The Euro-tribal churches bet their house on becoming relevant to this story, on being its religious curators by reinterpreting the Christian story in its terms. Now, we are awakening to the awareness we've lost our souls. Lamentation involves a devastating recognition:

> The roads to Zion mourn,
> for none come to the festival;
> all her gates are desolate;
> her priests groan;
> her virgins have been afflicted,
> and she herself suffers bitterly
> . . .
> because the Lord has afflicted her
> for the multitude of her transgressions;
> her children have gone away,
> captives before the foe.[6]

5. Kingsnorth, "Abbey of Misrule," *Into the Desert, Into the Woods*, Substack, July 7, 2023.

6. Lam 1:4–5 (NIV).

Lament is a door to discerning how God's severe compassion can give sustenance and guidance for the dark times ahead. Such lament isn't the final word, nor is the gathering darkness. The final word is apocalypse. In Scripture, apocalypse means an uncovering, a revelation of what lies behind the shadows. This apocalypse directs us toward hope because it reveals the workings of God in the midst of disruption. In the descending darkness, the Spirit of Jesus continues to weave another story, to put into place another future. Therefore, lamentation is informed by a patient waiting for the unveiling of God's future.

It's hard to lament when one's underlying conviction is that someone or some group out there has the right techniques to fix things. Apart from therapeutic and technological methods, there's little appetite for lament over the devastating social, political, and communal results of the road we've been on. Responses to the unraveling continue in the direction of trying to fix or revitalize a dying story. Surely, we still believe that we're smart enough to find solutions? The churches continue to expend energy rationalizing loss (selling buildings, amalgamating congregations, redistributing investment funds), working on new strategic plans, and analyzing trends in the hope they can innovate new directions that will manage a relevant future. The churches still look for guidance from within the very story that is unraveling, a story about management and control, about maintaining the professional status and identity of the clergy.

It can't be done. The road ahead requires a coming to terms with a devastation that is God's severe compassion. Something is happening to the Euro-tribal churches that is more than sociocultural displacement. Something more is required than political-economic–class analysis.

> My transgressions were bound into a yoke
> by his hand they were fastened together;
> they were set upon my neck;
> he caused my strength to fail;
> the Lord gave me into the hands
> of those whom I cannot withstand (1:14)
> . . .
> My children are destitute
> because the enemy has prevailed. (Lam 1:16)

We lament when established stories fail us.

When Stories Fail

What will root us as God's people when the story we've lived in can no longer hold us? Our ways of life, institutions, and forms of leadership are governed by the stories we hold as communities. These stories shape what we see and what we believe (our ideal narratives and convictions). They may, or may not, be healthy reflections of the actual reality in front of us. When a story that has shaped a people unravels, they and their leaders default to the habituated practices and convictions of that story. They work harder to make the story live again, not understanding why it isn't working now.

This is the current situation of the Euro-tribal churches. They are stuck in a dying story. Their leaders work harder at making the old story work precisely because it has worked for them. Julia Galef describes this default as a "soldier mindset." It is driven by the need to defend, to fortify, what we most want to believe and to shoot down people or perspectives that don't hold to our views. To admit that there is something about the story we're living in that's wrong is akin to suffering a defeat. When one is already overwhelmed, a sense of defeat is hard to accept. Understanding these disruptions requires us to discover new maps.[7]

When our current maps (the stories we have about how things work) no longer describe where we are, we need to change our mind about the story in which we're living. This is a big ask. The maps of our existing story were given to us through socialization, education, and credentialing. Our leaders are rewarded because they are good managers of the existing maps. The security these leaders brought to people and their institutions was, in fact, their excellence in maintaining the given maps. Recently there has been a great resignation of leaders who know the maps that made them successful no longer describe the landscape. Having no alternatives, they elect to leave the stage.

We place a high value on certainty, on our ability to make things legible so we can plan and direct outcomes. Our managerial skills are shaped around these convictions. We reward entrepreneurial leaders armed with the techniques and technologies of organizing success. This search for certainty and legibility turns up in many forms. It shows, for example, in our search for a model or method to fix the crises of our churches. If megachurch and worship bands were the answer for Baby Boomers, we become convinced now that "microchurch" will be the game-changer for another

7. See Roxburgh, *Missional Map-Making.*

generation. This unraveling requires a different kind of intelligence, however, one shaped by a humility that can embrace a moment of lament. It requires companions with whom to walk an unclear road to practice discernment. At the end of a story rooted in the conviction that we can make all things legible, a different imagination is needed.

Adam Grant's *Think Again*[8] illustrates this need to find another story amidst radical change. A group of elite firefighters were parachuted into a forest fire. They landed near the top of a mountain with the fire visible across the gully and began to make their way down the slope towards the fire. The plan was to dig a line in the soil around the fire to contain and direct it toward an area where there wasn't much to burn. The fire, however, had leapt across the gully and was heading straight toward them. With flames stretching as high as thirty feet in the air and rapidly advancing, it was clear that even containing the fire would be an impossible task. Realizing it was time to shift from fight to flight, the crew began to turn around and run back up the mountain slope. Just a couple of hundred yards away from the summit, with safety in sight, the fire continued to advance. The team leader did something that was not expected. Instead of trying to outrun the fire, he stopped, and then proceeded to light matches and throw them into the surrounding grass. His crew, no doubt thinking he had lost the plot, broke rank and didn't take up his command to join him. They didn't realize that he was building an escape fire. By burning the grass ahead of him, he cleared the area of anything that the wildfire could feed on. He then poured the water from his flask onto his scarf, covered his mouth with a wet handkerchief and lay face down in the charred area. As the wildfire raged directly above him he survived in the oxygen close to the ground. Sadly, twelve of the other firefighters perished. Only two reached the crest of the ridge. The team leader survived by recognizing the reality of the situation he faced and acting counterintuitively. Contending for what we have always believed isn't helpful when we find ourselves in a place we've never been before.

Finding Our Story in a Place We've Never Been Before

A people's identity depends on the perduring character of the story in which they dwell. Story gives us the ability to name who we are and how to act; it provides explanations for where we're going and how we relate

8. Grant, *Think Again*.

with one another and the other. It gives us common practices for how we connect with and relate to a broader community and to our environment. To lose one's story is to lose touch with ways of being human that forms a tradition and way of life over time.

As Christians we've been shaped by a particular story that took its current form around the midpoint of the last century, right after World War II. It is the story of a self-determining, individualized culture with techniques and methods to compel the world to become legible so that we can make it anything we choose. The Christian story has been shoehorned into this story. Stories formed us as communities. The more concrete the story, the greater the chance of a people's identity enduring through crises. The more the Euro-tribal churches lost touch with their story of God's agency in the world, the more they took on the methods and techniques of this seventy-five-year story. As it comes apart, they are adrift with little sense of another story beyond what this modern culture has given us. We're in a place we've never been before with few resources to address the question of what to do.

Scripture is a story about God's formation and vocation of a people. The Hebrew Scriptures are rooted in stories about useless, old, worn-out gypsies like Abram and Sarai and a chattel people facing shoah in Egypt. These stories coalesce around the stubborn conviction that this God chose this couple and these slaves for the sake of the world. This is a story about incommensurable hope that cannot be overcome in a dark world. It is a story shaped by God's acts of choosing, forming, and rooting these people in a geography. Israel has endured because they are this story. The feast of Passover is its central rehearsal, enacting and re-presenting their identity-forming story. Each year, over millennia, Jewish households come around a table at Passover to rehearse events that are still alive and fundamental to their identity. On the day of Passover, the eldest son ritually asks: "Father, why do we keep this festival?" to which the perduring response is read ". . . A wandering Aramian was my father . . ." (Deut 26:5). Critical to their enduring identity is the story's concreteness and particularity. It is earthed in an event involving real people in a real place at a real time. So it is with the Christian story as Luke, in the opening of his Gospel, makes clear:

> In the days of Herod, king of Judea, there was a priest named Zechariah of the division of Abijah. And he had a wife from the daughters of Aaron, and her name was Elizabeth . . . [I]n the sixth month the angel Gabriel was sent from God to a city of

> Galilee named Nazareth, to a virgin betrothed to a man whose name was Joseph, of the house of David. And the virgin's name was Mary. And he came to her and said, "Greetings, O favored one, the Lord is with you!"

The persistence of a people is linked to their being rooted in a concrete story. This is how we know who we are and where we are in the flux of history. This has been the case until the modern era when a very different kind of story emerged.[9]

The modern story, our primary story, abhors the concrete and the everyday. Its drive has been to dissolve place as the location of meaning and discount the ordinary as unimportant in terms of skill, knowledge, and a source of progress. It is a story committed to abstractions and universalized ideas (the state, the market, the people, freedom, liberty, equality, and so forth) that have no substantive reality. Rather than being rooted in the ordinary, everyday, local lives of men and women, "the very concept of the modern state presupposes a vastly simplified and uniform property regime that is legible and hence manipulable from the center."[10] The modern has decentered and diminished local, specific cultures and practices. Local life has been inexorably absorbed into the modern story where belonging is about abstractions (the "will of the people" or being for justice and so forth). These abstractions are unrooted ideals. The modern has shaped a new and unique kind of culture about people formed inside abstract, universalized ideals. Today, all this is taken for granted to the extent that we no longer see this imagination as a massive assault on concrete, everyday life. Language like the *people*, *state*, and the *market* are used as if they're actual, substantive realities when, in fact, they're abstractions in the service of other abstractions, such as power, success, and progress. On balance, we don't see how this story is the opposite of the Christian story, rooted as it is in a specific person who, stubbornly, turns up in a specific place among ordinary people.

This transformation of Western social, political, and economic imagination from the grounded to the abstract laid the groundwork for the uprootedness and rootlessness that now characterizes our societies. To be modern is to be without roots. Rootlessness is of this story's essence.[11] Over the last seventy-five years, we've put in place systems, institutions,

9. For an important and brilliant analysis of our loss of concreteness and story see Scott, *Seeing Like a State*.

10. Scott, *Seeing Like a State*, 35.

11. See Arendt, *Without Roots*.

and professional classes to legitimize and manage this deracinement—this uprooting. A rootless regime, to be successful, must suppress all that is local. We usually don't see this for ourselves, but we can see it through its effects on others. A painful example is colonialism. In Canada, for example, it is seen in residential schools that existed well into the twentieth century. One of their purposes was to take First Nations children from their homes, communities, language, and traditions, to make them rootless, so that they would become citizens of the state and its modern regime. In Britain, the Windrush Scandal was made possible because an abstracted bureaucracy saw colonial immigrants as needing to be moved (uprooted, deported) in order to serve them as "clients." The state lives so deeply in this technocratic story that it could not see them as people born as British subjects, in countries under colonial rule, and, therefore, having full British citizen rights under a law passed in 1948.

In the modern story, control and decision-making are distanced from the local and everyday. In this depersonalized regime, relationships are digitized in order to become transactional; covenant is replaced with contract. This is the normative way of modern societies. To live in this regime we create a new kind of person, the uprooted individual who has become a client with a managerial class of experts and professionals around whom the client is organized, codified, and managed. This normalized rootlessness of the abstract individual is our modern story that is failing us. Once this is seen, the painful rendering of Lamentations becomes a way of interpreting the situation of the churches in our unraveling. Euro-tribal churches hitched their wagons to this story. As participants in a rootless society, they created congregations for rootless people, symbolized by the penchant for massive parking lots for people attending the seeker churches. In doing so, churches have lost the story that formed Christian identity.

How Do We Respond?

How do we respond to this situation? What we face is not resolvable using the methods of the seventy-five-year story. In 2021, US states adjacent to the Gulf of Mexico entered hurricane season. Hurricane Katrina (2005) had revealed that the institutions created to address disasters could not deal with hurricanes in an era of climate change. The year 2021 brought Hurricane Ida. It wasn't unusual for hurricanes to bring heavy rains as they moved up the Atlantic Seaboard. This time, however, the flooding was catastrophic. Millions saw their homes underwater, deaths occurred, and systems failed. Storms like Ida were once the exception; now they come with fearful regularity. Experts in climate modeling were unprepared. Tripti Bhattacharya, assistant professor of earth and environmental science at Syracuse University, stated in a NPR interview: "We are moving into a world we've never seen." Echoing this, the governor of New Jersey made a stunning observation about the sewage and water systems. They performed, he said, exactly as they were designed to. The problem was they were designed for the world of a hundred years ago. They were built for a world that doesn't exist anymore. We're in a world we've never seen before.[12]

The British farmer James Rebanks tells a similar story. His book *Pastoral Song*[13] chronicles his awakening to the destructive effects of industrial farming. The book is a three-act play. The first act describes farming to the midpoint of the last century (the beginning of the seventy-five-year era). It was epitomized by his grandfather from whom his knowledge and love of farming came. The second act describes how farming was transformed from the 1950s onward by industrialization. In the forms of sophisticated GPS-driven tractors, chemical fertilizers, genetically modified seeds, intensive monoculture, technology promised to maximize efficiency and reduce the price of goods to a minimum. It is farming dissociated from the land, dependent on chemicals and shaped by experts with little relationship to the rhythms of people or land. It dismissed and swept away local knowledge. By the end of the millennium, the evidence was clear—industrial farming had rendered soils void of nutrients and made crops dependent on chemicals sold by experts. Local experience was lost. Workers were made redundant by farming methods needing few people. In Rebanks's words: "The countryside that feeds us has changed. It is profoundly different from even a generation ago . . . [T]he more we learn about this change the more unease and anger we feel about what farming has become."[14] The worse the unintended consequences of industrial farming became, "the

12. See https://www.npr.org/2021/09/03/1034058911/hurrican-ida-climate-change-northeast-flooding-rainfall.

13. Rebanks, *Pastoral Song*.

14. Rebanks, *Pastoral Song*, 15.

more people seemed to gravitate to charlatans with grand promises and ready-made scapegoats to focus all their anger on."[15]

Undergirding industrial farming lay the seventy-five-year story about the power of professional elites to manage and remake the world. Schools produced a professional class with little connection to the land. Their tools are chemical fertilizers, lab-produced seeds, and massive tractors designed for maximum efficiency. Land care was displaced. A story infused by the language of consumers, production, maximization, choice, taste. and options took over. Farmers, Rebanks observes, became strangers to the fields that feed us. Act three is about how he found a way back to sustainable farming rooted in the rhythms of the land and the local. Rebanks sees this as an essential journey for us all that will "take time and faith, and radical structural changes . . ."[16]

A parallel story has shaped our churches over the last seventy-five years. The churches industrialized, becoming enthralled with methods of success, strategies of growth, techniques of measurement, prediction, and the need to manage outcomes. They adopted the prescribed programs and strategies of so-called successful churches. Franchising and a myriad of successful models and schemes were applied to churches. Strategically located church buildings (close to highway intersections) draw people from a wide geographic radius on the basis of personal preference and contemporary, trend relevance. Similarly, cathedrals in the UK have seen an increase in their attendance through their ability to offer music and services that no longer exist elsewhere, given the closure of many churches. Church planting in targeted areas and resource churches in university cities are similarly seeking to connect with students and younger professionals. Consumerism reigns. COVID lockdown provided, for a time, consumer models around internet livestream church from the comfort of one's living room. Overall, none of this has staunched the decline of many of these churches. These expressions of church have removed believers from their neighborhoods.

Like industrial farming, a guild-like clergy has been schooled to professionally manage church institutions, in the assumption that the structures we have now will always be around and are essential for the church. For Rebanks, however, adjustment of the given systems is no longer viable. A different story is needed. In terms of farming it will

15. Rebanks, *Pastoral Song*, 170.

16. Rebanks, *Pastoral Song*, 191.

mean a radical shift from a story of farming that presumes the plow to be essential part of farming:

> [In] the past thirty years we have learned that plowing is ecologically disastrous . . . This news is staggering—and hard to take in for farmers . . .Our civilization rests on the plow (and the chemical tools of the post war period) and yet the plow is the problem . . . [T]hat means changing how we farm and thinking again about tools we have come to rely on.[17]

For the Euro-tribal churches adjustment is no longer enough. The story we need now must turn us toward the ways that God works in dark times. The contours of this story are in Scripture and the history of the church. Christians are not called to remove themselves from the places where they dwell but to form practices and structures of common life predicated on what Jonathan Tran describes as "the absolute value of God and the relative value of creation."[18] These communities respond by becoming communities that are able to discern what God is doing where they dwell. As Christians, the core practice of such a common life is doxological; it is focused around God's intentions for all creation. Christians are to become communities of hope discerning what God is doing among and ahead of them in their communities.

God's desire for us is to live doxologically, in the place to which we have been called. As creatures of the Creator God, we're called to live in reciprocal relationship with the Other where the Other is given as gift and each of us are given for the Other as expressions of God's own delight. As Tran states so well, "everything turns on the question of whether persons live into the gift-structure of creation or pursue distorted desires to the detriment of creation."[19] In the ending of the seventy-five-year story, the question for Christians is about their desires in the midst of their anxieties.

Disordered Desire

This chapter has briefly described a political, social, and economic story built upon systems of domination and exploitation. It is about the distorted human desire to manage and control all of life. The stories we choose

17. Rebanks, *Pastoral Song*, 246.

18. Tran, *Asian Americans and the Spirit of Racial Capitalism*, 14.

19. Tran, *Asian Americans and the Spirit of Racial Capitalism*, 15.

to live in are never simply a matter of dispassionate calculus. They involve a long, entangled series of historical events that came to shape our time and impact our choices as societies.

The stories we live in are about our desires. This is the point of the garden of Eden story. The late French, Catholic theorist Rene Girard (1923–2015) argued that most of what we desire lies in what he called the mimetic, that is, intrinsic to being human is the need to imitate or, put in another way, to want what some other person or group has. Luke Burgis expands on this: "Our power of imitation . . . allows us to build sophisticated culture and technology . . . At the same time . . . it locks them into cycles of desire and rivalry that are difficult . . . to escape."[20] To say that we live inside of a story is to say that our desires have been formed through the imitating of the structures, habits, and practices of that story over a number of generations. The story we live in tells us what is worthy of our time, what is worth having, and how we get the good things in life. Most often these values come to us through people we've looked up to as sources of our desires. Girard's argument about mimetic desire is much more complex than this, but this is sufficient to point out that the stories we live in are much more than rational choices or just the traditions we happen to inhabit.

The seventy-five-year story is a story of disordered desire that has produced an anti-doxological society focused around the conviction that we get the good things in life through our capacities to measure, assess, control, and manage outcomes. It is a story of desire in which God is of no relevance. We don't let go of our desires merely by being shown a reasoned argument for change or, even, by arguing how and why this story is destroying us. As we shall see, Jeremiah's reasoning about the falseness of the story in which Israel was living changed few minds. Desire is a powerful thing. Lamentations is a lament of conflicting desires around the loss of a story. When our life is formed through practices and skills imitated from those we've sought to emulate, we do not easily let go of them or be convinced we need to change.

When confronted with this story, the "aha moment" of leaders results in some form of the question: *What do I do?* While an important question, it is not the first one we need to ask. Something more difficult is required. Christians need to posit a coherent alternative to the seventy-five-year story. The chapters ahead offer proposals for what this

20. Burgis, *Wanting*, xvi–xvii.

might look like. It involves a long, patient journey of what we will describe as dwelling, discerning, and exploring. Hope in the coming dark times will emerge from out of this dwelling, discerning, and exploring. We don't need more proposals to innovate, adapt, plant, or double down on a tradition. We need to be formed in a different desire—the desire to know what God is gestating ahead of us in the places where we dwell. What does the Christian story look like in these dark times?[21] How do we listen to the movements of the Spirit in this place? How does God engage us when we're shaped by a story that deforms God's purposes for creation? Chapter 3 turns to these questions.

21. The term "dark times" is intended in a very specific way. It describes the way in which a story that has characterized modern Western life is unraveling with little sense of what might take its place. In this unraveling of such a big, overarching story we find ourselves increasingly struggling with multiple, cascading disruptions that are propelling us into a place we've never been before. It is in this sense that we use the phrase. We do not in any way whatsoever intend to communicate some gnostic world-denying perspective that views the material and everyday as evil or life-denying or something from which Christians are to flee. This is not about seeing ourselves as a faithful remnant in a sea of darkness. As Christians we confess that this is God's good creation—the world is good. It bears the word that Genesis ascribes to God—the Lord saw the creation and declared that it was good. Therefore, we confess that this is God's good creation and not a place from which we are to flee as some pure remnant in a dark world. This is a world filled with amazing and good people, a place that is blessed and at the heart of God's desire. At the same time this creation bears all the scars of an overreaching human agency that has and continues to wreak destruction. It is in this sense that we use the term "dark times"—we live in one of those times when that overreaching has created this dark space that, at the moment, is without resolution. God's people are called to faithfully reflect our Lord and Creator by participating in the reweaving of creation and the healing of our torn social fabric. We are called to dwell in the midst of the darkness in doxological ways that anticipate the One who has declared "behold, I make all things new."

SECTION TWO

God, God's People, and the Unraveling of Their Worlds

THIS SECTION TURNS TO the question of what the churches are called to do when they're confronted with a story that has colonized their imaginations. It proposes that asking "What do we do?" will only return us to the story itself. We need to ask a very different question if we're to discern the movement of the Spirit in this time.

CHAPTER THREE

Stories to Guide God's People in a Place We've Not Been Before

Introduction: The Sources of Our Stories

THIS BRIEF CHAPTER IS a bridge designed to take us from Section One to Section Two by examining the central questions leaders often ask when they awaken to the story we have described in Section One: *What do we do?* The next three chapters propose the question we now need to ask in this unraveling and then provide examples of how God has engaged God's people as they've been confronted by disruptions in other times. Chapter 1 proposed that the times ahead for our societies and, in particular, the Euro-tribal churches, are dark. A group of pastors and congregation moderators[1] were meeting in one of our "Leaders' Tables."[2] It was the first of four sessions. The question being addressed in this first session was "What's happening?" After viewing a video addressing this question, participants were asked to share with one another a critical leadership question the video was raising for them. Typical responses were:

- As a leader, I'm trying to sort out who we are as churches in our society—where are we going?
- How does the church go forward in these difficult times?

1. This term usually refers to the lay chair of a congregation.
2. See https://www.themissionalnetwork.com/.

- What will this new season of church look like and how do I lead in it?
- What's the future of the church? This is no longer clear to me.

What these questions illustrate is the depth of wrestling that's going on for many leaders just now. Not everyone is in this space. On the day we guided this Leaders' Table, someone posted on Facebook about the growing number of successful microchurches they'd been involved in planting over the previous month. While there are still many leaders who believe they've found the technique for making the church work, there are many more leaders asking existential questions. These leaders genuinely sense that the road just ahead of us isn't all light and success. Their questions press around the edges of this nagging concern that there are some hard days ahead and we are not prepared for them.

It would be naive and faithless to see our dark times as all there is or that there is little we can do beyond make the best of our own personal situations. These pastors participating in the Leaders' Table were, also, able to name the tensions that confront them in this moment of unraveling. They are well aware that a significant number of people in their congregations want these pastors to fix their churches. They are afraid to name this reality for fear of the pushback from congregation members. In this tension, they know they can't treat this unraveling as a minor hiccup amenable to a good strategy. In this situation, it is easy to succumb to the feeling of being caught between people's expectations and the reality of the situation. Such tensions can produce the sense that there's nothing we can do, that all is bad or lost. These responses lead some of us to withdraw into ourselves, into a remnant/exile mentality. On the other hand, some leaders are still doubling down on all the things they're currently doing and believing—that in execution of programs, better marketing, more research, or more complete data, they'll find the right innovation to turn the tide. Inside these responses lies a progressive belief that, while this might be a bit of a dark moment for the church, it's but a brief prelude before another era of abundance and success breaks upon Christ's bride. Our formation in the seventy-five-year story directs us to this response. We still find it hard to believe there isn't a strategic answer to these dark times. We remain convinced there is a method to instigate a fix. Such convictions are encoded into our lives and embodied in our practices. It's difficult to see alternatives. But there is another story that can shape our common life.

What Do We Do?[3]

What follows the "aha" response to the framing of the seventy-five year-story is an immediate question: "What do we do?" It is still difficult to resist looking for a response that offers tactics and strategies. What-to-do questions seem like the right ones to ask, but they come directly out of the now failing seventy-five-year story. *We can't solve the problem of the great unraveling with the methods that created it.* The consciousness that's led to the unraveling can't address the unraveling. We need another starting point. This chapter proposes we ask a very different question, one that is more faithful to our story as Christians: *When God's people have found themselves in places of great disruption, how has God turned up among them and what can we learn from this about our own moment as Christians?*

Another Story

There is another story to the one we're living in. That story is continually before us in Scripture and our traditions as Christians. Even though it has been colonized, it has not been erased. First Nations peoples of North America describe their own struggle to recover their stories from the overpowering ways colonialism has all but eradicated them. They speak about this work as recovering the grounded normativity[4] of their own story. It is about the ways their traditions and stories that undergird them become, again, central to all their communal practices in a colonized space. Something similar must now happen to our own story as God's people. The great narrative of God's purposes in the creation must be reclaimed not just as some postmodern nostalgic pastiche, but as that which shapes our everyday lives.

Those recording the story of the early church saw these little communities struggling to make sense of their identities within powerful, colonizing, civilizational forces (Greek, Jewish, Roman, etc.). The early Christians were keenly aware that they "were recording not just human

3. We have a process for leaders wanting to reimagine this other story in their contexts. The Leaders Table involves four sessions that build on one another. The first session addresses the question: *What is this new space where we find ourselves and how did we get here?* Material for that first session is drawn from chapter 1 of this book. It gives leaders a picture and new language for what we're experiencing.

4. See chapter 7 below for some discussion of this phrase in relation to First Nations peoples.

actions, but their providential design."[5] These witnesses were alive to the conviction that in all the dynamics of empire affecting these young churches, God was shaping another story. As real, destructive, and overpowering as the dynamics of empire were, they were not the story that determined them. The New Testament churches were continually attending to how the Spirit was working out this other story in the midst of empire. God's work in Christ for the world was their grounded normativity, their reading of the forces of empire confronting them. This is why they weren't daunted by persecutions or the disintegrative forces pulling apart the Roman Empire. They indwelt this other story, a different normativity. We confront the seventy-five-year story to the extent we discern the grounded normativity of this other story.

The direction of creation is doxological. Doxology and apocalypse are also the context for the lament we need to embrace at this moment. The tension facing Christian life just now is that, at the beginning of the undoing of a story, our captivity to that story has resulted in our losing touch with our own grounded normativity. In this tension we feel abandoned, disoriented, confused, overworked, and anxious. Our instincts are to lament our situation and our experiences of loss. This is not what lament is about. Lament comes out of a recognition that we've made secondary the One who makes all things new and, thus, we have lost the capacity to live doxological lives, lost a hope that does not need to manage the outcomes.

Resurrection, hope, and doxology come out of this other story. Another future will emerge beyond this darkening age because God has never ceased the work of reweaving a broken creation.[6] That said, resurrection and hope involve death, a grave, and, as the disciples acutely expressed at times, hopelessness. To see and hear, again, this other story requires us to lay down the control, tactics, and strategies at the heart of the seventy-five-year story in order to listen to how this other story has been worked out at critical moments in the life of God's people. We need to look at how God continually turns up when our worlds unravel. We see this in texts like Jeremiah and Lamentations as well as in the young church in Luke/Acts. Here and in other places we see how God gets in (to borrow a phrase from Leonard Cohen) inside broken, dark times. We ask the question of how the light gets in by asking about two

5. Ahmari, "Apostolic Empire," 45.

6. See Ephesians 1.

biblical narratives: *How has God addressed God's people when they found themselves in a place they'd never been before?*

Clarity Inside Mystery but No Control

The Easter narratives express our central conviction about the direction of creation in dark times: God has acted for all creation in Jesus Christ, death is not the end, but resurrection. God is acting in Christ for the healing of all things. Our vocation is to join with the Spirit in this reweaving of life. The place where we do that is where we dwell. Hope is in short supply right now across western societies. Too often Christians of Euro-tribal churches are like the bewildered followers of Jesus on the road to Emmaus. In their disorientation, they can't see beyond their grief and confusion over loss. The two on the Emmaus road had put all their trust in the outcome of a story that, for them, had catastrophically failed on the cross. Jesus was supposed to return the kingdom to Israel. Disillusioned, they left Jerusalem to return to their former lives. Similarly, today leaders know something has gone terribly wrong. It's crushing to realize that the story on which one has based one's life is failing. We are hungry for clarity of direction, of how to move forward. We keep looking for a strategy, method, or tactic we can take up to do something.

A pervasive disillusionment, a fog of confusion has settled upon the churches. There's a broad skepticism toward the institutions that have long undergirded our Christian lives. While writing this section, Alan was listening to a radio program about climate change. It involved an interview with Britt Wray, a Canadian writer working at the interface of climate change and mental health. Her book, *Generation Dread: Finding Purpose in an Age of Climate Crisis,*[7] addresses growing and overpowering feelings of climate anxiety afflicting generations who've known nothing except apocalyptic reports about climate catastrophe. They are generations living without hope, fearful there's no clarity around how to act. "Swarms of people are waking up to a sense that, if nothing changes, the fate of humanity will be like the slinky pushed off the top stair, with no good structures in place to halt its energetic descent. Nothing could be further from what people want, but many

7. Wray, *Generation Dread.*

feel powerless to stop this from happening."[8] This disillusionment is why we need another story. What's involved?

This book proposes three kinds of practices that must become the focal work of local churches: dwelling, discerning, and exploring. But while these practices, taken together, offer a way of being God's people, they're not strategies to help us predict, manage, or control the outcomes we want. They can provide clarity, but not certainty, and, probably, not the legibility we still desire. Only in the context of the mystery of God's actions amongst us can we journey in this dark time.

What does Scripture and Christian tradition say to us about hope in dark times? How does it respond to the question: *How has God addressed God's people when they found themselves in a place they'd never been before?* The next two chapters engage with four stories that address this question. Times of unraveling and crisis are more the norm for God's people than the seventy-five-year golden era that has shaped the Euro-tribal churches. Of the stories shared here, two are from Scripture (Jeremiah, Luke-Acts) and two from the shaping of Europe after Rome removed itself from that part of the world (Benedict and Celtic Christianity). Together they offer a picture of how these practices form communities of hope in a darkening time.

8. Wray, *Generation Dread*, 2.

CHAPTER FOUR

Signs of Hope in Dark Times

JEREMIAH AND LUKE/ACTS ARE written in times of massive unraveling for God's people. In each of these texts, God's people find themselves in places that were outside the story they had come to believe about who they were and how God was working among them and in their world. In exploring the reactions and experiences of these times we will discern some of the ways God's Spirit is calling us to live in our own dark times.

Jeremiah: The Covenant-God Is Acting

> "The time is coming," declares the Lord, "when I will make a new covenant with the house of Israel and with the house of Judah . . ."—Jeremiah 31:31.
>
> ". . . real politics is about the always unfinished business of creating structures, policies and human habits in which people can recognise each other's concerns sufficiently clearly and empathetically to guarantee a level of well-being for all."—Rowan Williams

Jeremiah tells Israel that their dark times are God's merciless compassion. Israel had broken covenant with God, yet God was acting in the midst of her failed politics. The One who called creation into being, who "came all the way down" and "pitched his tent right beside ours"[1] is the primary Actor in this catastrophic unraveling of Israel's life. For the

1. John 1:1–12.

prophet, Israel had forgotten its fundamental confession that Yahweh is Lord of all. In Jeremiah's telling, God was the primary actor in their collapsed world, even though Israel had opted for political, economic, and military alliances with Assyria and Egypt. In doing so, Israel had been colonized by the stories of power and success that undergirded these states. Israel had become convinced, even while continuing the ritual life of the temple and festivals, that her future depended on her skills to make agreements and manage power; Israel's balance between these two powers was her *realpolitik*. For Israel, these contracts were the signs of her brilliant innovativeness in the context of international power politics. The book of Jeremiah confronts Israel with another story—the Babylonian captivity was God's hard compassion intended to call them back to covenant life (Jeremiah 30:12–14).

Jeremiah had to tell Israel that before the promise of a restored covenant could be realized, Israel would have to dwell in a place of unthinkable, unmitigated, grave-like lament (Jer 30:3). Through this darkening experience, she could comprehend the depth of her faithlessness and conceive the hope Yahweh was calling her to embrace.

God Is Acting . . . in a Place We Haven't Been Before

Jeremiah is the story of God unraveling Israel's world to reorient her back to God's covenant agency. For generations, Israel's *modus operandi* had been bent toward the powers that surrounded and beset her. Her energies had been taken up in managing the political dynamics of living between empires. In that situation, she reshaped her story, coming to assume it was her acuity and agency, her capacities to manage and manipulate her geopolitical world that had brought success. Israel had assumed her own agency and power were sufficient to order and manage all relationships. Success lay in the capacities of her leaders to manage their desired outcomes. Babylon shattered this story.

The prophet's words of promise present an alternative story (Jer 31).[2] They address Judah's crises. Babylon was besieging Jerusalem. Captivity was inevitable. Chapter 1 of this book proposed that the dominant story we've lived in is a political, social, and economic story built upon systems of domination and exploitation, of power and control and

2. "For behold, the days are coming when I will restore the fortunes of my people Israel and Judah . . . I will bring them back to the land that I gave to their forefathers and they shall possess it"—31:3.

driven by disordered desire. It is a story that results in an anti-doxological society. Both Judah and Israel had embraced a political and economic story of power and control. They had come to be shaped around this story of distorted desires; a story that broke covenant with God. As long as Israel failed to see God as the primary actor in its unraveling, there would be no doxological community.

Jeremiah tells of a conflict between Israel's established orthodoxy and the prophet who tells a radically different story. Judah's leaders (elites with no separation between the political and the religious) interpreted what was happening (the invasions) in ways that squared with the desires of Jerusalem's population. They presumed their economic security depended on their ability to manage relationships with the surrounding empires. They constructed theological interpretations about why Yahweh would be faithful to the covenant promises. Their conviction about Yahweh's faithfulness was being put to the test as Chaldean armies transported Judah's elites to Babylon. The official story of the leaders was that Judah would face short-term pain in the geopolitical squeeze between empires, but Yahweh, faithful to the covenant, would deliver them if they kept temple worship and festival days. In terms of the geopolitical and economic situation on the ground, this orthodoxy proposed that Israel, with right tactics and smart innovations, would be looked after by Yahweh. The people wanted from their elites words that fit their desires for how God would work and how the elites would lead.

The prophet was unpopular because he spoke in a different voice about the upheavals. He announced that the orthodoxies of management and control, of right liturgy and ordered institutions, weren't going to save them. The promises of the elites that everything would return to the old norms were, said Jeremiah, lies that held no hope. Things were going over the cliff and the elites could do nothing about it because they inhabited the wrong story. It's as if Jeremiah were saying to us that all the consultants in the world, all the thriving congregational planning and all the innovative dreaming of elite leaders, will not fix the Euro-tribal churches. That game is over.

Jeremiah, in the crises of invasion and its interpretation, was jailed in a war zone for disagreeing with the official story—that the incursion was a one-off event. With smart politics and right liturgy all would be well. Jeremiah announced the Chaldeans would overthrow the king, lay waste Judea, destroy Jerusalem, and take the elites captive. All this, he claimed, was not simply the nasty work of bad actor states, it was the action of the covenant God. Jeremiah wasn't thrilled with having to tell the story, but in his bones lay this sense of God calling him to speak it.

The deportation created a state of hopelessness and lament ("how do we sing the Lord's song in a strange land"). Lamentations is Israel's dark awakening to her faithlessness. But the book of Jeremiah isn't just a story of hopelessness and lament. This crushing sense of loss and acute lamentation were to redirect Israel to an alternative future. In this context of lament, God instructs Jeremiah to make a foolish public act—purchase a piece of land that was now worthless (Jer 32). The prophet was acting hopefully in front of a people plunged into lament. Jeremiah went through correct legal proceedings (a public demonstration before a people who could make no sense of these actions). He offered a *drama*, an "act" of God's hopeful future. Before all the people he performed another story: God was in the midst of catastrophe working out a different future. God's covenantal promise would not be broken. The land purchase was an act of hope when there was no material reason for hope. It was announcing another future right in the midst of the unraveling and lamenting of the elites. As Walter Brueggemann points out: "[T]he public act . . . put Jeremiah on public record as claiming that there is indeed life after Babylon." The narrative is clear that while this is a carefully performed economic, legal act, it is far more than an economic or legal transaction. "It is a land deal freighted with enormous theological significance." [3]

Jeremiah is often misapplied to the Euro-tribal church's situation. It is used to wrongly describe the Euro-tribal situation as exile. These churches are not in exile in any sense that connects with the experiences of Jeremiah and Israel. This misdirecting metaphor creates a misreading of our context and a misapplication of Jeremiah. The book is concerned with the source of Israel's identity—God, and God's covenant agency in a world of many powers. It addresses the question of Israel's covenant faithlessness among the nations. Jeremiah is the story of God's covenant love in the midst of despair and loss. This covenant love isn't a kindly emotion for getting through hard times. It calls Israel to embrace a different future from the one they chose among the powers, a counterintuitive space. Who buys a worthless piece of land when everything is so dark? Hope is not to be found in the usual places, with the usual people, using the usual methods.

3. Brueggemann, *Commentary on Jeremiah*, 302.

Babylon—God Acting in the Most God-Forsaken Places

Babylon presented the possibility of Israel reorienting herself around a different imagination after her world had imploded. Israel had ended up in what was, to all appearances, the most godforsaken place (Babylon) in the world. Israel's theological frameworks told them the gods of Babylon had won and Yahweh was defeated. Manufacturing fixes were useless in Babylon. Everything that happened to them screamed that Babylon's story of how the world worked was the triumphant story (a reading of the world from the perspective of power politics). This is why they lamented: "How do you sing the Lord's song in a strange land?" Captivity made it clear that their songs and worship forms had neither life nor power in this faraway place. Prior to the deportations, it had seemed to the leaders of Israel there were pathways for innovating and managing their situation of being squeezed between rival empires. They thought they had the formula for managing this situation. Ritual, negotiation, and contract were the means. God would reward their skills in the marketplace of power. They had made a Faustian bargain. In so choosing, Israel set aside covenant relationship with Yahweh—their identity as a people among the nations. They lost any sense of God's agency because they were convinced that, like other nations, they could build the kingdom through their own agency.

The book of Jeremiah is secondarily about exile. It is focally about God's agency and covenant. Exile was their context, as unraveling is ours. Loss and disruption were the context where their questions of identity, vocation, covenant, and agency had to be confronted. Would Israel trust and desire Yahweh or their own skills at managing the nations and strategizing outcomes? Would they discern God's ways of acting in exile or trust in their own skills to manage the end of an era? Babylon signified that Israel had chosen the latter. This most godforsaken of places was where God was acting to reawaken Israel to its identity. But to be clear, at the start of this unraveling, Israel's elites had no imagination whatsoever that God's hopeful future could be in such a god-forsaken place.

Just as the prophet saw that God was acting in exile, the Euro-tribal churches are invited to discern the Spirit's acting in their unraveling. But such discernment doesn't come from new tactics for discovering strategies to fix things. In each case, the situation requires readiness to embrace the darkness for quite some time. The question with which Jeremiah confronts the Euro-tribal churches is whether or not they will embrace this emerging darkness to see what God is doing. Israel had to come to see that God was acting in a godforsaken place. That meant seeing their situation from outside of and against their established narratives and institutions. It was to be a shattering awakening. Babylon required relinquishment and reorientation. The Euro-tribal churches confront a similar possibility. Jeremiah points to patterns of practice that can shape us in our dark times. These counterintuitive practices are not strategies for returning to old familiarities. Israel failed to embrace this moment. We are confronted with a place we've never been before. Jeremiah makes it clear there will be no quick fixes. The wrong thing to do, Jeremiah tells us, is to try to extricate ourselves from the unraveling. A hopeful story only emerges within the unraveling and the lamentation, not in strategies of fix, escape, or return.

Practices: Embracing God's Agency in Dark Times

If Israel was to reorient its life around God's agency, it would need to let go of imperial dreams. It would need to dwell in what seemed the most godforsaken of places. This was a terrible, disorienting, and counterintuitive invitation. It would undermine her whole understanding of who they were as a people and what God was doing in the world. To recover her identity in God's story, Israel had to take certain actions. First, remain in Babylon rather than return to Jerusalem. Nothing about that decision could have made sense. It stood against all her convictions. Everything screamed that they should escape Babylon. Second, she needed to take on specific practices for living in Babylon. These practices are outlined in Jeremiah 29. Their origins are in the Deuteronomic codes of covenant formation and in Israel's originating story of God's acting—the exodus. Exodus, desert, and Covenant undergird these Jeremiah 29 practices. They were to be the basis for living faithfully in dark times.

Jeremiah is replete with references to Deuteronomy, the text of covenant. The prophet lifts up the story of Josiah's discovery of the Deuteronomic texts that lay out covenant practices. Herein lies that other story that could reorient Israel in her collapse. Dwelling in these practices, Israel could rediscover her story and see what God was doing beyond exile. Jeremiah 29 summarizes what was involved. It comes in the form of a letter from God to the exiles as they debate their options. Some (Jeremiah and his community) offered an anxiety-producing option: submit to Babylon and enter an uncontrollable situation as the basis for discerning God's purposes. The pro-Egyptian elites in Jerusalem and Babylon advocated the opposite: alliance with Egypt and revolt against Babylon to control the power balance. This was a period of confusion and unrest. Egypt continually stirred up discontent among smaller states that, in turn, thought Egypt's assistance would result in a successful revolt against Babylon. But beneath the geopolitics lay this other struggle around Israel's identity and God's agency.

The Jeremiah 29 letter counters Israel's orthodox strategies. It would have been a letter few wanted to hear. The word of Israel's elite's to the exiles and those left in Jerusalem was that the Babylon situation would soon be fixed and Babylon left behind. A return to normal was ahead. The covenant God would not let Israel's shame persist. The evil Babylon would not prevail. That story told people that their established perceptions of God and what it meant to be God's people were right. Their default story didn't need to change. This focus undergirded the managerial elites, and confirmed the roles of the clergy and its guilds. Jeremiah 29 contradicted this story of nation, contract, management, technique, and power. The exiles had to choose stories. "Jeremiah writes that the exiles had an alternative: turn toward a different interpretation and some basic communal neighbourly practices. In those practices they would enter a new imaginary."[4] For the captives, embracing Yahweh's alternative story involved several things:

First, embracing the reality of a dark time.

This would have been the most difficult, counterintuitive step to take. Recognizing that we are not going to fix a situation but need to reorient our lives around another story is a hard task. It was, for them, a readiness to embrace the grave. They had to die to the hope that they could fix their situation before anything else could happen. Lamentations spells this out in no uncertain terms. The Euro-tribal churches are still not at this place. These churches recognize their perilous state but continue to negotiate ways of fixing and remaking what they have. They still read themselves as dominant, having power and still capable of controlling outcomes. In Babylon, Israel had to lay down these assumptions before they could discern what God was doing. In Jeremiah the determination

4. Branson and Roxburgh, *Leadership, God's Agency and Disruptions*, 96.

to *return* to Jerusalem indicates that this first step was not accepted by a majority of the exiles.

But those who did let go of this desire were banking on God's faithfulness in dark times. What may have made this risk tenable was some sense of responsibility to their ancestors (their grounded normativity) and their children (apocalyptic hope). Settling in Babylon meant that some chose to live in a story different from the official ones of Jerusalem. They opted for a story that began with the words, "My father was a wandering Aramean." It was rooted in a tradition that went back a very long way. This story helped them believe they were part of a great train, a movement of God from before and into the future. It would sustain them in Babylon.

Members of the Euro-tribal churches now have few of these narratives in their bones. The seventy-five-year story has erased such an understanding of what it means to be a people. *Ours is an individualism that throws out tradition as an impediment to progress. Ours is a generation that occludes our children and children's children in favor of the self-actualizing individual in the immediate.*

Second, choosing to see God as the primary agent.

The opening sentences of God's letter to the captives is an invitation for them to make such a choice. Its introduction—" . . . to all the exiles whom I have sent into exile from Jerusalem to Babylon"—makes it clear that this exile is the act of Yahweh, not Nebuchadnezzar (Jeremiah 29:4). The captives had to rightly grasp what had happened to them to know how to respond. If we can't interpret the agency behind our unraveling, we'll never see what's at stake. It will mean we fail to embrace the practices we need. The unraveling of the Euro-tribal churches is a function of their tacitly accepting modernity's wager (see chapter 1) and, therefore, buying wholesale, technocratic forms of leadership that colonize its life. If one believes the situation confronting these churches is primarily about cultural/social dynamics in the realms of politics, economics, race, gender, or the methods of change, then the response will be straightforward—develop new methods, tools, and techniques to manage the situation. If this unraveling has a different source, then an altogether different set of responses will be required. How will the Euro-tribal churches lay down their default tactics and strategies to hear

God in their disruption? Discernment isn't innovation. But discernment has atrophied into technique.

Third, discerning God's actions called for a changed posture toward the Babylonians.

Jeremiah 29 introduces simple but demanding practices. They require a reorientation of Israel's perspective on and attitudes toward the Babylonians. Jeremiah 29 is a call to stop hating the Babylonians and desiring their extinction. Why did Israel hate the Babylonians? The answer is straightforward—the humiliation of slavery. Israel had been rendered as nonhuman chattel living at the whim of the Babylonian gods and, therefore, the Babylonian king. Being made nonpersons rubbed Israel's nose in her most significant story—Egypt and exodus. The deportation left the Israelites free to go about their lives. But this is to miss the point of what Nebuchadnezzar had done to Israel. Exile presented every reason to hate the Babylonians because they had turned Israel back into slaves rather than the free people of God. These texts make it clear that if the captives were to grasp the bigger story of God's intentions for them, they would need to do the unimaginable—dwell in Babylon and love the other who was their enemy. In these practices lay the hope of recovering their identity as God's people.

Fourth, seeking the welfare of the city.

Every instinct in the bones of the captives was to work for the destruction of Babylon. In God's economy, Israel was to seek the welfare of the city. They were given practices for doing this. They would dwell in the city (enter its life, become a part of its people, remain in it). It was a counterintuitive practice for a people formed around hating Babylon. They were to do that not by settling into enclaves of affinity transferred from Jerusalem to Babylon, but by building houses in Babylonian neighborhoods. These actions were about more than wood, brick, and mortar. They involved a fundamental theological orientation of their world. It meant a reimagining of God and themselves as God's people. We cannot take lightly this call to settle and build houses. This is far different territory from neighborhood walks or sitting in coffee shops. It is about being in, with, among, and for the other.[5] It is about identification with the neighborhood as the place of discerning what it means to be God's people. This is clarified in the instructions to plant gardens and have families. Israel is to seek the common good of this godforsaken place.

In these practices Israel would rediscover its identity and vocation. Notice how this alternative story isn't about strategies for fixing their situation or returning to a prior place of success and power. These practices take away the status and power of the Jerusalem elites. They are practices that anticipate a way of living in a dark time.

For Brueggemann, such covenantal practices involved two "crucial and difficult moves, *relinquishment* and *receiving*."[6] *Receiving* has to do with remembering and deciding to embrace the primacy of God's agency; *relinquishment* involves laying down the need to predict, manage, and control. In Babylon, Jerusalem's institutions were no longer viable. Israel's sense of being a privileged people in a privileged place was gone. This had precipitated the crisis. Privilege, certitude, control, and the assumption of sustainable institutions had to be relinquished. Letting go of one's own agency is a terrifying choice. Embracing these practices meant being grounded in God's agency.

The Euro-tribal church and its leaders are called to such a vocation. Jeremiah tells us that this vocation must be rooted in the conviction that God continues to be the primary agent in our world even as the story we have lived in unravels. The prophet proposes the shape this vocation needs to take. We encounter the same themes in the New Testament. There we encounter the young churches confronting an unraveling of their expectations, of the story they so quickly created about how this Jesus movement would work out. These young communities were trying to discern how to be God's people when the stories they'd formed unraveled. Much of this had to do with Jerusalem and Rome.

Luke/Acts—When Our Stories Fail

Jeremiah and Luke—Bookend Stories

Luke/Acts is another window into this question of how God acts among us when we're in a place we've never been before. Luke is addressing

5. Later in this chapter we will discuss the importance of dwelling.

6. Brueggemann, *Hopeful Imagination*, 3.

Christians whose world had been torn apart. This might be an unexpected reading of Luke. Luke/Acts was, in all probability, written between the seventies and late nineties of the first century.[7] This places this two-volume accounting of the expanding mission of the young churches into the catastrophic events of the late first century. In this interpretive context, Luke/Acts is a bookend to Jeremiah. Jeremiah was written out of the catastrophe of 597 BC when Israel was deported to Babylon and Jerusalem laid waste. This unthinkable event was something that supposedly could not happen to the people of God. It undercut so many of their assumptions about who God was, how God was acting in the world, and who Israel was as God's people. Babylon was the theological unraveling of Israel's identity.

Luke/Acts reflects early Christian interpretations of their post-Jerusalem situation. The two volumes were written out of catastrophe. Jerusalem had been burned to the ground, the Temple destroyed and a second, unimaginable exile had come about. Christians could interpret these events through the words of Jesus who had prophesied about the Temple that not one stone would be left standing on another. There was, therefore, already a narrative with which they could make sense of 70 AD. One must not, however, understate the shock these events must have been, not just for Jews but Christians. It would have taken time to reframe the understanding of Christians in relationship to Jerusalem, the temple, and God's chosen people.

The year 70 AD created a second diaspora of both Jews and Christians that was more devastating than the first. Explanatory frameworks about God's purposes and the identity of God's people were desperately needed. The razing of Jerusalem, the massacre of populations, and the dispersal of all Jerusalem's populations would have raised unprecedented questions for both Jews and Christians about their identities and how they would carry on. For Christians, Jerusalem's destruction undercut that first generation's expectations of how God was working in Jesus to bring about the kingdom. The events of 70 AD upended the story this young Christian community had constructed after Jesus' ascension. The dominant assumption of the disciples was expressed in their question to Jesus prior to his being taken up into heaven: "Will you now restore the kingdom to Israel?" (Acts 1:6). In this question lay a whole set of assumptions and expectations. They had a story about how God was forming the

7. There is some debate around the dating of Luke/Acts. Some argue for a dating prior to 70 AD, but on balance a dating somewhere between 70 to 90 AD is commonly accepted.

new community of the resurrected Jesus in Jerusalem and around the temple. At the ascension, Jesus' instructions were to await the Spirit in Jerusalem. At Pentecost, the huge conversions of diaspora Jews congealed into a story about the power and inevitability of Jesus as the fulfillment and completion of God's reign centered in the Holy City.

But 70 AD shattered that story. Suddenly, this young Christian community was confronted with the unimaginable—the dissolution of their story of what God was doing in the world through Jesus and the Spirit. Other factors were at work. As Luke's account in the early chapters of Acts makes clear, the Spirit was already dispersing this Jerusalem community (the dispersion of Christians from Jerusalem through persecution, the initial conversion of gentiles in Antioch, Peter's dream of the clean and unclean animals followed by his encounter with Cornelius and then the Jerusalem Council). By 70 AD small household and synagogue communities of Jesus were spreading around the Mediterranean and Asia Minor. In Roman cities, these communities were confronted with new questions about their identities. They needed to understand such things as their relationship to the synagogues, the extent of accountability to the Law within increasingly gentile contexts, how to deal with the reality of Rome, what rules and forms of authority they would need.

The destruction of Jerusalem and the temple created a situation in which these Christians struggled to interpret what had happened. A big piece of their story had gone wrong. If they could be wrong about critical elements of Jesus' story, what else could they have misunderstood? The crisis of 70 AD required a rethinking of what it meant to be communities of Jesus. It would be difficult to overstate their crisis of identity. Through the words of Jesus and in their own experiences (Peter with Cornelius and Paul with Lydia) they began to form a different explanatory framework around the mission of God for the world.

While new frameworks were debated, immediate questions had to be addressed. With their certainty undermined, how would they know what to do? Having expected the imminent return of Jesus in Jerusalem, where would their confidence now lie? What were these little Christian diasporas, spread around the empire, going to do with influxes of Jewish-Christian refugees from Jerusalem?

Luke constructed a theological response to the Jerusalem crisis and the spreading of God's mission to all the world (Acts 1:8). What became clear was that the Spirit, not the plans of apostles in Jerusalem, was spurring a movement that was becoming more gentile than Jewish. Luke's two volumes addressed the question, *What happened?*, by telling the story of how the Spirit was revealing God's work of reweaving a broken world. Luke/Acts engages the question of identity and of how the church can know its vocation. How would these diaspora Christians know what God was doing in such disruption? Without this knowledge, how could they know who they were? The events of 70 AD and the dispersion from Jerusalem seemed to negate the story they'd accepted and experienced in the early successes in Jerusalem after Pentecost. How were they to interpret the fact that little had turned out as expected? Rome had not bent its knees. Society had not become the kingdom of God. The state was not to be the curator of a Jesus movement. Luke's storytelling invited these Christians to revisit the questions of their identity and practices.

Galilee: In a Disrupted World, Discernment Comes in Unexpected Places

Luke has a number of responses to the question of how we know what God is doing when we find ourselves in a place we've never been before. The early birth narratives are such explanations. While locating the narratives of Jesus' birth squarely within the power and politics of the state and of global power politics, he makes it clear that questions about how and where God is working can't be answered from places of power, whether political, economic, or religious (all blended in together at that time). It is striking that in these initial chapters, answers to the question of how we know what God is doing are being given through stories about the weak, the blind, the old, and women, with no claims on knowledge. It is people living on the edges of civil and political life who receive visitations from God. John the Baptist announced the kingdom in the desert. Established clerisy of Jerusalem had to travel into the desert to hear what John had to say.

The story of the sending of the seventy (or seventy-two) into the towns and villages of Galilee was another example of how Luke addressed this question of knowing what God was doing in the midst of great disruption (Luke 10:1–12). In his accounting of Jesus' journey to the cross, Luke proposed a relocation of Christian life in the context of 70 AD. When writing this story, the downfall of Jerusalem was a recent, traumatic event whose implications were still being felt by these small Christian communities spreading across the Roman world. How would these communities make sense of the Jerusalem catastrophe? What would be the implications for living in Roman towns and cities, among the power of Rome, when they claimed a Jewish rebel as their leader? Luke's response was that the locus of Christian life was not Jerusalem or the temple. The geography of the kingdom had changed. This was a theological earthquake that went to the heart of how Christians can know (what is God doing in the world) and where this Jesus movement was going (eschatology). Luke reframes their understanding of these questions. This Jesus movement would be centered in dispersed communities everywhere; there would be no center, but, like seeds, small communities of Jesus would spring up in all kinds of towns and villages. Such a decentering of Christian life was an unimagined disruption right at the beginning of the movement.

Jerusalem, like Rome and Babylon (or Washington or Moscow or Westminster or Beijing or . . .) represented a center of power. For Luke the answer to the question of what to do in a great disruption isn't located in such places. It is found in towns and villages, in places like Galilee, the mongrel, messy, multiethnic demography where peoples clashed and intersected, where strangers, interlopers, and armies kept disrupting the settled worlds of Jewish people and demanding their loyalties. These are the places where little communities of Jesus discern what God is doing through the Spirit. Where this movement is going (theologically, eschatologically, or, in terms of modern pragmatic functionalism, the strategic outcomes) can only be discerned in these places. The question of what to do in crises isn't addressed from the temple where Jesus' disciples had centered their teaching. What does this say about pulpits, pews, and preaching? Temple rhythm was ill-designed for forming a people in an unraveling. The locus for discovering what God was doing would be households and meal tables in towns and villages. All of this harkens back to what the exiles in Babylon had to painfully discover. In Babylon, households and tables became the new centers of communal and religious life. Rather than established leaders (the Twelve or the clerisy classes), the future was going to be discerned through the *seventy*—nameless men and women without pedigrees; ordinary men and women of the towns and villages. For Luke, Christian communities caught in disruption discern the Spirit not through experts or even the *ordained,* but in ordinary people in their everyday rhythms of work and table.[8]

8. This raises important questions about the current construction and roles of the ordained within the modern church.

Luke 10: Discernment Is About Place and Practices

In response to the post-70 AD crisis, Luke crafts a different story to address questions of *what to do* and *how to know* when confronted with massive disruption. An example of this alternative story is Jesus' instructions to the seventy. They offer a pathway for moving from the Jerusalem story to one discerning what God is doing beyond the assumed centers of action and decision-making.[9] These are the practices Christian communities would need to discern what the Spirit was doing among them. The practices in this passage parallel those of *Jeremiah* 29. Their purpose, in a post-70 AD situation, was to point these dislocated communities to how they discern God's action. They are summarized here:

1. **Rooted in the Local:** In response to the question of what to do when we find ourselves in a place we've never been before, Luke tells a concrete story of Jesus at work. Luke eschews the abstract for the concrete. The Christian story is not about generalized principles based on abstract ideals (love, peace, joy, justice, etc.). Nor is it located in our inner affections and feelings (Schleiermacher's response to the unraveling of the Christian story in the nineteenth century). In disruption, we discern what God is doing only as we are rooted in real, concrete places with real, concrete people. We discern the work of the Spirit among us as we are rooted in the local and with the other.

2. **Formed with and by ordinary people:** Luke locates the continuation of the Jesus story in ordinary people, not elites. He is clear who the primary actors will be. The naming of the seventy, for example, isn't a random number picked from the air as if there are seventy-odd people hanging around Jesus and he just decides to send them out. The seventy recalls Israel's formation in the exodus. Luke 10 is the reconstitution of the elders in the desert. Luke is deliberately reframing the Jesus story in the light of 70 AD. In this post 70-AD era, these elders are, in all likelihood, Galileans. They are unspectacular, ordinary, and, in the parlance of the day, uneducated and unformed people, whom the elites despised, expecting little to nothing from them. (The question at Pentecost concerning the disciples—"Are

9. The great gift of unraveling and disruption, of liminal space, is that the whole notion of "center" (and, therefore, periphery) is exploded. It no longer exists. The anxiety of the clerisy is that they were trained for and developed their habits within the framework of center-periphery.

not all these who are speaking [lowly] Galileans?"—indicates this). Discerning the meaning of 70 AD couldn't be done by the elites of Jerusalem or the temple. The kingdom Jesus inaugurated is rooted in ordinary people. Jesus' reconstituting of Israel is to be among unknown men and women, not the famous or the gurus. This harkens back to Israel's own formation story with Abram and Sarai, a barren woman and an old man, which Luke reenacts in the Elizabeth and Zachariah birth narrative. Dispirited, confused Christian communities could not have missed the point Luke was making—the answers to their questions would not be found amongst established experts or Reverend Doctors. Discerning what God is doing means looking in a radically different direction where we dwell deeply in the local and among ordinary people. As Luke states about the Jerusalem and temple responses to the disciples: "The members of the Council were amazed when they saw the boldness of Peter and John, for they could see that they were ordinary men with no special training in the Scriptures."[10] It is about a bottom-up, outside-in movement of those who, by the standards of their time, are without power or authority (fishermen, carpenters, shepherds, tax collectors, cloth merchants, tent-makers; those who Paul describes as the "offscouring of the world").[11]

3. **From Affinity to the Other:** Luke answers the question of discerning what God is doing when our story fails us by locating his response in Galilee. He is saying something about the geography of knowing in relation to discerning what God is doing. It is likely that the majority of the seventy were Galileans. Jesus is probably sending them into their own towns and villages. An indicator of this is in the specific instructions he gives them. When they enter a town, they are not to stop to greet anyone on the road. This refers to a specific Jewish custom around familial obligations. If you meet a relative on the road, they are obligated to invite you to their household and you are obligated to go for three days and nights. Jesus' instruction to not greet anyone on the road was breaking one of the more basic social obligations and choosing not to get entangled with relatives, suggesting that most of the seventy were Galileans entering into their own towns and villages.

10. Acts 4:13.

11. 1 Cor 1:27–28.

4. **Formed by a Clear Set of Practices:** Jesus' instructions regarding how the seventy were to enter their towns and villages was a way Luke responded to the question of how to know (discern) what God was doing in the upheaval. In Luke, Jesus gives to these disoriented disciple communities a set of practices that echo Jeremiah 29. The instructions are specific practices of common life. God's purposes will be discerned to the extent that these disciples dwell with the households and join with the rhythms of their life. The way forward after 70 AD was to be discovered in local communities. The "do not stop to greet anyone on the road" instruction was a radical, countercultural practice about where and with whom disciples would spend their time. Jesus' practices break social convention and connect these young communities to the exiles in Jeremiah 29. The disciple is pressed from relationships of affinity toward the other; the neighbor rather than like-minded family, friends, or associates. The instructions to "take nothing with you" was about disciples becoming vulnerable and interdependent with the other; learning to *dwell with* more than *doing for*. They were to leave behind their means of self-support to become interdependent with the other, joining the economic and social life of the households in the community.

Discerning what God is doing in the unraveling is addressed by Luke in terms of practices:

1. **Dwelling** rather than camping for a while or raiding to get others into one's camp.
2. **Receiving hospitality** more than giving hospitality—be a guest more than host.
3. **Laying down our power** and control in all situations.
4. **Joining the economies** of the local.

In the biblical narratives we have engaged, what emerges is a pattern of practices that form communities of God's people in discerning how the Spirit is guiding them in disruptive times. It is, however, not only in the biblical narratives that we see these rhythms and practices of Christian formation. They continue to turn up in the unfolding traditions of the church. As examples, we turn next to the early centuries of the church in the context of a failing Rome and the emergence of a new series of disruptive crises remaking society. We look at Benedict and the Celts.

CHAPTER FIVE

Benedict and the Celts

In different ways, Jeremiah and Luke/Acts each address the question of how we discern what God is doing when we're in a place we've never been before. Continuing to reflect on that question, we turn to two stories of how God's reweaving of the world was being worked out in other times of breakdown: Benedict's and the Celts were communities trying to shape Christian life in a crumbled Roman Empire and an emerging West.

St. Benedict and Darkening Times[1]

The period in which Benedict lived is another example of an era in which Christians found themselves in a place they'd never been before. He is a transition figure living between the end of an era and the beginning of another, much darker, time. The glorious light of Rome had dimmed. This darkening of the West created a search for ways of living when long-established societal forms were coming apart. Benedict was born (480 AD) in the midst of this dissolution of the Western Empire. Rome was in a slow moving crash. What was later to become the West was collapsing into a dark time that would last for centuries. This collapse of Roman life, culture, and order, devastated the everyday life of people across a disappearing empire. A central challenge confronting

1. There are a multitude of books about St. Benedict and his Rule as well as the Celts. Within these books are conflicting accounts of how Benedict speaks to our precarious moment. One of the more recent books that informs our writing in this section is Patrick Henry, *Benedict Options*.

Christians was how to remake society in such a desiccated time. It would be Christians, shaped by the gospel, who saw part of their vocation as reimagining society after the "fall."[2]

The awareness of dark times would not have been alien to Christians shaped by Scripture. Much of the desert monasticism of that period involved individuals going into the desert to wage battle with the forces of darkness and, more to the point, encounter the light of Christ. Benedict was familiar with this biblical reading that harkened back to the Prologue of John's Gospel. Christ brings into the darkness the light of God's life and the darkness cannot not confound it. The desert monastics entered the desert to embrace the light of Christ that the darkness of Rome could not confound. This was the world from which Benedict experienced the dissolution of the empire and sensed the darkness descending.

Whether Benedict thoroughly understood what was happening in this dissolution or not (who can fully grasp the unraveling of their own time?), he instinctively recognized that something massive was happening to the Christian lands of the West. Furthermore, he saw that the once powerful institutions of Roman society were no longer providing a way of life for people in that dark time. Equally, he must have realized that the structures and institutions of Christian life formed since Constantine would not sustain or shape Christian life in the dark times ahead.

Benedict would mold an institution within which Christian life could reweave the sparse threads of a frayed society in a descending darkness. This institution was shaped by a set of practices (Benedict's Rule). Together, the institution and the Rule would, over time, contribute immensely to the remaking of a post-Roman West. Benedict formed an experiment in living as God's people in a place they'd never been before.

Benedict's response to the forming of Christian identity when worlds unravel had two sides. On one side was this God-given imagination that was Benedict's genius. On the other (the side that is too easy to miss or ignore) was his awareness that the institutions of Christian life formed within the empire could not carry Christian life forward. Discerning hope in dark times would require other kinds of institutions. *The institutions and practices we have lived in as Christians in the modern West cannot carry us forward in this new dark time.* The forms of religious life embodied in denominations, congregations and clergy guilds have run their course; they cannot carry us into this new dark

2. This was the way St. Augustine framed what was happening to Rome and the empire. It was the label that stuck as a primary Christian interpretive frame.

time. We need other kinds of institutions and leaders. Furthermore, current forms and assumptions of the modern state and its economies are hollowing out so much of the life of the local that they cannot be the forms that address these coming dark times. The vocation before the churches is not that of renewing or fixing the churches but how to form places of hope in the midst of a failed politics and destructive economic imagination. The God of Scripture has an economy, a shalom, a way of life. In the practices of God's story, we form communities of hope. Today, people's lives are determined by the narratives of modern capitalism rather than God's economy. As a result, our social, religious, and political lives have been greatly diminished.

Benedict's institution was not birthed out of nothing, but it did not happen in a well-planned straight line. There was no big conference, study group, or strategic planning process led by professionals and elites. It was the result of quiet experimenting, of trial and error by ordinary people suffering on the ground in disappearing local communities. The story is told of Benedict's experiment in monastic life that had monks trying to poison him. He was wrestling with trial and error, with being misunderstood and making mistakes. He crafted something very old into a new institution. The desert tradition went directly back to Jesus and the Old Testament. When John turned up in the wilderness crying out for repentance and readiness for the light that was coming, the Gospel writers were harkening back to older traditions such as the exodus. From a long tradition, then, Benedict experimented with an institution for the formation of Christian communities that could thrive in dark times ahead and, eventually, reweave the tattered threads of social life. This institution would be the monastery, but it would not be in the desert, out, away from the towns and cities that were about to fall apart. Benedict's imagination was similar to that of Israel in Babylon. In that city, confronted with the ending of their world, Israel had to let go of the institutions of Jerusalem with its temple and the priestly roles built around that centralizing institution. What took their place were other forms (institutions) for being God's people in a strange place.[3]

For Benedict this involved practices of liturgies:

3. The precedent was already present in the form of the synagogue—a decentralized community rooted in the local around which Israel rebuilt its common life after Babylon.

- the keeping of the "Hours" centered around Scripture and prayer,[4]
- the household (which meant how people worked together for the common good),
- and the meal table.

These became new centers of life. But even more than these practices and rhythms was the locating of these monastic communities among the people in their fragile communities. This would be a different kind of monasticism. For Benedict the breakdown of societal order called for such a remaking. Something similar to household, synagogue, and monastery needs to happen in our time if we are to address the crisis confronting both Christian life and our society. Our structures of congregational and denominational life were designed for a time that has all but passed. Millions of pounds and dollars are still being spent trying to resuscitate these structures. But they can't sustain God's people in this place we've never been before. These structures:

- Are proving themselves incapable of reweaving the torn life of our societies within market capitalism and the modern state.
- Were formed for a society of middle-class, self-referenced, autonomous individuals who have dominated the modern West over the past century.
- Are not capable of reordering God's people for the dark night ahead.
- The leadership roles created to sustain these institutions (congregation and denomination) are no longer capable of forming God's people in this place we've never been before. The professionalized clergy invented after World War II and given substance in seminaries were not formed for these in-between times.

Benedict understood these things about his own time. He risked an experiment in new institutional forms for making locally based pilgrims in a dark time.

4. See, for example, https://www.newarkabbey.org/spirituality/the-liturgy-of-the-hours.

Crisis Requires Dwelling and Discerning, Not Strategy and Innovation

The language of *dark ages* evokes another time. It is a pejorative, modern myth proposing that the bright lights of Graeco-Roman culture were extinguished as a Christian-made dark age descended upon the West from the fifth century until the Renaissance and Enlightenment. That myth with its arrogance was a simplistic way of dismissing how Christianity brought light and hope after the retreat of Rome. It is true that in the fifth century a dark time descended over the West as Rome retreated into an ever smaller center around the imperial city. Into this vacuum flowed tribal groups from the north and the east, accelerating the unraveling of society and the emergence of a precarious world none had expected or seen before. It would be small clusters of Christian communities spread across this crumbled West that would reweave the shattered fibers of social life and birth an amazing period of art and writing.[5]

At the beginning of our own new millennium the American urbanologist, Jane Jacobs, wrote *Dark Ages Ahead* (2004).[6] Her insights were perceptive. She foresaw the deformities the machine age was creating and anticipated the coming of our own dark times. As we confront the unraveling of our environment, our economies, our churches, and society itself, we confront a precariousness for which our established, professionalized class of leaders with their methods and tools are woefully inadequate. The past seventy-five years promised prosperity and progress; but, what we have been bequeathed is a precarious world.[7]

In asking about a different story for our time, Jeremiah and Luke/Acts show us how God formed a people in their unravelings. With Benedict, we see how other Christian communities responded to the unraveling of their world in the fifth and sixth centuries. Contrary to common myths, Christians brought a hopeful imagination that witnessed to another story. What they did will surprise a culture saturated with the narratives of technique, control, and method. Our churches reflect the practices of a society that prioritizes human agency and has little desire to imagine how God is the Agent in our world.

Rome's withdrawals shattered social cohesion, making irrelevant the governance, roles, and leadership that had undergirded its

5. Holland, *Dominion*.

6. Jacobs, *Dark Ages Ahead*.

7. See Brindle, *New Dark Age Technology and the End of the Future*.

long-established institutions. They became incapable of addressing the new situation. The social, cultural, and economic implications of Rome's retreat were most devastating to ordinary people in disintegrating towns and villages. Elites and common people alike found themselves in diminished situations that could not be fixed from within the narrative of the imperium. There would be no easy solutions for addressing this social disintegration. It would take several hundred years to live into other ways of living that could remake the torn social fabric. This is what the ending of an era involves. It implicated everyone and was devastating, rewriting the order of things and precipitating a dark time. It was in this space that some Christians, like Benedict, formed institutions and structures to build communities of hope and remake their world.

For those small, dispersed bands of Christians there were few obvious maps. But there were stories to attend to in Scripture and everyday practices to guide their discernment. From the fifth and stretching into the tenth century there gradually emerged a period of immense creativity. A focal space for this reweaving of the social ecology were the monasteries, especially those formed around Benedict's Rule.

Responding to a Dark Time

The challenges of engaging an unraveling social order and retaining our humanity are immense. The quest to find a way for living that offers hope is an urgent one. We are entering a liminal time that may last for several generations. In his dark time, Benedict created a Rule to shape a way of life for the institution he was creating. The Rule would form a common life that opened the possibility of another future. Alasdair MacIntrye put it well in *After Virtue*:

> A crucial turning point in that earlier history occurred when men and women of good will turned aside from the task of shoring up the *imperium* and ceased to identify a continuum of civility and moral community with the maintenance of that *imperium*. What they set themselves to achieve instead—often not recognizing fully what they were doing—was the construction of new forms of community within which the moral life . . . might survive from the coming ages of barbarism and darkness.[8]

8. MacIntrye, *After Virtue*, 263.

Here are themes that move from Jeremiah, through Luke/Acts to Benedict. Whether Israel in Babylon, or early Christian communities after 70 AD or Benedict after Rome—each formed local communities of practice within the rubble of a failed story. These communities were not trying to sustain the imperium (whether Babylon, Jerusalem, Rome, or the modern state with its market capitalism). The *pax* Rome offered could not live with the shalom of the kingdom. These little communities could not be God's people and be shaped by the narratives of an imperium. Benedict's monasteries and Rule were ways of addressing it.

We know Benedict (c 480-547) through his Rule and the history of his life written by Gregory the Great (c 540–604). Benedict lived in Italy as the imperium was coming apart. An age of anxiety had been shaking Rome's identity for a long time.[9] Even then there was speculation about the causes of what Augustine called a *fall*. The standard argument was that the embracing of Christianity, a religion of the poor, slave, and weak that disregarded the gods of Rome, was the source of this fall.[10] For E. R. Dodds the most potent factor in this age of anxiety was that people had stepped aside from any sense of a common good.[11] They had lost confidence in the politics of everyday life and turned in on themselves. With this turning inwards, there were religious movements that turned aside from the material and the everyday into a spirituality of abstract ideals and the infinite. Attendant with this anti-materialist anxiety came a hedonism that Christians reacted to in their move into the desert practice of a solitary Christian life.

For three centuries Rome (249–604) was continually fighting or negotiating to keep the Goths and Greeks at bay. Benedict was cognizant of these tensions as well as the libidinous way of life that occupied the upper classes and filtered into all the other classes. He chose, early on, to leave the city for a life in the caves like many others. But his vocation would take another trajectory.

Pope Gregory the Great (540–604) was himself a descendent of Roman nobles. He lived in Rome some hundred years after Benedict, amid its continued unraveling. As pope, he was preoccupied with questions of stability, order, and the identity of Christian faith in society-wide disruptions. How should Christians live as God's people in a changing era? By the time Gregory became pope, all pretense of a glorious

9. Dodds, *Pagan and Christian in an Age of Anxiety.*

10. Augustine's *City of God* was a direct engagement with this prevailing position.

11. Dodds, *Pagan and Christian in an Age of Anxiety.*

Rome was gone. The city remained important but it was no longer the imperial city it had once been. Its future would be continued diminution. It was an era characterized by widespread capitulation of church leaders and institutions to Roman society's intermixture of paganism and Christianity. Reactions to this loss of Christian identity had led to desert monasticism. It was ascetic and solitary, shaped by heroic monks living with severe rules. This reaction to Rome's excesses resulted in a division between the material and spiritual worlds. These monastics had huge appeal as a world-denying, solitary spirituality in an age of anxiety. Gregory's challenge, however, was how to renew Christian life in a failing society. Rome lay in the past; it was unclear what lay ahead. There were tensions between the material and spiritual, as well as culture-wide anxieties about survival, good and evil, judgement and a dark world. How would Christians address these tensions? Benedict's institution and his Rule would play a significant role in shaping a response.

Benedict's Rule

For Gregory, Benedict's Rule offered a way to address the question of how to live hopefully in a time of unraveling:

> His "rule" for which he's famous, a slim book describing how to live the best monastic life, is just one of many such attempts to create a pathway for an individual to dedicate their life to God, but what made Benedict's rule different was its emphasis on merging the individual with the collective, on taking the ascetic practices of the solitary monks of the eastern Mediterranean and then forming a single corporate identity in which the community would progress . . .[12]

Gregory seized on Benedict's imagination in the Rule to shape his own reforms of the church. His *Regula Pastoralis* was his way of doing that. Peter Brown puts it this way:

> Gregory knew the *Regula*, the *Rule*, of Benedict and wrote the only account that we have of Benedict's life. Yet Benedict was not close to him. He was a figure of the now-distant past. He had died around 547. Benedict's monastery at Monte Casino

12. Gabriele and Perry, *Bright Ages*, 58. Note: what has to be carefully balanced here is the language of the individual. Those living in Benedict's time did not have the sense of individuality that is so strongly embedded in modern societies.

> no longer existed. It had been sacked by the Lombard war band of Duke Zotto. The story of Benedict's life came to Gregory, like the ghostly bells of a sunken city, from a world before the furious impact of the Lombards. But this didn't matter. In Gregory's opinion, to read Benedict's *Regula* was to seize the essence of the man.[13]

It is easy to romanticize Benedict, especially when we're so fearful of what is being lost and are searching for some anchor for stability. There are things about Benedict's monasticism that would not, and probably should not, be carried over into our era. The ordering of monastic life was intensely regimented, in terms of the ways monks were thrown together and the rules of obedience put around them. Even at the beginning, there was resentment. But there is much in Benedict's Rule that can provide us with insight into how to form Christian identity in our unraveling. It's important to remember Benedict was forming a community, a school for beginners, in an era of change he'd never experienced before. These monastics were *beginners*. His Rule was, deliberately, a school for beginners searching for direction at the end of an era. The Rule was a practical guide in how to live daily life as God's people.

We won't address our disruptive time through current forms of congregational and denominational life. Some form of a "monastery" shaped by a rule has to take the place of these associational, contractual social structures. Our current forms of clergy, trained to manage branch plant associations of expressive individuals, need to be replaced by something like Benedict's "abbot" or "abbess." As MacIntrye wrote in a famous quote:

> What matters at this stage is the construction of local forms of community within which civility and the intellectual and moral life can be sustained through the new dark ages which are already upon us. And if the tradition of the virtues was able to survive the horrors of the last dark ages, we are not entirely without grounds for hope. This time however the barbarians are not waiting beyond the frontiers; they have already been governing us for quite some time. And it is our lack of consciousness of this that constitutes part of our predicament. We are waiting not for a Godot, but for another—doubtless very different—St. Benedict.[14]

13. Brown, *Rise of Western Christendom*, 210.
14. MacIntyre, *After Virtue*, 244–45.

Benedict's institution and Rule build on directions already identified in Jeremiah and Luke/Acts. Taken together, they address the question of how to shape Christian life in the midst of societal disruption. In the Rule, Benedict offers a realism around how Christians should address our unraveling.

First, it offers a way of shaping Christian life that is available to ordinary people over against the elitism of so much current "spirituality." Benedict understood that asceticism, while admired by many, was the way of the few with no real sustainability relative to the challenges confronting fifth- and sixth-century Europe.

Second, it embodied a way of life that could sustain communities through dark times. Its practices made possible the formation of anticipatory communities of Jesus. Formed eucharistically around work and prayer and rooted in local life, these communities may not have grasped their significance, but these little structures of Christian life (originally there were no more than fifteen to thirty members in each) were the engines for the emergence of a different world.

Third, its structures provided a way of forming communities in a dissolving society. Part of Benedict's genius was how he saw that an alternative to the empire had to involve a common, local life rooted in communities. This parallels Jeremiah's instructions to the exiles to settle in the place where they were and, in that place, build a community among the people. It parallels Luke's instructions to the seventy. They would address the post-70 AD situation to the extent they dwelt in the local. The Rule expresses this in its instructions about stability. Benedict would have seen the upshot of the disruptions undoing societies across the old Roman world. The instability and economic implosions resulted in flows of rootless people crisscrossing each other in search for some place of security. There had existed within the old Roman order thousands of towns and cities that acted as centers of civilization, commerce, learning, artisanship, and a solidarity of common life. The collapse of this order was devastating. A world needed to be reimagined that could address the disintegration that ensued. For such a reimagining would require communities of people living in stability with each other and their context. Benedict knew that in every one of us lies the belief that the grass is greener somewhere else. Like a good abbot, he knew there could be no reweaving of life, no discerning of God's movements, without stability. What a powerful word in our darkening moment! We are societies uprooted from place, where people have lost much sense of their interdependence; they're feeling alone and cast adrift. The singer-songwriter Carole King, put voice to our situation in these words: "So far away. Doesn't anybody stay in one place anymore? . . . I sure hope the road don't come to own me."[15]

Fourth, written against the backdrop of eremitic monasticism (the spiritual formation of monks seeking a life with God by living alone within a set of harsh practices), Benedict invited ordinary people into a common life around work, table, Scripture, prayer, and common practices. This common life was not to be out in the desert but around the devolving centers of social life and power. A deeply entrenched material/spiritual distinction was broken down. This common life was expressed through rhythms of work and prayer that were woven into the same cloth. Rhythms of belonging, stability, work, and prayer were the basic ways of witnessing to Jesus' reweaving the life of a broken society. The community was the witness. What is fascinating to think about for our own moment is that, originally, Benedict's communities were small and composed of what we call *lay* people. They were composed of around thirty to forty monks with their abbot/abbess. What sustained them was their common life, their rhythms of prayer and work. They were not congregations built around a paid professional clergy. That model could not have sustained the kinds of communities needed as witnesses to the kingdom in a broken, unraveling world. They were more like the ancient household, which was made up of extended economic groups of relatives and others built around work and practices. Such a change of imagination could have huge implications for us, as it has become increasingly clear that current forms of congregations with their paid professional clergy are unsustainable. Our own unraveling points us to locally based communities gathered around practices and table, shaped by an abbot (who very likely will not be full-time). We are at a tipping point where full-time, professional clergy are about to disappear.

Fifth, the first word of the Rule is *harken*—listen. The word is about one of the most critical elements constituting this other story of how God meets us in a world that no longer works. Harken takes us back to the

15. Carole King, *Tapestry*, 1971.

original question asked in each of these stories: in a time when our stories have been dissolved and our understanding of our life as God's people is unraveling, how can we know what God is doing? Part of Benedict's response is in this first instruction. These were to be communities of listening and discernment. At the core of their life was the practice of communally listening to the Spirit, which could only happen as people were dwelling with one another and in the community where they were located. Right at the gateway to a dark age Benedict made dwelling, listening, and discerning central practices of his communities across a crumbling West. He seemed to grasp that in the dark times ahead, Christians weren't going to quickly solve/fix things, but they would need ways of being encountered by God. It was in dwelling and discernment shaped by listening that a hopeful future would emerge.

A central element in this dwelling and discerning was *lectio divina*—the communal act of listening with one another through Scripture to what God was saying to them. *Lectio* has a pattern and rules but, above all else, is about how a community hears the Spirit through one another. It was nothing like the approach to Scripture that emerged after the sixteenth-century reformations. Here Scripture was interpreted through professional clergy. In Benedict's communities, *lectio* was carried out in the midst of the rhythms of dwelling (communal life and work) with one another in stability. This long-term practice of listening to God through Scripture enabled them to learn how to discern the Spirit in uncertain times. This form of lectio became a central practice in discerning ways of reweaving a common life. It drew a community into communion with the One who was *making all things new.* Through this Benedict formed communities whose practices in dark times were being formed in everyday practices of discernment. Benedict had seemed to realize that hope emerges from the communal reading of Scripture far more than from professional and expert teachers. We will say more about this later in the book.

We are asking about the story we need to live into at the beginning of another dark time. We wonder what to do as God's people and as leaders as we enter this time of precarity and unraveling. The Spirit makes all things new through a communal embracing of practices—the small, slow, hesitant act of dwelling/listening/discerning as we confront a time we cannot change or wish away with pious platitudes, new methods, or the rationalization of our existing institutions with strategies to fix them.

Celtic Saints: Discerning God's Story in a World of Action

Another example of Christians confronted with a disruptive world was the Celts. Celtic Christianity was forged on the anvil of change. Along the fringes of a collapsing empire, Celtic Christians shaped ways of being God's people among the pagan cultures of Ireland. Their forms of Christianity took root and flourished in the midst of cultural disruptions. While Rome never annexed Ireland into its empire, its influence was present through commerce and religion. Rome's retreat did not directly affect the Irish and its religious influences had little influence in peripheral places like Ireland. Ireland saw a unique blossoming of Christianity. Celtic Christianity did not keep this faith to itself but turned it into a missionary movement. Through these missionaries, the light of Christ spread back across a darkening Europe. Celtic Christianity gave expression to a culture and way of living that was in many respects closer to the early church than many of the ways Christianity had been institutionalized in the Roman Empire. A form of Christianity emerged that was not shaped by a centralized uniformity and conformity. Planted at the margins of the empire was an imaginative way of living out the faith in times of change. Its brilliance was that it did not try to abolish the cultures in which it dwelt nor impose strictures over societies. Rather, it embraced and, where appropriate, celebrated and redeemed those aspects of culture alien to central Christian virtues.

A creative wisdom in the forms and practices of Celtic Christianity speaks directly into our unraveling. Like Benedict's, their response to being in a place of unraveling was the formation of a monasticism around a common life that could navigate the uncertainties of a world that had come apart. The Celts open windows into how we can shape Christian life in our darkening time. Here are some indicators of the ways they formed Christian life in their disruptive times.

1. Materiality

First, it was rooted in the material, in the basic earthiness of creation, in the rhythms of the everyday, and in a conviction about the importance of a common life. It was, for example, a Christian way of life formed around the rhythms of the seasons with their shades of darkness and light, birth and death, creation and re-creation. Often living close to the waters, the ebb and flow of the tides shaped these rhythms. The waters communicated to them that there were journeys to take with the tide as they went out on missions guided by the winds. Just as much, there were inward journeys to take in the rhythms of prayer and daily office. Prayer engaged heart and mind, words and feelings, images and symbols, giving room for intuition and encouraging imagination. These forms of Christian life now seem quaint and strange, at odds with our digital lives shaped as they are around media and event—distanced from ordinary, grounded local life and the rhythms of seasons. This being grounded in the rhythms of the earth was the glue that bound them together, giving them hope and sustenance on a journey beyond the familiar into the unknown and unpredictable.

2. **Peregrinatio**

A second element of their Christianity is expressed in the word *peregrinatio*—it means journey. It was this language that gave Celts the ability to embrace their disruptions not as crisis or calamity, but as the means of journeying with the Spirit out from zones of comfort and predictability. *Peregrinatio* was the invitation to adventure, to wandering. It was a word with affinities to language like exile, displacement, and exploration. Abram's story was paradigmatic for shaping the life of these communities. He was invited by God onto a journey from his known, familiar, predictable world into an unknown future. In this *peregrinatio,* the only certainty was that of trust in God. Abram's imagination resonated with the Celts. It helped them understand that their precarious times were precisely the places in which the Spirit would guide them into God's future.

Peregrinatio was rooted in another of the Celt's convictions about how to live as God's people in troubled times. They believed their relationship with God and one another was covenantal. Covenant was about relationships of commitment to one another. It was about choosing to dwell in place together believing that God was the One shaping their common life. Their relationships were not the associative, transactional relationships that pervade Euro-tribal churches. Pilgrimage was a common way of life for the Celts. This wandering, to which God had called them, was for the love of Christ. The characteristic of Euro-tribal churches is like that of a gentry atop a pyramid or at the center of a circle (hence their colonizing). Gentry assume place, role, privilege, whereas travelers receive from the other, as guests. Our leaders are more like managers and caregivers of settled communities. The forms of life we create make us insular and vulnerable in a disruptive unraveling.

3. Paradox

A third characteristic of Celtic Christianity lay in how they wove the threads of life's paradoxes into a rich tapestry that became a way of living in the everyday. These Christians were at home with paradox and mystery. This way of life encompassed, for example, the paradoxes of stability and movement. They experienced God as immanent and transcendent—in nature and the everyday and yet also as holy, high, and exalted, as Redeemer. God is at home with us in our daily life, yet God also calls us to pilgrimages where we step out beyond the bounds of our security and control. The realm of the Spirit is close at hand, continually touching our world in many ways and yet can't be reduced to the created order. Their Christianity was both monastic and missional, chaotic and creative, simple and ordered, down to earth yet open to transcendence and mystery. Here was a Christian life opened toward the supernatural while rooted in the ordinary and everyday.

4. A deep connection and appreciation of ordinary life

A fourth characteristic was a deep connection to and appreciation of ordinary life. The Celts believed God's kingdom was found in the present. This might be expressed in the belief that God is found where we *touch grass* (a meme some are using to call us out of virtual reality and reconnect with the material) rather than virtual worlds of disembodied ideals and identities. The Celts believed that God was actively present in the everyday. Christian life was about attending, listening, and discerning what Jesus was doing on the ground, in the community, in the everyday. This is a far cry from the *believing* of most Euro-tribal Christians today. The Celtic focus on the interior life, the "landscape of the heart," gave expression to a faith that had connections to time and place, recognizing the elements of earth, wind, fire, and water. For the Celts, creation wasn't a process God began and occasionally intervenes in. Creation was God's and God was continuously at work in it. This conviction pressed them into a relationship in which the whole cosmos, at every point, was dependent on the self-giving God whose nature is love and who calls us into community and relatedness. In such a robust, holistic spirituality, there was no sacred and secular divide. This broad comprehension of God's engagement with the world helped the Celts to thrive in the difficult times that came with Rome's retreat.

5. **Reality of God's presence in the world**

Fifth, Carl Jung observed that the rational humanisms of the modern West dismissed what it deemed primitive religion and, therefore, lost touch with the primal and universal in being human. This is part of what makes us so ill-equipped to confront the unraveling. We've dismissed God from the stage and, most of the time, are completely unaware that we have done this. The belief in God's active presence with and for us finds its replacements in such abstract ideas as progress, the state, the individual, and the market. Now, however, we are awakening to the ways in which these replacement ideals are failed realities. The pieties and certainties of the modern order have been breached, leaving us without an alternative story. We are ill-prepared for what lies ahead. The fantasy that technology and management will create a new world without God is being shattered before our eyes. At the center of the Celtic vision was the conviction that God was present and active in their world.

The rhythms of Celtic spirituality were shaped around this conviction that God was present in their communal and inner lives. Creation was the stage for the sacred. For the Celts, the earth we inhabit is where our human longing for connectedness, community, and interdependence are worked out. This was God's world and God was active. The modern progress story is the opposite of this that has produced a soulless society cut off from the reality of God's presence. A burgeoning interest in spirituality, without a return to church, suggests our hunger is a disenchantment with the barrenness of secularism.

6. **Orientation to the relational**

Sixth, their way of life was founded upon the monastic "one thing necessary." This one thing, set into their practice, was to seek God and love their neighbor. This orientation was hospitable in its DNA and welcoming in its expression. It was shaped by kinship and companionship that shunned party factions and tribal spirits. Celtic Saints laid great emphasis on the "anamchara" or soul friend. They valued their families and tribal affiliations. They had systems of fostering and mentoring one another. The primacy of relationality moved them away from the dogmatic structures of power embedded in Roman Christianity.

Their ways of expressing community are seen in the forming of the clachan settlements. The religious and secular, believer and unbeliever, lived side by side. In the enclosures of such communities was the powerful symbol of the open gate and a welcome for the stranger, the traveler. It was a place of refuge for the wounded and sick. While traditional monastic communities were closed, Celtic monastics lived openly among believers and unbelievers.

Celtic Christianity was formed in marginal places but had a deep impact on the towns and cities of Ireland. It was formed more among the outsider, those closely bound to the land, with an awareness of the elemental forces of nature. Faith was formed in the furnace of struggle, dependency, and the vulnerability of the changing seasons. One's identity could not be seen in isolation from one's neighbor.

7. Time was more than chronological or limited (finite and running out), but a sacred gift

Seventh, the Celts were in tune with an understanding of time as *kairos*. For the Greeks this was not so much about linearity as much as the opportune or critical moment. Jesus used this meaning of time when, at the beginning of Mark's Gospel, he came into Galilee after a forty-day desert sojourn with God and the powers to announce: "the time is filled up, the kingdom of God is at hand" (Mark 1:15). For the Celts, this meant the world was pregnant with God's presence so that all things can be made new. This made them into communities of hope shaped by the conviction that their time was a moment that brought the mystery of seeing what God was doing in creation.

This imagination is all but absent in the Euro-tribal churches. The hand-wringing and confusion we see all about us is not about a sense of hopefulness, of participating in God's moment, of the Abram-like adventure to which we're called. What most of us see is loss and an anxious need to shore up the institutional walls.

8. Life as creative imagination

Eighth, connected to this understanding of time was the creativity and genius of their arts, music, poetry, and jewelry. Their illuminating of the Gospels[16] reveals imaginative, highly intelligent people. Schools and libraries were much in evidence. Building upon the foundations of desert monastic wisdom, the Celts imagined how to integrate their faith into the landscape of a disruptive world. The Scriptures were the interpretive lens through which to view the happenings of the world around them.

16. See, for example, *The Book of Kells* (produced around 800 AD).

The Celts had the imagination to dream, envisage, and implement ways of life that reflected God's loving purposes for the world. The ultimate literary source for them were the Gospel stories. Across Ireland can be found ancient stone crosses depicting scenes from the Gospels. The Celtic saints mirrored in their time what Jesus did in his day—healing the sick, feeding the hungry, praying, valuing friendships with both men and women, calming the sea, evidencing miracles of intervention, provision and protection.

9. **Celtic spirituality is deeply incarnational**

Ninth, the notion of presence permeated the Celtic spirit. It involved living with others, worshiping and working as communities alongside and with people. The source of this spirituality was the incarnation. An incarnational posture made the Celts present to people through hospitality, care for the other, listening, peacemaking, and healing.

10. **They were not about extending diocesan structures but planting and expanding communities**

The Celts did not formulate strategies for planting churches. They shared faith and ordered themselves around practices that established monastic communities. They saw the transformation of culture not by imposition but by engagement. In contrast to the monastics who withdrew from society to save their own souls, Celtic monks pursued both godliness and engagement with their world.

11. **Their conceptions of leadership recognized the inherent dangers of power and status**

Mutuality and accountability between abbots and bishops enabled them to have authority without being authoritarian, holding elements of hierarchy without being hierarchical. The distinction between authority and power was recognized. While women were generally excluded from positions of authority in the Roman Empire, women were equal to men in the Celtic church.

Like the Benedictines, a key element of their spirituality was prayerful discernment. In keeping with these monastic traditions, they drew inspiration from John the Beloved. The image of John leaning up on the breast of Jesus in the upper room symbolized a call to listen to the heartbeat of God. Contemplation, listening, and discerning informed their actions. In our time of frenetic activism, large strategies, and programs, which we pray that God might bless, this monastic tradition calls us to first seek God, listening to his heartbeat that we might be directed by his Spirit in living out this good news in our neighborhoods.

The chapters in this section have looked at the question of how God engages God's people when they find themselves in a disruptive place. They have identified practices common to God's people across eras of disruption. We've proposed that the question we must ask in our time is not that of tactics or strategies. It is: *How has God engaged communities of God's people when they found themselves in places of massive disruption?* It is through stories from Scripture and our early traditions that we've sought to address that question. Section Three asks what these practices say to us as we enter a dark time.

SECTION THREE

Practices for Forming Communities of Hope

Section One presented a picture of the unraveling now reshaping Western societies and their churches. It proposed that the response of the churches when confronted by this unraveling is not to turn again to the default question: *What do we do?* Such a tactical question will only keep us colonized by this seventy-five-year story with its promises of fixing things through management, control, outcomes, and predictions. This story has broken down.

Section Two proposed a different starting point with a different question. It turned to Scripture and tradition to address the question of how God has been engaged with God's people in other times of social disintegration. Through an engagement with Jeremiah, Luke/Acts, Benedict, and the Celts, it proposed that there is a common set of practices running through the experiences of all these groups. These practices, furthermore, underline a more fundamental posture of Christian life that has, in the modern period, been lost or reduced to some form of inner, personal, spiritual experience of God. What has been largely evacuated from the discourse and practice of these churches is any sense or practice of God as the primary agent in our world.

Section Three turns to the question of what these practices tell us about how Christians might form communities of hope in this time. What does all this mean for leaders of Christian communities now confronting another period of darkness? This section responds by describing three central practices that we must recover as communities of God's people in order to appropriately engage with the mission of God.

These practices have been introduced as dwelling, discerning, and exploring.

CHAPTER SIX

Forming Communities of Hope in Dark Times

Leaders Respond

LEADERS HAVE SEVERAL IMMEDIATE responses when they first engage the seventy-five-year story outlined in chapter 1. For some it is an "aha" moment. They're being given language that makes sense of what they're already feeling but haven't had words to express. Others question details of the story. They want to add their own nuances but, overall, the story makes sense of their experience. Some get the themes being named in this story but suggest its roots go back long before the middle part of the last century. They're right! The roots of this seventy-five-year story are, like a tree system, disparate; they can be traced a long way back through multiple systems and centuries. While well aware of this broader history, we want to focus attention on what has been happening to the Euro-tribal churches over the past seventy-five years—since the end of World War II. Some, however, don't believe the situation is as critical as we have described it. They see a lot of room for current systems and methods to make a difference.

This unraveling has unique characteristics on each side of the Atlantic. For Europe and the UK, it started many, many years before it was experienced in North America. There is, consequently, less anxiety and hand-wringing in the UK and Europe about the crises and the fact of their displacement in the culture. This is because they have been unraveling for a long time. What we have described in the first several chapters can be described as old hat for those who understand the history of the churches in the UK and Europe through the long twentieth century. Much of the church's attention in Europe and the UK has focused on trying to come to terms with their unraveling. In North America it still feels very new and critical, driving continued attempts to fix the situation.

At the end of this seventy-five-year story, we are presenting a framework within which to have a conversation about where we find ourselves. Some church leaders, on hearing this story, are overwhelmed; for others this is no longer news, but the fact of their situation. Feeling overwhelmed is a normal response to crises. For the deported elites of Israel, their being overwhelmed was expressed in the lament: How to sing the Lord's song in a strange land? Implicit in that question is an immobilizing fear that we can no longer sing the Lord's song. A lot of leaders are experiencing this lament firsthand. The seventy-five-year story gave them tools and methods to successfully manage their world, but these tools and skills are no longer working for most leaders.

Others have a strong resistance to the notion that contemporary or traditional leadership frames and skills are out of touch with what's happening in the unraveling. This seems too stark, too critical in terms of their own identities. Because our desires have been formed by this seventy-five-year story of success and progress, we resist suggestions that it has stopped working.[1] Some, finally, are not sure what all the fuss is about. They can plant and grow churches as easily as ever; it's all working, where's the problem? Reactions to the assessments we have offered are varied.

Being God's People in a Dark Time

Our original question was: *How do we form communities of hope when we find ourselves in a place we've never been before?* This question must now be restated in a more urgent way: *As we confront cascading crises across so many fronts, what does it mean for God's people to form communities of hope?* The default of fixing our institutions is so powerful that the originating question can leave us inside a reassuring world of our own agency where we are continually chasing new tactics for putting the church back

1. This issue of desire and resistance will be addressed in terms of the practices introduced later in this chapter. René Girard addressed this kind of resistance through his notion of mimetic desire, which accounts for the pervasive resistance people have to addressing the stories within which they live. See Cayley, ed., *Ideas of René Girard*, and Burgis, *Wanting*.

together. The question can beguile us into imagining that the challenges before us are still about fixing or adjusting our institutions.

This latter question expresses the urgency of our moment for the churches. If the Euro-tribal churches continue to focus on fixing themselves or climbing aboard the latest movements (in times of crises many movements will cry out for our attention), they will become irrelevant. Christians cannot avoid their participation in the unraveling of our social fabric, of the fragile ecologies of common life. Leaders must not trivialize this dissolution of common life and the common good. Neither should we continue to focus on anxious, reductionist strategies for fixing the churches. These defaults of the modern era still shape the approaches of church leaders to this crisis of meaning and identity. Arguments go something like this:

> Yes, we're confronted by the crises of a huge unraveling of the churches. Here's an analysis of what has happened . . . It's a terrible mess. But, in this disruption, God is already planting the seeds of a new future, renewal is just around the corner if we can just design the right tactics (read modernity and notions of progress here). What we have to do is analyse the context and see the seeds (for example, the move from a hierarchical to a network society, joining an organic, networked, globalized world, and so forth) to see what God is doing. Then, we can develop a new kind of organic, networked discipleship, change our forms of leadership and rediscover (renew) the church God intended all along.

Implicit in this oft-repeated narrative is the conviction that we don't have to be stuck in this dark time[2] but, with the right analysis and data, we'll see the trends and map the methods for moving past the unraveling. Such moves are sourced from our own agency, our convictions that we have the smarts, the analysis, and the methods to fix this.

Our proposals move in a different direction. We propose that this unraveling has no fixes. There is no renewal or revival to be operationalized. God has brought us to this place. It's not primarily the result of sociocultural, political-economic forces (they are certainly present),

2. This recognition of a dark time emerging has been named by people like Jane Jacobs (*Dark Ages Ahead*) and, more recently by the well-known leadership guru Margaret Wheatly (see her 1994 bestseller, *Leadership and the New Science)*, who suggests that its too late to rectify past mistakes and that some kind of breakdown is unavoidable. See also Singh, Thompson, and Curran, eds., *Reimagining Leadership on the Commons*, xxiv.

but, as Lamentations makes clear, it is God's judgement on the church's incapacity to live in God's story. This is a shocking claim. It's easier to believe that God's plan for renewal is just around the corner and that with a bit of confession, a lot of data, a mix of strategy and prayer, we'll fix the situation and move forward. We propose this is not the situation into which the Spirit has brought us. We're in a place that cannot be fixed with analysis or data, or even workshops on clergy burnout. Something radically different is required.

When God's people found themselves in massive disruption, what was the Spirit doing among them? The four narratives we examined in Section Two suggested patterns of behavior that, taken together, point to a way of forming communities of hope. In each story, the Spirit was reorienting God's people away from themselves and their own agency to see/remember God as the primary agent in an unraveling world. This reorientation was never to be (although in numerous instances it did become) an invitation for God's people to turn in on themselves, or to turn God into a spiritual resource for their inner life, or create enclaves of the righteous few in a wicked world. The reorientation directed them away from themselves into their communities with a renewed trust in God.

How do we discern God's actions? What does such discernment involve? How does the Spirit encounter us in this epochal unraveling?[3] As we try "to make sense of forces that feel completely out of our hands and beyond our collective control,"[4] the four narratives we've engaged with point to forms of hope and action shaped by the Spirit. That hope is schooled by practices. The coming dark times will require new institutions and practices. Just as the institutions and leadership of Jerusalem were not formed to engage the realities of Babylon, the institutional and leadership forms of the seventy-five-year story cannot carry us forward. We will need to discern institutions that can provide stability and the capacity to risk. The urgency of forming such alternative institutions is apparent in the desiccation of social belonging, the breakdown of the demos, and the increasing number of congregations that are going over the cliff. Rather than nostalgia for some simpler time, this is an awareness of how profound the unraveling is in its effects upon our communities. We have created an environment in which we treat one another as commodities.

3. We address these questions in chapter 8.

4. Moyles, *Lookout*, 297.

People and nature have become:

> fungible objects to be moved about on the basis of maximum return on investment. Its distinctive feature is that the very substance of society is turned into a market, with fluctuating prices setting value on human beings, land and food. This is what we refer to as a market society. It is unsustainable as the organizing principle of society, leading to human and ecological degradation, powerlessness and inequality.[5]

Benedict concluded that a gospel life wasn't possible from within the institutions and structures that had formed him. He left behind the status of the institutions in which he'd been formed as the son of wealthy Roman elites. Initially, he retreated from the world to join the movement of monks and hermits who saw the only hope of being Christian in removing themselves from a corrupted society. This had become a default practice for Christians seeking to live a faithful life with God. Discipleship came to be interpreted as a world-escaping, inner spirituality. Retreat and isolation were a common way of dealing with the anxiety of social implosion. For Benedict, that retreat was not God's way of healing the torn social fabric of a darkening empire. Amidst moral decadence, where political and economic powers vied for ascendancy, Benedict instituted a lay experiment shaped by a Rule that would form communities alongside and within a desiccated society. This is what we need in our own time.

Benedict's experiment would form an alternative institution, a way to a life embodied in gospel practices. These tiny communities were initially lay-based and they would, eventually, transform Western society. In a similar time and in parallel ways, the Celts were forming institutions within which to shape practices of Christian life that would contribute to the remaking of Western societies. The Spirit is calling us to create institutions formed around postures and practices that seek the common good of society and the creation.[6] These are not strategies or methods for turning things around and delivering renewal. They're ways of journeying in darkening times.

5. Glasman, *Blue Labour*, 19.

6. This notion of the common good isn't a nice idea pulled out of nowhere. The common good goes to the heart of Catholic Social Teaching. For a deeper appreciation of this central set of Christian practices see https://ccsww.org/about-us/catholic-social-teaching.

Postures of Hope

> pos·ture: *a particular way of dealing with or considering something; an approach or attitude.* Oxford Languages

The word *posture* makes us think about our bodies. Alan began a new exercise regimen years ago where his trainer started with instructions about changing his posture. Lucy, his trainer, told him to imagine his head attached to a sky hook pulling his neck up from his body. To do this, Alan regularly and awkwardly reminded himself to take on this posture; it wasn't natural for him. After a time, his posture began to change and it stopped feeling awkward. But it was about reorienting lifelong habits. Lucy's point as a trainer was that she couldn't develop healthy practices in Alan's body without first changing his lazy posture. This section proposes some of the postures needed to take on the practicing of Christian life in a dark time.

1. **Attending to established defaults and obstacles to Christian postures**

- Being aware is about paying attention. Benedict's Rule expresses this posture in its opening sentences: *Harken, my son, with the ear of your heart, hear the precepts of your master.* Harkening is paying attention. You will read a lot about this posture throughout the rest of this book. It is so basic and fundamental that little else can be achieved without it. Further chapters will point out the ways our attention as Christians in the West is continually redirected toward technique and our own agency.
- Harkening is about turning towards what's in front of us to notice what it is and ask what it means. It is training our eyes and ears to see the default patterns shaping how we're automatically engaging our world.
- Our culture, for example, reads almost everything individualistically, rather than corporately. We read New Testament texts from this individualist perspective. Our default assumption is that texts are directed to individuals rather than a community.
- We assume experts or professionals have the answers.
- We assume everything that happens is the result of our own agency, that it is self-evident we are in control.

- We have little imagination for considering that God's Spirit is at work in what's happening about us.

These are current examples of postures determining what we attend to and how we interpret our world.

If the big story we've lived in misdirects, then our postures will regularly misinterpret and misdirect how we see the world. If our established methods of working and managing our lives are misdirecting us, then what we harken to will also be misdirected.

When we first recognize the defaults of the seventy-five-year story, it can leave us disoriented, with little sense of what to do. We are, for example, aware of how our driving habits contribute to climate change, but we may not know how to change our patterns of car use. Seeing our default patterns can be overwhelming. Such recognition brings a desire to quickly fix habits and patterns. When that doesn't happen, we get discouraged. Our default postures keep telling us we ought to fix our situation when, in fact, it's not that simple.

Like Israel in Babylon, we're invited to see another way of being God's people. This takes time because it calls for developing a posture of paying attention to what is going on about us. Benedict was aware that this is hard work. This is why he focused attention on the role of the abbot or abbess. These are leaders who gently offer practical directions to the community in seeing with different eyes.

2. **Embracing the reality that we're in a place we've never been before**

The disorientation of Babylon left Israel feeling it was impossible to act. *How do you sing the Lord's song in this place?* The exiles had to come to terms with the reality they were in a place they'd never been before (except for their forefathers and mothers in that other story located in Egypt). Further, they needed to recognize that what had happened to them was more than the result of geopolitics. It involved the hard reality of their own forgetting and failure before God. While a continual stream of people tried to get back to restore Jerusalem, some recognized this catastrophe as their own making. Psalm 137 is a psalm of lament expressing their tragic sense of loss and confusion as well as an awakening to the fact they'd forgotten God's covenant with them.

Israel could not imagine herself in Babylon. It was like asking someone to describe the taste of green. We, too, have anxieties about being in a place we've never been before. Right up to the present moment, too many leaders still can't come to terms with the fact that Christian life as they have known it in congregations is over and can't be fixed. We're now sailing on uncharted seas, subject to unknown currents, driven by winds we can't see. Coming to terms with this is more about our emotional than cognitive state. Seeing no return brings a terrifying feeling of abandonment. We want to believe this awful place can be escaped. Our posture needs to be one of embracing this unraveling, not trying to escape it. Counterintuitive as this sounds, laying down tactics will enable us to discern God's hope.

3. **Making a path as we walk—being open to testing and experimenting**

Our default response to the unraveling is to ask: *What do we do?* Our assumption is that we can figure out what's wrong and construct a new road. On a journey without maps, a counterintuitive posture is required. No Israelite could have imagined that hope involved dwelling in Babylon. No innovative exercise would have got them there. Finding hope in a place we've never been involves a journey that leaves behind the familiar. Abram and Sarai journeyed with no idea where it would lead them. Their hope was in the God who went before them. As we awaken from the deformed story that has defined us, we're in a place where there's no road. What practical actions do we need to take? How do we invite people onto a journey where we have to make the road as we walk together? The Spanish writer Antonio Machado wrote a poem about this hope at the start of the twentieth century. Spain had lost its empire in the Spanish-American War (1898). The loss was devastating for Spain's elites. For hundreds of years their identities had been constructed around their sense of being an empire, of being in control, and being important in the world. It was all suddenly taken away even though it had been years in the making. The result was a crisis of meaning and identity. The majority of Spain's elites lamented, they wanted to build a new movement to restore the empire. One among them felt the loss, but knew there was no restoration. In fact, there was no way forward along those well-trod pathways. Machado's poem expresses the posture for being in such a place:

> Walker, your footsteps
> are the road, and nothing more.
> Walker, there is no road,
> the road is made by walking.

Walking you make the road,
and turning to look behind
you see the path you never
again will step upon.
Walker, there is no road,
only foam trails on the sea.[7]

4. **Reorient our lives around God's agency**

The direction modernity took was that of a secularized rationalism that has no need for the transcendent, for God's agency. The Italian philosopher, Augusto Del Noce (1910–1989), describes this in his book *The Crisis of Modernity*. Carlo Lancelloti, in his introduction to the book, summarizes Noce's assessments of modernity and Marx's influence: "all of Marx's thought is a consistent development of the radical *metaphysical* principle that *freedom requires self-creation*, and thus the rejection of all possible forms of dependence, especially dependence on God."[8] This story is like a compass continually pulling our attention to this secular North Pole. In so doing it renders any sense of God's agency invisible. We dwell in a world with little to no reference to God as Agent. A critical posture of leaders is to reorient our attention to the One who is the Agent of the world.

The Christian story is of God's involvement in the world. We confess in our liturgies that God matters, but our practices of leadership and daily life are void of this agency. Reorienting a common life around the triune God who is acting in the world is an essential work of a gospel community. Such communities participate with Jesus in reweaving the broken threads of human life and the creation. This means joining with the One who is acting in the world. Our participation in the reweaving of political, social, economic, and environmental life comes from a posture directed toward God as Agent.

The Russian Orthodox philosopher Nikolai Feyodorovich Federov declared: "The Holy Trinity is our social programme."[9] Created in the image of the trinitarian God, we are persons in community; we live not as individuals, isolated from one another, but as people in community. Miroslav Volf proposes that the posture of the church needs to be that of:

7. Machado, "Walker, Your Footsteps."

8. Del Noce, *Crisis of Modernity*, xii.

9. Quoted in Fletcher, *Disciplining the Divine*, 98.

> A people whose social action and social practices image the Triune God's coming down in self emptying passion in order to take human beings into the perfect cycle of exchanges in which they give themselves to each other and receive themselves back ever anew in love.[10]

Our being formed for the sake of the world is rooted in a commitment to discerning the agency of the trinitarian God and a posture of shaping our common life around God's Agency. Our question about how we function as God's people can't simply be about the pragmatics of tactics, methods, and strategies. We function as God's people when we come together to ask the question of *what God is doing among us: how do we join with what the Spirit is doing where we dwell?*

In the seventy-five-year story, agency is embedded in autonomous, self-making individuals with the power to predict, design, and manage outcomes. This posture relegates God to brief moments when nothing else seems to work. Henri Nouwen told a story of being a ship's chaplain. The ship was in serious trouble. Nouwen asked the captain if he could pray for the situation. The captain's response was quick and blunt—he had not yet reached that point of desperation, thank you. *God as agent is the Hail Mary of Christian life—when all else fails, pray.* By contrast, hope is birthed in communities that are steadily discerning where and how God is working ahead of them in their communities.

These postures are about how we orient ourselves as communities. They're not meant to be a new burden we lay on ourselves and our people. As little bands of God's people, we are, taken together, such a mix of desires. We long for God, sometimes we want to pick up a backpack and head out onto the road with others. At other times, we just want to be left alone, to stay still, not wanting to hear any more exhortations or new projects. Sometimes, like the liturgies we speak, we long to know the mystery and wonder of God; at other times, not so much. This is where, among us, clay and spirit intermingle, and where God turns up and acts. These postures are not markers against which we measure people to determine if they're true or fully devoted or passionate disciples. There is no room for that kind of abstract, idealistic nonsense on this road. These postures are invitations, they are how, in the muckiness of everyday life, we start a messy journey. What overshadows all of this is love and companionship. It is love that invites us to embrace all my people, not just the

10. Volf, "Trinity Is Our Social Program."

ones that fit our expectations of succeeding. It is only in the midst of such love that we can become companions making a start on the road.

5. Embracing Humility

> I love my fellow travelers on this journey, and I am sad to see the church in disarray. I hope that people return to celebrating the liturgy once the pandemic subsides. But the church is always on the verge of failing, and recognizing this allows for some hope that God, not we, will do something new. As Thomas Merton wrote, "Hope then is a gift. Like life, it is a gift from God, total, unexpected, incomprehensible, undeserved . . . but to meet it, we have to descend into nothingness."
>
> William Cavanaugh, *Christian Century*, "How My Mind Changed," June 16, 2021

What we mean by humility here is somewhat different from the personal humility that's a central part of an individual Christian's approach to life. Unquestionably, the journey into which we are inviting Christian communities in the practices we outline is one that calls for a posture of personal humility. Deciding to shape one's life around these practices will call for a personal laying down of many habits and assumptions that have come to shape life across the West. For example, dwelling with others in our local neighborhoods requires a humble walking with and listening with the neighbor as a way of life. Each of the practices we describe here invites us into a posture of humility.

The humility we want to describe in this section, however, turns our attention in a bit of a different direction. Here, the posture of humility we're trying to get at can be expressed, first, by referencing Albert H. Van Den Heuvel's 1953 book *The Humiliation of the Church.*[11] The two words, *humility* and *humiliation,* come from the same root. They have the same source in the word *houmous*, or earth. In each case, though for different reasons, the words describe that which is low, or close to the ground—rooted in the houmous of the earth, the mud out of which God created human beings.

Van Den Heuvel's book describes the humiliation of the church. As a Dutch theologian, he was describing the situation of the churches in Europe at the midpoint of the twentieth century. This humiliation had to do with a number of movements that had been remaking Europe for

11. Van Den Heuvel, *Humiliation of the Church.*

more than a century. There had been a thorough disestablishment of the churches in which they were inexorably moved from the center to the periphery of society. Everywhere on the continent, churches of all stripes had been diminished.[12] Connected with this was the ever deeper penetration of secularization.[13] These forces combined to create the situation that Van Den Heuval described as the humiliation of the church. These dynamics have been well documented in many books since that time. Europe has been shaped by this humiliation and the unraveling of the churches for a long time. This same humiliation came to North America only gradually and long after it had become a clear reality in Europe. It is now complete in Canada. While one can still find areas where this is not the case, this same humiliation process has established itself across the United States in the once dominant Euro-tribal churches. The reality is, however, that in North America in the second decade of the new millennium, these churches are only just faintly awakening to their humiliation.

Our concern here, in terms of postures, is not to contribute to the analysis of the situation but to ask about the relationship of this humiliation to humility. The loss of place of these churches commenced in North America sometime after World War II. The decentering, however, did not come into the conversations of these churches until the late 1970s to eighties. Over this same period, as awareness of the church's humiliation was slowly emerging following the booms that followed World War II, the seventy-five-year story became the dominant story shaping North America.

The fact that these two dynamics were developing at the same time has had massive implications for our understanding of the unraveling and our practices as churches. Along with the erosion of the church, we are immersed in these powerful narratives of human agency, technique, the power to predict, and the capacity to manage the outcomes we desire. Thus, side by side, these two dynamics are continually interacting

12. Building on Van Den Heuvel's insights, the Canadian theologian Douglas John Hall wrote these words in 1989, just as North American churches were awakening to their own humiliation: "[I]t is pretty obvious to anyone who cares about the church's future that the vast changes which have been occurring in Christendom for nearly two centuries have accelerated since World War II, and that a great question-mark is written over the Christian future—not just the distant future, but the future that is already impinging on the present" (*Future of the Church*, iv).

13. Secularization theories became a central method for explaining this humiliation of the church. In retrospect one wonders if this is, in fact, a satisfactory explanation. A more helpful reading of the situation is found in Cavanaugh, *Migration of the Holy*.

with one another. The increasing anxieties around the church's humiliation are continually filtered through this other, powerful narrative conviction that with the right technique, the right data and methods (innovation, adaptations, agility, and so forth), we can turn the humiliation around. We can fix the situation.

To state the point in another way: the humiliation of the churches brought with it an abandonment of humility. Humility would involve the painful recognition that we, Euro-tribal Christians in North America, have been brought down, all the way down to the mud and dirt of the earth. Our posture, however, has been to refuse to accept this situation because the seventy-five-year story keeps telling us that we are agents with the capacity to manage this situation and the techniques to turn it around. Rather than embracing a humility that sees the humiliation as the place God has brought us, these churches have been on an endless quest for methods and techniques to reverse the humiliation and, therefore, fix the church in relation to its societies.

A radically different posture is needed for this moment. Humility means coming to terms with and embracing the humiliation as a critical step in our being able to listen to what the Spirit is saying to the churches.

The next section looks at the practices that can direct us in this way.

Practices of Hope

The stories we've attended to in Jeremiah, Luke/Acts, Benedict, and the Celts point us to a series of practices that shaped their responses to their unraveling times. These practices are everyday actions in a world that has broken down. We form communities of hope as we live into these practices. Taking on these practices is like moving from the house we've lived in all our lives to one in another location. Initially, they will cause us to feel out of place, no longer at home. The changed geography, architecture, smells, visuals, and people around us will make us feel out of sync. We'll make comparisons between this new situation (not good) and the world we've known (the best). We'll feel awkward, out of place, and, at times, angry. These are natural responses as we adopt new practices.

These realities give leaders pause. We need to understand the kind of oversight and care they need to give to a local community of God's people. Like a wise abbot or abbess, we will invite our people into these practices with great patience. We will gently guide them into tiny steps of engagement, creating spaces where people feel safe and loved. These practices are not about starting a movement; they're about how a community rediscovers hope together. The practices are not goals, strategies, outcomes, or a dashboard for discipleship effectiveness. They're the ways in which an abbot/abbess invites God's people into this making of the road as we walk along it. No leader should present to others an aspirational life that cannot be lived. Benedict's Rule was designed to create schools for beginners. He wanted to form a school for the service of God. What is wonderful about this posture is that of beginners embracing practices that gently called them into a way of life. That is how we want our proposals around practices to be understood, for here is the central work of the leader. Benedict learned to do this by trial and error. He wasn't perfect. At one point his novices tried to poison him. All did not run smoothly.

The practices we are proposing are about some specific forms of church. They're not about a false dichotomy between old and new or tradition and innovation. They're not about style or forms of worship (traditional or contemporary, micro-church or cathedral, high or low liturgy, Orthodox or Evangelical). Our purpose is to name the practices for forming communities of hope in our dark times. The three practices we identify are:

1. Dwelling
2. Discerning
3. Exploring

Each of these three terms expresses an overarching practice within which are different activities. Following this summary of what's involved in each practice are succeeding chapters that offer a detailed description of each practice.

Dwelling

Dwelling is about how we form life together as a community of God's people and with our neighbors. Just as Jesus is described as coming and pitching his tent right beside ours, or, moving right into the neighborhood, this is to be our basic form of life (John 1). This practice is about how we form a Christian community committed to the people and the place where we live. Dwelling is a disruptive practice for those raised in narratives of individualism, self-expression, and the freedom to live unencumbered lives. Dwelling calls us to a different kind of discipleship. There will be little discernment without this dwelling and without discernment we have no idea what God is doing in the unraveling.

Discerning

In a place we've never been before, our first priority is to attend to what God is doing in the place we live so that we can know how to act. This is what we mean by discerning. Rather than defaulting to the usual tactics that leave us primary agents, discerning moves in a different direction.

Discernment is not an easy practice to place at the center of a community's life, especially when people feel disoriented and confused. The desire for a leader or expert to tell us what to do is strong. The default to strategy is deeply embedded in us. Discernment steps away from usual methods of decision-making. It's shaped by the question: *What is God doing here amongst us and in our communities?* Attending to this question is not the work of professional leaders or a select group. It's the work of all the people. Discernment comes from a community that is prayerfully dwelling in Scripture, listening to the stories shaping its life and that of the neighborhood. Within these interconnected relationships, we begin to prayerfully ask what it is that the Spirit is calling us to do amidst the disruption: we become healers of the common good and weavers of the broken world.

Exploring

The seventy-five-year story proposes that its methods will give us certainty. Beneath the details of planning, visioning, collecting data, and defining outcomes is this belief that if done well we can have a level of certainty about outcomes. This default story is mostly about our need to be in control, to make our worlds legible in order to predict and manage our return on investment. By these criteria, Abram and Sarah were fools.

This "certainty" is folly. This is why we need to embrace a different story about how we know what God is doing in the world. In this other story, there are things we can be confident about as God's people. We know God is with us. The Spirit of Jesus is present and at work in the places we dwell. We can trust that Christ is working among us and in our communities. A leader attends to how he/she is assisting their people to turn their attention to these realities. This is done through the normal liturgies, but it is also done through the telling of stories that point to where God is present and at work in people's lives. This regular telling of stories is critical to creating an environment of expectation among our people.

Even as cascading crises beset our world and a new dark time approaches, we are confident that the One who declared *all will be well* is present among us and in our communities. As we dwell with one another, in Scripture, in our neighborhoods, and in our stories, we will begin to detect the outlines of what Jesus is doing and creating. There are no certainties. It is about learning to trust and risk and explore. In this, we build new kinds of muscles—communal ways of hearing the Spirit together.

This is what exploring, experimenting, and testing is about. As we listen with and through one another and in our communities we tentatively begin to say "it seems good to the Lord and one another that we . . ." In this exploration we take small risks to test and see if, perhaps, our hearing guides us into ways the Spirit is at work ahead of us.

Summary

This chapter began with a question *How do we form communities of hope in a place we've never been before?* We've begun to address it in terms of several postures and three practices: dwelling, discerning, and exploring. The following chapters delve into each of these practices. Before turning to that discussion, we address a core need leaders must recognize when embarking on this journey. The seventy-five-year story was built around the ideal of the professional who acted, under most circumstances, alone. The journey we are proposing cannot be taken alone. It requires companions who walk this road together. The next chapter describes those companions who travel with us.

SECTION FOUR

Leading Communities of Hope in Dark Times

CHAPTER SEVEN

Traveling Companions

"No man is an island."—John Donne

A person standing alone can be attacked and defeated, but two can stand back-to-back and conquer. Three are even better, for a triple-braided cord is not easily broken.—Ecclesiastes 4:12

Companionship—one who eats bread with another, one who accompanies another.

Introduction

Forming communities of hope where we've never been before is not a journey we take alone. We were never created to be John Wayne-like leaders but somehow, along the way, we've created a leadership culture around the notion of the powerful individual,[1] the hero who saves the day. It's a terrible lie. The Lone Ranger and John Wayne are part of a powerful,

1. We are well aware that over the past decades a long list of books have been written about this reality. Books and coaching methods on the likes of servant leadership or team leadership have abounded. But, in retrospect, they have remained largely ideational and aspirational. The reflection of too many leaders at local, regional, and national levels continues to be that of soldiering on, mostly alone, as individual leaders. It's not that there's anything wrong with the suggestions offered in these books. What they tend to miss, however, is what we have sought to describe in chapter 1—an overarching story that has shaped and determined our culture for generations. This story runs in the background as the real default system of our societies and, therefore, our churches. These deep-seated patterns of life and leadership carry with them a sense of inevitably—it's just how things are; we can make adjustments but we can't basically change it. This chapter sets the context for how we can move our aspirations into concrete practices.

paradigmatic, self-reliant, destructive myth about the individual that distorts Christian life and leadership.[2] One doesn't need to lift up Ayn Rand or the neoliberal individual to see how destructive this has been to our society, how corrosive to character and community this embracing of the individual has been to us all.[3] Until the modern era, societies never understood themselves as individuals in the way that term has come to shape modern life. John Donne was not only a poet, but also the dean of St. Paul's Cathedral, London, in the seventeenth century. In one of his sermons he spoke the oft-quoted, "No man is an island." Undergirding that sermon was the belief that human beings belong to and are connected to each other. That connection reflects the nature of God and makes for the well-being of a society. It's a story all but lost in our era.

This modern story of individualism is contrary to Christian imagination. That it became the dominant form of leadership for the church says a lot about how the modern story has colonized us. When this individualism was married with market capitalism, it created a deadly cocktail damaging to persons and society. It is a theologically abhorrent mixture. At this moment, far too many church leaders find themselves as individuals, anxious and alone, confronting a place they've never been before. Far too many are discouraged and confused.

A different leadership is needed to form communities of hope. The seventy-five-year story presents itself as reality and therefore unassailable. What's shaped us, just is. This just-isness can make us feel helpless, having to carry on with managing and strategizing as individual leaders. To not be doing, making, or progressing is to fail in our vocation and, therefore, our identity. What is lost in this form of leadership are the arts of waiting, receiving, and belonging with others. This is what is producing so much weariness amongst leaders.

How we address this situation is integrally connected with how we are being accountable with others. We are too often alone in leadership, struggling to hold everything together, fearful that people will find out that we actually don't know what to do or how to plan right now. In an expanding period of social and economic precarity, we see a growing inability in people to make it on their own. We witness, for example, an increase of single parents (usually mothers) dependent on food banks, struggling alone to make ends meet and keep something close to family

2. See Du Mez, *Jesus and John Wayne*.

3. See three books by Richard Sennett: *Fall of Public Man*; *Corrosion of Character*; and *Culture of the New Capitalism*.

afloat amidst the demands of jobs (usually low-paying) and children. We've created a society where people are without the support of others or extended families that once made it possible to manage through hard times. Somewhere along the way, since the end of World War II, our remaking of society around the individual has torn apart the threads of belonging and commitment to one another. We'll never get them back with this individualistic leadership ethos.

The late UK philosopher Mark Fisher, in *Capitalist Realism: Is There No Alternative?*, compared gangster movies between 1971 and 1995. While this perhaps is not the best text for talking about God's people, Fisher makes an important observation. Earlier gangster movies (1970s) were made by the likes of Martin Scorsese and Francis Ford Coppola (*The Godfather* and *Goodfellas*). At the center of these stories are families shaped by codes of obligation and belonging. There were street addresses, houses, big tables around which the family gathered. By the 1990s, Michael Mann's film *Heat* (1995) discarded family, accountability, and belonging in the dustbin. A new set of relationships have taken hold in this post Thatcher-Reagan neoliberal world that promised a new dawn for Britain and America. It was no longer a society, but individuals freed to make themselves. The main character in Mann's film is Neil McCauley. Fisher describes McCauley and the differences between these movies:

> McCauley is no mafia Boss; no puffed up chief perched atop a baroque hierarchy governed by codes as solemn and mysterious as those of the Catholic Church and written in the blood of a thousand feuds. His crew are professionals, hands-on entrepreneur-speculators, crime-technicians, whose credo is the exact opposite of *Costra Nostra* family loyalty. Family ties are unsustainable in these conditions . . . McCauley's crew is held together by the prospect of future revenue, any other bonds are optional extras . . . The arrangements are temporary, pragmatic and lateral—they know they are interchangeable machine parts, that there are no guarantees, that nothing lasts.[4]

"There's no long term!" There's the message of our seventy-five-year story. Such a different story from that of Ruth and Naomi, a story of covenant love, of a belonging that cannot be broken.

> Ruth said, Do not urge me to leave you or turn back from following you; for wherever you go, I will go, and where you

4. Fisher, *Capitalist Realism*, 31.

> lodge, I will lodge. Your people shall be my people, and your God, my God. Where you die, I will die, and there I will be buried. Thus may the Lord do to me, and worse, if anything but death parts you and me.[5]

These changes to who we are as societies came on the tides of neoliberal capitalism with its spellbinding, Mephistophelian promises of a world for all who were ready to uproot in the name of progress and paychecks. This brave new world is now the culture of our churches, our clergy, our denominational systems. What is terrifying is the way more and more of us see this as just the way things are, the way the world works, rather than a deliberately cultivated narrative that bloomed in the late 1970s. For most of us this is the only story we know. It is an inevitability, it is reality, and there are no options. So the Ruth story is quaint, a nostalgic dream of older people, who don't understand this global, connected multiverse. This lack of connection and belonging is killing us. It's created an epidemic of loneliness, making it seem impossible to find the way back to God's story of belonging together.

Loneliness, *Sola Pastora,* and Companions

Loneliness is a crisis across Western societies.[6] Alexis de Tocqueville, the nineteenth-century French social theorist who coined the term *individualism,* argued that individualism and collectivism, as value systems, had to hold one another in check for the best values of each to complement one another for the well-being of society. That tension has broken apart as we opted for the individual.[7] We have produced, in the language of T. S. Eliot, a wasteland in which, as caring pastors, we try to shore up spaces of sanity for our people. But it hasn't worked. Our social structures are broken, our churches, like other institutions, are running as fast they can "patching up the tired and the stressed and the broken so that we can re-engage in the very forms of neoliberal work,

5. Ruth 1:16–17 (NAMSB).

6. From the North American perspective, the literature on this crisis is growing. For one excellent example, see Trish Harrison Warren, "We're in a Loneliness Crisis," *The New York Times,* April 20, 2022.

7. For an excellent theological discussion of this, working with the notions of *separability/distinction* and *situatedness/relation,* see Pally, *Commonwealth and Covenant.*

family and entertainment that made us tired, stressed and broken in the first place."[8] Leaders are lonely.

There is no way out of this without the accompaniment of companions. Whenever we name this for leaders, there is overwhelming agreement. But there is also an impotence around how to act. Our seventy-five-year story has confined us to a narrative where there seems to be no other viable options.

Our training systems became highly effective at preparing leaders to be and to serve individualized, expressive, neoliberal selves. Convinced we had the techniques to make whatever world we want, self-reliance, self-competency, and self-development became the characteristics of effective leaders. Loneliness is the result. The phrase "it's lonely at the top" does not express what we desire but the effects of a culture of the self-made individual, the hero, the alpha, responsible for all things.

The idea that loneliness is the price of achievement that cannot be altered must be challenged. Loneliness among leaders is about a lack of meaningful connections and of accountability rooted in deep relationships. It is driven by a terrible cultural lie—as a leader it's up to me, and no one else, to make something happen. This lie produces continual anxiety around being good enough. It is expressed in how leaders schedule their days, piling on responsibilities and meetings that are exchange of information with little connectivity. This anxious need to fill days with busyness and be seen as indispensable is the outworking of an erosion of identity that gets more destructive without companions.

We can't engage this new space as a *sola pastora* leader and expect different outcomes. The accountability of companions is part of getting perspective when our world is unraveling. Fellow travelers protect one another from getting lost in their own echo chambers. Companions are confidants, not just to listen with us, as important as that is, but to stand alongside us. They bring perspective, discernment, challenge, and support from outside our immediate situation. Companions share honestly what they are seeing in one another. Far more than merely support groups for caring conversations, they're a covenant company holding up one another in the work of forming communities of hope.

8. Garry Deverell, "Wait without Hope," https://uncommonprayers.blogspot.com/2022/11/.

A Covenant Company

Covenant companionship means figuring out together how we form such communities. Companions are directed by the question of how to be attentive to the practices and the actions each needs to take in their contexts. They're regularly connected through rhythms of listening to and questioning one another. They assist each other to discern simple actions each can take in discovering how to walk this road. Such companionship is different from most clergy/pastor groups that are focused on emotional support or strategies with outcomes. While companions do care for one another, that caring is directed to discerning concrete actions and staying accountable. Companions protect one another from blind spots and stubborn defaults, potential threats and attacks. A phrase used by early Methodists and instrumental in the Methodist Revival of the 1700s in England was "watching over one another in love." We need companions who guard our hearts and watch our backs in a covenant company.

In times of unraveling, things hidden get revealed. Continual disruption, the experience of "permacrisis,"[9] can unmask that which we have sought to cover and deny. Crises reveal where our systems of leading aren't working. What we're discovering about the state of our society, our churches, and our leaders makes the need for companionship paramount.

Companionship and the Celtic Tradition

The encouragement of the apostle Paul for those guiding Christ's people was to *keep watch over one another and the whole church.*[10] Ecclesial systems incorporate these words into ordination vows. While their wisdom needs no explanation, denominational systems, outside of formal regulations, have little capacity to cultivate such a way of life. Watching over one another is to safeguard our lives. Right now, most leaders know that if they fall it will be the rules, regulations, and policies that take over; "there will likely be no one there to catch me if I fall—I'm on my own."

The rhythms of life among the Celts nurtured a different way. Individualistic leadership was countered through mutual accountability. Church systems still carry this language in roles like that of the bishop

9. "Permacrisis—an extended period of instability and insecurity, esp. one resulting from a series of catastrophic events." Declared the Collins Dictionary Word of the Year, November 1, 2022. See https://www.bbc.com/news/entertainment-arts-63458467.

10. Acts 20:28 (NIV).

or pastor, but these roles have changed radically in terms of relationships with one another. It is mind-numbing to hear bishops describe how much of their time is consumed in management and administration, in putting out fires or in endless study groups and strategies aimed at fixing decline. There's little room for the companionship and soul-friend accountability that the Celts had with one another. Such companionship doesn't come from denominational strategies, study grants, or seminary programs.

The Celtic tradition placed great emphasis on soul-friendship. "Indeed we each need one special friend, who may be called a friend of the soul. We must open our souls completely to this friend, hiding nothing and revealing everything. And we must allow this friend to assess and judge what he sees."[11] The Celtic Saint Brigid is attributed as saying that anyone without a soul-friend is like a body without a head.

The *anamchara*—"friend of the soul"—is a true friend, a traveling companion. Discerning soul-friends, what we're calling traveling companions, is the way leaders must travel in the unraveling. In such relationships, we rediscover mutual trust and respect, we learn to speak truth in love to one another, which means telling the truth about what's happening to us as leaders in our congregations and contexts.

Traveling companions create relationships where leaders can be honest and understood, without pretense or posturing. Such life-giving relationships provide settings where we're understood and loved, where it's safe to be real, and where it's okay to not be okay. To be at home with another person is a great gift: to have friends where the unconditional love of God is experienced is life-giving, healing, and illuminating. To not have to weigh things up before sharing what's on our hearts, or having to calculate how trustworthy the other person is, liberates a leader. Being with someone who mirrors to us God's unconditional love, whose concern is for one's well-being, awakens a leader's life to the potential and realization of God's loving purposes for their lives. A soul-friend is concerned with the leader's well-being, their relationship with God, themselves and others.

Traveling companions provide appropriate accountability to one another. This much-neglected discipline of accountability has led to innumerable casualties in the lives of leaders and those whom they serve. A common trait of leaders who have fallen prey to the dangers of money, sex, and power (life's major issues) is a lack of companionship

11. Pelagius, *Letters of Pelagius.*

and accountability. Leaders may know many, with their address books full of contacts, associates, and others with whom they are in fellowship, but such lists are no substitute for covenanted relationships of transparency, trust, and accountability.

Such companionable relationships can deliver leaders from the binding sense of obligation from their own and others' expectations. The paralysis of being consciously or unconsciously governed by a sense of "oughtness" is one that many leaders suffer. Traveling companions help one another deepen their self-awareness. True friends help each other recognize those things that they are blind or deaf to, or reluctant to speak about.

The cultivation of traveling companions never replaces the need for a leader to be at home, alone with God. The monastic tradition talks about the "one thing necessary," the seeking of God, alone in the cell. Alone with God, leaders encounter themselves, the landscape of their hearts, their desires, good and bad, and are open to the love and grace of God. Being alone and together are two sides of the same coin. Both speak of companionship with God and others. Perhaps one of the greatest deficiencies when it comes to training leaders is that both these aspects have suffered as professionalism, allied to learning people skills and managing programs, have taken precedence. If leaders are to navigate the challenges of an emerging new context, it is essential that they possess a rootedness and stability in God and help in the formation of companions. Thomas Merton aptly expresses the connection between being alone and together: "The more I become identified with God, the more will I be identified with others."[12]

Companionship is a vehicle for discerning with others the person I need to be as a leader in this new place. It is a matter of the heart and a trust that God will not let our foot slip. Good leadership flows from a life lived well, and we need companions to live life well in disruption. Companions walk with one another in the practices of dwelling, discerning, and exploring. The proposals offered in this book depend on leaders journeying together as companions.

Companions discover how to dwell, discern, and explore with their people. John pastors a well-established congregation in a medium-sized city in the central section of North America. Graduating seminary and being ordained over a decade ago, he's done a good job managing

12. Merton, *New Seeds of Contemplation*, 65.

his program-centered congregation. Over the last several years he sees that, while things appear to be going smoothly, cracks are showing in the story shaping the congregation. It's getting harder to sign people on to programs that once easily attracted them. The narrative of being warm and friendly as a church is wearing thin. COVID presented tough challenges, but John's management and pastoral skills served the congregation well. While some people (especially the seniors who comprise the bulk of the congregation) chose not to return to Sunday services and weekday programs, there are signs of a gradual uptick in attendance (live-streaming of services has created a new online congregation). While giving is drifting downward, it hasn't fallen precipitously. But John is seeing a new kind of dis-ease among some in the congregation. There's nothing clear, but there's now a feeling that things are out of sync and no one knows why or how to name it. People are less clear on where things are going as it becomes evident there isn't going to be a return to the ways things had been just a few years earlier. People don't know what things are going to look like going forward; they're feeling the dis-ease and turning to John for answers.

John, as pastor, struggles with these expectations. He understands why people are turning to him for answers. His training and ordination set him into a role with those expectations. He's always felt he needed to come up with a plan to guide a congregation. But he's no longer convinced that a pastor-managed, program-shaped church will address the disruptions he is seeing all around. He no longer believes that what he'd been taught about leadership can engage the unraveling. But he has no idea how to say these things to the congregation, particularly when they're looking to him for answers. John is wrestling with these tensions. He is experiencing an unraveling of his own identity as a pastor. He wants to lead his people in a different way, but isn't sure they'll buy into the directions he's trying to articulate. He knows the congregation is entering a time in which the established forms of life can't be sustained. Does he articulate this to his people?

Where does John start in a congregation shaped by affinity and attractional programs? He has participated in a Leader Table where he was introduced to the three practices discussed in this book. The practices of dwelling, discerning, and exploring make sense to him. They resonate with instincts that have been fomenting in him for quite awhile. But John is legitimately concerned that the congregation won't get what the practices are about. He fears they won't make sense to a people focused on reversing declining membership and budgets. Dwelling, discerning, and exploring don't connect the dots of growth and finances.

For John an underlying issue is that he doesn't know how to introduce these practices to his people. His question is: "How do I invite my people to step into these practices when they seem so outside people's expectations of church?" He's not clear on what to do when people resist these practices or ask questions he hasn't anticipated. John is aware that he's embarrassed about not having answers for people about why they should take up these practices and how they engage people's expectations of being a congregation. He's the professional who's supposed to know what to do. He's supposed to be a competent leader.

So what did John do? First he engaged these challenges in a companions group. There he was introduced to the practice of dwelling. Dwelling, at first, meant becoming willing to be open with other leaders wrestling with the same questions. Here's a safe space where he isn't alone, where he can risk admitting this "not knowing," and receive the supportive accountability of others. As a companion, John is recognizing he needs to address his own anxieties as much as those of his people. In his community of companions, almost for the first time as a pastor, John is understanding what it means to dwell with others in a place of trust, honesty, and common support. This dwelling is slowly opening his eyes to his own role in the congregation and to the question of how he dwells with his people rather than being the solution-giver or rescuer. Companion conversations are about what's happening in the congregation and in us as leaders, about how we communicate and the practical actions we'll take in forming a community of hope. The next several chapters dig into these three practices.

CHAPTER EIGHT

Dwelling

And I heard a loud voice from the throne, saying, "Behold, the tabernacle of God is among the people, and He will dwell among them, and they shall be His people, and God Himself will be among them."—Revelation 21:3

Introduction

THE FOLLOWING CHAPTERS DEVELOP the three practices of dwelling, discerning, and exploring. These practices emerged from our initial question: "How does God turn up among God's people when they're confronting a time of unraveling?" They propose a different way of leading and being God's people. Rather than focusing on the default question of the seventy-five-year story ("What do we do?"), we propose a way of leading fundamentally different from what Paul Kingsnorth describes as the "machine age."[1]

Dwelling is a core practice for forming communities of hope. Communities of hope dwell with and attend to the stories of the people in their communities. We may agree with the need to form such communities but the question of *how* can feel overwhelming. Dwelling is, in fact, the first response to the question of how. It is a multifaceted practice involving dwelling in Scripture, with one another as God's people, with the people who comprise our neighborhood, and with creation. Dwelling is a core Christian practice because this is the primary way in

1. See "Following Christ in a Machine Age," https://mereorthodoxy.com/following-christ-in-the-machine-age-a-conversation-with-paul-kingsnorth.

which God has covenanted to be with us. This dwelling runs through Jewish Scriptures and is expressed as an eschatological summing up of God's purposes in Christ in John's vision on Patmos—the kingdom's fulfillment is God dwelling among us.

The seventy-five-year story has misdirected the attention of the God's people from this dwelling. Ask people for images that describe their understanding of Christian life and dwelling won't be on the list. And yet, from Genesis to Revelation, dwelling is a key descriptor of God's relationship with us and God's intention through Christ for all creation. Ask the biblical narratives what it is that God does, and the response is that God chooses to dwell with, among, and for the world. In the Jewish Scriptures, God is the One who creates, covenants, delivers, leads, and commands. But the Jewish people confess these actions of God because, above all else, God is the One who chooses to dwell with us. Revelation 21:3 is not some aspirational picture of a future, it is a summary of the whole of biblical theology. It is the rendering of the meaning of the incarnation of Jesus Christ. It is the eschatological exclamation of what God has always been doing and where all creation is going—God dwelling among us.[2]

In a place we've never been before, it's imperative we grasp that forming a people of hope is about dwelling—dwelling with God, one another, and in our communities. Dwelling isn't a *spiritual* practice for the ordained or a special group set aside to be *religious*. It is to be the way of life shaping all Christians in their contexts. Dwelling involves a series of practices that, taken together, define what it means to be God's people in a fallen world. Lesslie Newbigin described the vocation of church as being a sign, foretaste, and instrument of God's workings in Jesus Christ.[3]

- The church is the sign that God's kingdom is present in the world;
- It is a foretaste of the eschatological fulfillment of God's redemptive work that has already begun;

2. There is a literature on this question of God dwelling with this us in creation. Much of it is focused on temple literature in terms of the physical construction of the temple, its purpose, and how it points to God's intentions for human life in creation. Linked to this there are rich studies on the creation and Edenic narratives that are, in their essence, about creation as being God's temple (see Beale and Kim, *God Dwells Among Us*). The beginning of Genesis with its expanding days of creation is about creation as being God's temple, the place of God's dwelling with us. The Edenic narratives expand on this as well as presenting a rationale for why this expansion of God's dwelling through all creation has to confront human sin and rebellion.

3. See Newbigin, *Open Secret*.

- It is the Spirit's means (instrument) of bringing about this kingdom.

When we introduce dwelling to church leaders, it is met with reticence, as if we're introducing another to-do item on top of all the to-dos being foisted on leaders. But dwelling is neither a new idea nor a technique. We know the burdens leaders carry, the expectations on them and their sense of failure and guilt. One pioneering couple participated with a dying congregation in reimagining its future in a dynamic city. Working with a developer, they tore down the old church building and replaced it with a multistory housing complex with low-rent apartments and condominiums. On the ground floor was a new church facility with offices, meeting rooms, and worship space. Also on the ground floor was a social enterprise business in the form of a coffee house and bakery. Several years into this creative project, key leaders were sharing how they found themselves driven by the all the demands of this creation, to the point where they had little family time or time to connect as couples. This pioneering project was depriving them of the possibility of dwelling with one another, their children, and the other people close to them. The enterprise wasn't wrong, but dwelling with one another and other people was being squeezed out.

At the center of the Christian story, God in Christ comes all the way down to dwell with us, the whole lot of us. As Eugene Peterson's rendering of John's Prologue puts it: "God moved right into the neighborhood." Christians are those who dwell with one another and in their neighborhoods. Without that, we have no clue about what God is doing amongst us.

Our worship liturgies confess that God was incarnate and revealed in Jesus. While this confession is at the heart of Christian identity, in late modernity, we have

> ceased to know how to be able to affirm that this *very same* real world of sensible human embodiment in space and time into which Jesus came should even today continue to be the site of God's real self-revelation . . . as it was then. We are thus apt . . . to understand theology today as needing to exercise itself as a discipline "between the times" of what is seen as two specific and definite "realities" of God's self-revelation: a past reality in the incarnation of Jesus Christ in a human body, and a future reality in the final judgement . . . The reality of theological reference and authority has come to be located everywhere but in the present: in the reality of the distant past, in the reality

> of an extreme future, or in the utterly intangible "reality" of a radical beyond.[4]

Practically lost to us is the experience of God's actual engagement in our everyday reality. We've trained leaders who, liturgically and confessionally, draw us to facts of the past (incarnation and resurrection), as well as a weekly rehearsal that Christ will come again to call creation back into its doxological purposes. But in the present, clergy function as professionals and experts forming congregations around vision, strategy, management, and outcomes. Accompanying these activities is a vague sense that the Spirit energizes and blesses our actions. Euro-tribal churches confess *what has happened in the past* (the incarnation) and *look to a future* (the final judgement), but in the actual, material, everyday world in which we live, its practices and methods are taken from sources and frames that do not require God's agency in any way. There is little expectation of God actively present where we dwell. That God dwells among us is a confession of what God once did in Jesus and an anticipation of what will be again. What if we took seriously that the places where we carry out our lives as Christians is, literally, the space where God dwells *now* and is at work?[5]

Dwelling: How Do We Sing the Lord's Song in a Strange Land?

Babylon

The captives in Babylon could only see the disruptions that had overtaken them. Therefore, they asked themselves a question: "How do we sing the Lord's song in a strange land?" Their self-understanding was that they couldn't. They were brutally honest about their reading of the situation, even if terribly wrong in their conclusions. They knew their world had imploded. There was no room to pretend. Their question was the

4. Davies, Janz, and Sedmak, *Transformation Theology*, 2.

5. We recognize the challenge and complexity in this claim because ours is a time that has domesticated God in Christ into an intimate friend whose principal role is to care for our needs and guarantee our self-development. This is a deep and profoundly difficult characteristic of contemporary Christian identity in the modern world. While pressing this lost awareness of God's presence dwelling with us in the reweaving of a shattered creation, we strongly acknowledge that this dwelling is about the One who is mystery, who is Other and cannot be reduced to the categories of our needs, plans, vision statements, or strategies. This is a challenging path in a culture whose defaults are all about the self or the power of control and outcomes.

anxious recognition of an impossibility: God could not dwell with them in that god-forsaken place. Babylon's gods had seemed to render Yahweh powerless. The world of Jerusalem's deported elites had collapsed. Their theologies, narratives of success, and programs of management made no sense in Babylon. Their anger knew no limits. Their response was visceral: "O Daughter of Babylon, doomed to destruction, happy is the one who repays you according to what you have done to us—he who seizes your infants and dashes them against the rocks" (Ps 137:8–9, NIV).

What were they to do in the extremity of that situation? A word from God came through Jeremiah the disgraced prophet. For the priestly classes, this was a word that suggested the end of their identity and the eradication of their roles. Babylon rendered the priestly classes meaningless. Jeremiah's letter offered the captives an unimaginable choice: *dwell* in a god-forsaken place or join the planning for a return to Jerusalem to re-establish role, status, and control (Jer 29).

Many chose to stay in Babylon.[6] It meant taking on a way of life that would overturn their assumptions of what it meant to be God's people. It meant letting go of existing institutions, structures, and roles. They would need to experiment with new institutions, structures, and roles. Priestly identity had imploded with the destruction of the temple and the deportations. That clergy class lost its forms and the means for practicing its roles. More than any other group, the priestly classes must have experienced the pathos of the question of "How do we sing the Lord's song in a strange land?" A clerical elite had their role made redundant. The exiled community had to experiment with new roles and structures for gathering, covenant-keeping, and engaging with Scripture.

Priestly classes and an incipient rabbinic movement were different ways of addressing the crisis. The priestly class led the charge to get back to Jerusalem and rebuild the past. This is where their identity lay. Without this drive to return, remake, fix, and get back, they had no identity. Incipient rabbinic movements formed around a different outlook. Their questions would have been about how to form a community of hope around the Scriptures, so that they could listen to God in the midst of this disaster. Initially, a rabbi was not an occupation, or a designated, official role in a structure. At the beginning, it carried the connotation of

6. Many of the original deportees would have been too old at that point for the journey back to Jerusalem. A good many would now be people born in Babylon and thoroughly embedded in its culture. Still others would be less than interested in returning to the arduous work of rebuilding.

elder such as we see, for example, amongst First Nations peoples today. There the elder is the one who carries the memory, the stories of their people, and is the bearer of traditions. An elder walks with the people as interpreter and translator of meaning. Rabbi was about being a sage, one immersed in the traditions, stories, and the Scriptures amidst the people. Their focus was their dwelling in the Word. This was not like the modern roles of clergy, pastors, preachers who engage Scriptures with more Enlightenment methods of interpretation. Rabbinic communities did not see Scripture primarily as a body of rational truths to be explicated to congregations. Instead of explication, they would form a community of God's people as they learned to dwell in Scripture.

Furthermore, for the exiles to form rhythms of common life in Babylon, they needed relationship with the Babylonians to thrive in a seemingly god-forsaken place. Therefore, they needed to listen to Babylon's stories to understand life in Babylon and make sense of their own story. Dwelling with rabbis in Scripture and with the Babylonian stories enabled them to form a counter-story of God's future, which became written in the early chapters of Scripture.

Benedict and Dwelling

Benedict, confronted with the unraveling of an empire, had been one of its cultured elite. He was born after the sacking of Rome (410), and the trauma of that event must have played a central part in his formation of a monastic community. As a desert monk, he'd been part of an exploration into how to dwell as God's people in Rome's unraveling. Benedict lived in the outworking of the collapse of Roman institutions. He experienced the breakdown of social and economic life. People were thrown into precarity. Leaders, civic and religious, had little sense of what to do. Benedict witnessed huge numbers of people cast adrift with no social, political, or spiritual systems within which to find safety or discover direction. He understood the crisis as one of religious life. His small, lay monasteries were a response to the crisis of common life. Rather than seeking the light of Christ in the desert, he sought to discern the light of Christ in the descending darkness of Roman society. He would explore a form of common life that would, in years to come, crystallize into a socioeconomic-religious reweaving of society. His communities were formed around a Rule that brought order to the chaos through practices. At the heart of these practices was dwelling.

The Celts and Formation

Celtic Christianity can appear paradoxical when it comes to the question of the self and dwelling. Embedded in the mindset of Celtic believers was a readiness to launch out into the unknown to find their place of resurrection. The idea of finding one's place of resurrection originates from Abram and Sarai's call to leave the security of their homeland and journey to "a place that I will show you" (Gen 12:1). Their story was inspirational to Celtic believers. One of the archetypal images of early Irish Celtic communities was that of monks casting themselves off into the ocean. They traveled in coracles and were taken by the currents toward an unknown land from where they wandered, seeking their place of resurrection. Their form of dwelling came through wandering, moving from what once was to what was to be discovered. It required courage to let go of long-held traditions to find the place of God's appointing.

> We see monks moving into hermitages deep in the forest, heading off in their coracles or currachs, or walking across the countryside in faith and expectation. Many monks found their way to Europe, establishing communities of faith throughout the continent. The inspiration of Abraham's journey led Irish monks to recognise the divine call within themselves to leave the security of home and to travel to where the Spirit would lead them.[7]

Finding the place of resurrection meant they'd discovered home where they settled physically and spiritually. Dwelling in that place, their purpose was to become aware of the connectedness of all things and the thin veil between the eternal and physical realms. This dwelling was the realization of something of the kingdom of God "on earth as in heaven." Their place of dwelling was a place of homecoming without yearning to be anywhere else. There they discovered how to discern and discover what it was to be human in being connected with both God and neighbor.

The life of Gobnait illustrates this dwelling. Leaving her homeland of County Clare in Ireland, she journeyed looking for her place of resurrection, eventually settling and establishing a community in County Cork, on a small hill overlooking a river. There, embracing her call to a

7. Molloy, *Globalisation of God*, 163.

life of prayer, she established a community that cared for the needs of the poor, prayed, worked in the fields, and kept bees. Gobnait is famed as the patron saint of bees and beekeepers.

Beehives only survive if a colony works together. Each bee fulfills its distinct role, working for the benefit of the whole colony. It's an insightful and beautiful image of the community Gobnait formed. Her sixth-century community was a dynamic example of dwelling together, being self-sufficient, and benefiting the wider communities around them. Like the Benedictine communities, these expressions of dwelling offered hope to a depleted culture.

Dwelling and the seventy-five-year story

Dwelling is not a tactic for creating what attractional, affinity-based churches call community or fellowship. Gestating through the sixteenth-century reformations and coming into full bloom in the first part of the twentieth century, was a radically new understanding of what it means to be human. Along with this came new forms of social, political, organizational, and economic relationships. With the unraveling of medieval society there emerged a drive to secure the rights of the individual above all else. Social, religious, and political life came to be organized around a new sense of individual rights. It became a paramount value that society should create systems that allowed individuals to be free from all forms of external determinants in order to pursue their own interests. Self-interest became paramount. It increasingly shaped religious language and economic self-interest. A good society did not depend on an ethic of the common good that binds citizens in covenant, but in securing individuals' right to be free to pursue their own economic ends independent of others.

This form of society came to its full life in the seventy-five-year story. That story had been gestating for several hundred years, becoming a central tenet of the modern story after World War II. It's now possible to see how this story, so seemingly promising for human thriving at its beginnings, has torn apart the bonds of belonging and solidarity upon which human thriving depends. The seventy-five-year story is a counter-story to the scriptural vocation of dwelling in covenantal love. As we've argued, this is the only story the generations now living have known. When individual rights define what it means to be a society, what emerges is not a Benedict, but a Bezos. We now inhabit a world in which the likes of Bezos, Musk, and Zuckerberg embody a capitalist plutocracy carried via social media, paired with a proletariat that is increasingly unable to dwell in the places they were born or with the families in which they were formed. Somewhere along the trajectory of this story, we became societies in which our children and grandchildren cannot live. The churches have been so lulled into this story that they cannot see how it has dissolved societal life. Dwelling is how the church becomes again, in Newbigin's words, a sign, foretaste and instrument of God's redemptive work. What is involved in this dwelling?

The Four Elements of Dwelling

To understand what we intend by dwelling we dig a little more into its meaning. *Dwelling* is an ancient word. It relates to the Hebrew *shakan*. Its sources in English have a difficult etymology. It has variant meanings (for example: dust cloud, trickery, keeping attention fixed, moving). It carried the idea of moving in circles that, gradually, migrated to mean staying in place. These different movements are neither opposites nor contradictories. They're ways of reaching for imagery to express a dynamic interaction of a relationship that is at the heart of dwelling. In this sense, dwelling, which is rooted in God's creation, is about relationality; and relationality is about knowing (this is the meaning of the phrase: "Adam knew Eve"). Dwelling is intimately related to knowing—knowing God, one another, and the creation.

This primitive meaning of dwelling as movement in circles (not away from one another but eternally with and around) brings to mind Andre Rublev's fifteenth-century icon of the Trinity. In that image the Trinity, three in one together, are seated and, at the same time, signifying movement with one another. That expresses what we intend with the word *dwelling*. It is about staying in place with others but, at the same time, it expresses that relationality occurs as people risk the dance of life with each other. In dwelling, the dance of listening, hearing, and knowing is called into light. Dwelling is how the darkness is defeated. In Leonard Cohen's evocative poetry, dwelling is how the light gets in.[8]

Dwelling involves the act of choosing to stay in a place and with a people (to perdure where I find myself and with the people of that place).

8. Leonard Cohen, "Anthem," https://www.youtube.com/watch?v=c8-BT6y_wYg.

As Cohen intuitively grasped, this dwelling was not in some perfection or among those who have it together or are in control. It will always be amongst the cracked, the ordinary, the mundane. To dwell is to decide to be a permanent resident of the place where I am and among its people no matter what. Dwelling is a longitudinal choice to not move on. It is not a step in some other plan nor a strategy for doing something for people. Dwelling is the heart of the dance that forms communities of hope in a dark time. It is that first step in the relationality required for knowing God, anyone, or anything. It calls us into spaces of risk where the possibility of the new creation might emerge.

To dwell is to be radically freed to be oneself. In dwelling, there emerges the terrifying recognition and possibility of redemption. Dwelling precedes acting. It is the arena for the formation of communities wherein people realize their call for the sake of the world. It promotes the flourishing of all; it is the basis of the common good.

Dwelling is essential for the subversion of top-down directives and the centralizing control that is distant from local neighborhoods. Top-down leadership that seeks to instrumentalize a vision that comes from the few to the many is inadequate for our moment. Power and decision-making held by the few and trickled down to the rest often seems, at the beginning, like a powerful movement attracting many like the perennial Pied Piper. But these moments rarely effect any transformation and more often than not fail to return people to the imagined times they have lost. They are only able to function where communities have lost the capacity to dwell with one another.

In our story, congregations became affinity groups based on sameness and tentative connection to one another. Their leaders did not remain where they were for very long. In North America, the average stay of a pastor or clergy person was about four years. The point is not to assess the varied internal and external forces creating this, but to indicate there is little cultural expectation that a leader dwells (stays and commits to life longitudinally) in a place with a people.[9]

9. The data for non-clergy is very different but also complex to analyze. Home owners tend to stay in the same place for around thirteen years. But it's difficult to imagine the measure of home ownership represents a normative standard any longer. Increasingly, younger generations are unable to own homes and are being turned into high-rise nomads, where it is not unusual for someone in their early thirties to have moved twelve to fifteen times already. These new forms of life exacerbate the disconnections between people. Furthermore, the very notion of neighborhood has been weakened in the wake of neoliberalism. In the North American context see Dunkelman's *Vanishing Neighbor*.

Forms of Dwelling

1. Leaders Dwelling with Their People

Beneath so many of the *how?* questions (methods, processes, programs), leaders are asking a more fundamental question about how they dwell with their people. While dwelling with one's people sounds obvious, it involves a reorientation of priorities and attention. A pastor in one of our Companion Groups shared that he gets the dwelling, discerning, and exploring, but that the people of his congregation would never get these practices and, even more, weren't interested. The pastor's companions challenged his posture, suggesting he was diminishing his people before he even shared with them. The truth was he didn't know them that well and was making untested assumptions. That encounter in his Companion Group began a painful journey of asking how he might dwell with his people. This dwelling journey begins when we choose to love our people irrespective of what they get or don't get, no matter how demanding of solutions they may be. Stepping into a space of receiving and loving our people is the beginning of dwelling.

Alan remembers when someone in his congregation confronted him. This lay leader was angry. In a shaking voice he said to Alan: "We are not your project." Alan was stunned. Irrespective of how he saw himself not making people the object of his plans or vision, he instinctively knew this person was right. Alan had to step back to process what had happened and what it all meant for him. This stepping back took a number of months. He knew the man was right, but he was confused. Gradually, Alan came to see that he wasn't dwelling with his people, loving them for who they were, but leading out of the goals and strategies focused on those in the church who wanted to join his vision. We all need to know we're loved before all else. The people of a congregation have to know they're not and never will be our project, no matter how noble or right we might think that project to be. Both of us authors can look back and regret how long it took us to embrace this way.

Dwelling happens when we know it's okay not to have to change people. Leaders confess how liberating it is to finally lay down that terrible "ought." This dwelling is expressed in the desire to hear the stories of our people. Stepping into this space enables us to see where the Spirit is already at work in our people's stories. In our people's own stories, in their capacities to listen with one another, to dwell together in Scripture and with their neighbors, lies the clues to how the Spirit is at work among us. Dwelling is like midwifery; it is the key to calling forth our people's stories. Leaders are not called to change people, but create places where people trust they can hear the Spirit through each other.

Dwelling is born of the conviction that the answers to the questions of what to do in this unraveling are among our people, not in data, futuring, or innovating. Dwelling is how we see that it is among our people that the Spirit is weaving their future as God's missionary people. A leader is like a detective of divinity, listening for the ways the Spirit is at work among a people. We can only do this as we dwell with our people.

Nick is a pastor who's a natural entrepreneur. He can innovate all day long. At the end of a day, Nick has created another list of ways to connect with people in the neighborhood. He naturally encounters neighbors. Without planning or innovating, his home fills up with people from the community. Seeing that the people of his church weren't signing on to be with people in their community, he decided to take that journey himself, leaving the congregation to its own internal concerns. However, Nick was challenged to rethink his Lone Ranger ways. What if he was dismissing his people too quickly? What if he created a small experiment where he dwelt with some of the people in the congregation? He would invite them to listen to God together and, from that, discover how to be with people in their neighborhood. So began another kind of journey for a wonderful entrepreneur who was learning how to dwell with his own people. The culture of a congregation starts to change as we embrace dwelling with our people. It's a fantasy to believe we change a group's culture through strategy, programs, or vision statements. The way of dwelling invites you to love your people where they are, not in what you want them to be.

Dwelling is an inglorious work. It is about being with our people without agendas. It is about the risk of relationality, of coming all the way down to pitch our tent with our people in all their beauty, mendacity, anxiety, and glorious presence as images of God. Everything depends on this dwelling with our people.

2. Dwelling with one another

In his Prologue, John writes about the Word, Jesus, dwelling among us. Dwelling is how God was incarnate in Jesus, entering our common life as vulnerable and dependent. In Jesus, God chooses to be identified with a people and place. A primary characteristic of a local group of Christians is their dwelling with one another.

The triune God is involved in a mission and the church, empowered by the Spirit, embodies and participates in that mission.[10] In its life with one another, a congregation is a sign, instrument, and foretaste of God's future. In its life together, the congregation is a *sign* that God's redemptive reign in Christ is actually, concretely present where we dwell. When people see a congregation, they're meant to experience a *foretaste* of where God is drawing all creation to its eschatological outcome. A local congregation is, therefore, the *instrument*—the means by which the Spirit is bringing this redemptive future into all of life.

Newbigin describes the local congregation as the "hermeneutic of the Gospel."[11] He believed that a local community of Christians is an embodied explanation of God's redemptive work. Newbigin draws upon the work of Michael Polanyi.[12] Polanyi was addressing the debates around the relationship between modern science and the question of how we know (epistemology). Over against a reductionism that argued the only knowledge we have is empirical, Polanyi proposed that knowing requires relationship. Relationships require trust, which, in turn, involves the risk of being in relationship with another.[13] For Newbigin, this knowing is grounded in God's self-revelation in Jesus Christ. In Jesus, God enters the risk of a deep, vulnerable relationship with the other.[14] God's self-revelation is an emptying of power through which Jesus reveals God's nature as that of risking love toward the other. It involved an emptying of power, a coming down and dwelling right among us. In Jesus, God risks dwelling with us. We know God, therefore, because Jesus risked revealing God to us. What is presented to us in the birth narratives of the Gospels is

10. Newbigin, *Open Secret*, 110, 113, 150.

11. Newbigin, *Gospel in a Pluralist Society*, chapter 18.

12. Michel Polanyi (1891–1976) was a Hungarian Jew who, in 1933, escaped the Nazis and went to England. He became professor of physical chemistry at Manchester University. His most well known book is *Personal Knowledge*, published in 1953. It was this book that significantly influenced Newbigin's missiological reflections around questions of how we know. For an in-depth engagement with the question of knowing and the importance of *Personal Knowledge* in Newbigin's work, see Weston, *Humble Confidence*.

13. For further reading on this question of modernity and how we know, see Scott, *Everyman Revived*, and Meek, *Little Manual of Knowing*.

14. See Roxburgh, *Joining God in the Great Unraveling*, chapter 10.

that all knowing is dependent on this risk of relationality with the other. This is what we mean by dwelling with one another.

The Spirit calls us to practice this dwelling with one another. Right now, congregations, reflecting our broader culture, are little more than affinity groups based on familiarity and the religious goods and services on offer. Congregations are echo chambers of affinity. Ann Snyder, editor-in-chief of *Comment* magazine, writes:

> [I]n an era of seductive ideological culs-de-sac . . . the restoration of the human . . . is going to require renewed commitment on our part to the way of the cross, and to welcoming the voices and communities who are especially intimate with that cross. It will require a renewed commitment to cultivating those *patient* spaces where bewilderment, grief, and hope might find their footing and yield a wiser way of leading. And it will require . . . a more explicit rejection of the false narratives suffocating human hunger for communion: West-to-the-Rest narratives that manipulate Christianity into sponsoring racist, nationalist projects; anti-human narratives that hear "Christianity" only as a euphemism for colonialism, oppression, and hypocrisy; and technocratic narratives that worship scientific rationality at the expense of a transcendent telos.[15]

The crises confronting our societies cannot be addressed by affinity groups formed around issues and ideologies. We need communities that take on the hard, long-term commitment of dwelling with one another across differences.

Furthermore, dwelling is how a congregation listens to God. This will mean forming communities that live in proximity to each other. Driving to belong to a group of Christians is not about dwelling but finding an affinity group. Dwelling is about becoming rooted in the lives of people where we live. Dwelling is about geography. All of this might sound counterintuitive to most Christians. Relationships are built around cars and highways and, therefore, affinity. Modern transportation gives us the power to go wherever we want and be with the kind of people we choose.

We propose that dwelling in the place where we are makes congregations a sign, foretaste, and instrument of God's redemptive story. The work of a leader is to shape a people around this dwelling. For some, this sounds romantically unreal. People argue that we can't be naive about recapturing

15. https://comment.org/committing-to-the-wrestling-way/?utm_source=tinyroofnail&utm_medium=email&utm_campaign=february-frenzy.

the past. We're not trying to do that. We're not nostalgic for some other era. We look at the endless reporting of multiple crises besetting our societies. Not all these are caused by the kind of living we've fallen into over the last hundred years. But a lot of the contemporary crises are the result of the way we've constructed life around the individual and forms of living that remove us from difference and the other. We've created social forms in which people are closed off from one another by the design of our housing and transportation. So, yes, we are proposing the remaking of congregational life around dwelling. Yes, it is radical and, from where one stands at this moment, delusionary, but we are called to make a beginning, to take small explorations in forming such communities of Christ followers, as did the Celts and Benedict in other times.

This dwelling is a starting point in the reweaving of the frayed strands of our societies and communities. It challenges the dominant notion that we are individuals, free to go and be when and where we choose, to live uprooted from relationships of accountability. Dwelling is the decision to stay put, to settle in for the long term, choosing to love the place and people where one lives.

There is always a groovier, more contemporary church just over the hill. But Benedict knew there could be no real engagement with his own dark times without a people committed to place, to one another and to the people of that place. Likewise, Celtic communities provided the means of being rooted in their relationship with God and place. Such communities will speak to the cascading crises of our time.[16]

The modern story has colonized us with the lie that social mobility provides freedom, whereas dwelling means failure and loss of status. The church will grasp its vocation in a place it's never been before as it chooses to dwell. For some, there is a call to go, to reach out and serve others beyond their neighborhood, but that should be the exception, not the norm. The missionary call to embrace the Great Commission to "Go" should not be interpreted through our modern lens of individualism, nor to the exclusion of dwelling with those outside the walls of the church within our neighborhoods.

16. We are well aware of the counter-arguments that we live in a networked, social media, globalized village and, therefore, place and the local are no longer that important. We will engage these arguments in the chapters ahead.

3. Dwelling with God

Dwelling together opens us to ways of dwelling with God. Over the millennia our tradition has given us a rich resource of Christian practices. These can be found, for example, in the Daily Office[17] and the Jesuit practice of Examen.[18] The dwelling journey with one another is, then, shaped around us taking on these practices of daily life that root that life in God. Here, dwelling is intended to redirect our attention, to reshape the ways in which our lives (individually and in common) become redirected in a society satiated with the self, isolation, and power.

If there is any place where the classic skills of pastoral life are essential, this is it. We need leaders who can patiently and faithfully guide people into the practices of Christian life. It is only in the regular, daily attention we give to such practices as the Daily Office and Examen that we can begin to shape a community whose attention (gaze) is turned toward God. This is no small work of leadership. We have argued that ours is a society shaped by a story that has determined life can be lived well without God. Modernity's wager tells us we can be good Christians in our personal, private religious lives. Here, apart from vague moral commitments in the rest of life, Christian faith is worked out privately, on our own. If, as we claim, it is the case that God, through the Spirit, is at work ahead of us in our neighborhoods reweaving the broken threads of human society and of creation, then the most important work of a congregation is in discovering those practices that turn its gaze and attention toward God. This is what makes these practices so essential to any renewal of Christian life today. This turning of our gaze toward God is not some form of escape from the world, but on the contrary, the only way we regain the sanity of seeing God where we dwell in order to join with the Spirit there.

17. Many Christian traditions have their own version of the Daily Office. We are shaped by that of the Northumbria Community. You can get information about the rhythms of the office at https://www.northumbriacommunity.org/offices/morning-prayer/.

18. The Daily Examen is a form of regular prayer and accountability with one another based on the Spiritual Exercises of St. Ignatius Loyola. The Daily Examen is a technique of prayerful reflection on the events of the day in order to detect God's presence and discern his direction for us. There are multiple websites that offer information and guidance around the practice of the Examen.

4. Dwelling in Scripture

Dwelling is how a local community of Christians listens to God through Scripture. Leaders form communities that attend to God. An important way to do this is through a common dwelling in Scripture. This is not about the preaching of the trained or teaching of professionals. It is more than what is known as Bible study. Dwelling is a way of listening to God's word as a people. This dwelling is an ancient practice of the church. In it, we're not seeking to master a text or be an expert in exegesis. It is about how God's ordinary people hear God with and through one another.

Rowan Williams asks: "What would a church life look like that saw itself as shaped primarily by the Word in such a way that the relation to God's call was the single determining factor in holding a community together?"[19] Dwelling in the Word is a central way of addressing the *how* in William's question. The vocation of God's people is to discern and join with what God is doing in the world. Dwelling in Scripture together creates space for the Spirit to shape our discernment. In the practice of dwelling, we slowly and repeatedly read and attend to a specific text as a way of listening to the Spirit. Dwelling is the work of the people attending to a text together. It is a way of letting Scripture reshape our listening through one another. We come to a text with an expectation that the Spirit is addressing us through one another. As we listen through one another, we discern how the Spirit is awakening us to where God is acting.

Dwelling does not come to us easily. We still look to the professionals to tell us what Scripture is saying. We are still driven by the desire to find solutions and formulas to the challenges before us. We still desire measurables and metrics so we can act. Dwelling in the Word is a different kind of practice. We are discerning what God is doing when we dwell in Scripture as a community.

Dwelling in the Word isn't the Bible study in which many congregations have been shaped. In Bible study, a passage is analyzed to get the clear, precise meaning of the text and then, perhaps, we ask how to apply it to our personal life. Bible study is important. It is about teaching and is usually led by a pastor or someone literate in the Bible. Getting it right is the end of the teaching/study process. It's left to the individual how to apply its meaning. Dwelling has a different goal and a different method. Rather than coming to a text for information (commentaries, study guides, experts), we come with others to wait with each other before the text in

19. Williams, *Way of St. Benedict*, 57.

a spirit of receptivity. Dwelling is about the posture of waiting to receive from God by listening to one another. If Bible study is about how we read the text to get it right, dwelling is about letting the text read us.

Dwelling in the Word invites us to step outside our normal ways of working with Scripture. At first, dwelling doesn't feel *normal.* Our default is to want someone to tell us what the text means. We want experts in the room (pastors, for example) because they know the truth. Dwelling takes time before it becomes a familiar practice. Some, with a strong sense of their own agency, push back because dwelling doesn't deliver the usually expected outcomes. There is a deliberate method for Dwelling in the Word. This method is a way of guiding one another into a receptivity to God's presence.[20]

The three action elements of dwelling we've proposed are about formation in a local congregation. The next section introduces a fourth—dwelling with our neighbors.

5. Dwelling with the Neighbor

Dwelling in our neighborhood is a key practice for engaging the question: *How do we discern what it means to be God's people in this great unraveling?* It is the combination of these practices that create the space for what we are describing as discernment. What is involved in the neighborhood dwelling? The act was small and simple. In the scheme of things it wouldn't change the world, but it was a moment of God's grace in neighborhoods that have lost much of the sense of grace and belonging. Alan realized that he needed to stop traveling if he was to dwell in his community. He assumed this would be an easy transition. It wasn't. Changing well-established patterns is no easy task. For one thing, Alan's car always seemed to head out of the neighborhood to the places he was used to and preferred. It was a huge shift to park the car so he had to be in the neighborhood. Furthermore, people are fine with garden and front porch conversations, but wary of anything that suggests deeper connections with one another. Alan gradually realized that dwelling with neighbors was more than a project. It was going to be a long journey, not a one-off church event. One day, close to Christmas, he learned that Phil's birthday was December 24. He and Phil had spent

20. Information on the method is found at https://www.themissionalnetwork.com/ and Roy's website, https://www.thecommonscooperative.com.

time in the back alleyway talking about the neighborhood but it was always a distant friendliness. Still, Alan had grown to appreciate Phil a lot. Learning about the birthday, he went to a well-known chocolate and bakery shop nearby to buy Phil some "birthday baking." Christmas eve, Al knocked on Phil's front door with his gifts. It was a holy moment. Phil was completely surprised. This little act of care touched Phil quite deeply. Alan, reflecting on Phil's response, realized that, like many, Phil has little sense of the neighborhood as a place of grace. He was quite overcome with something he probably couldn't name—a simple act of grace that had no strings attached.[21]

What makes a neighborhood a community is its sharing of life together. This is a basis for human flourishing. As God's people, we're needing to learn, all over again, how to dwell with our neighbors. Forming communities of hope requires we dwell in our neighborhoods. But, it's not a church program, something we do to recruit for the church. This dwelling practice is about how we follow the One who pitched his tent right beside ours. It is how we begin to answer the question: How do we sing the Lord's song in a strange land? In response to the question: *How do we know what God is doing when our assumptions have been torn up?* Jesus sends his disciples into the neighborhood to dwell with the households participating in their social and economic lives. While we no longer dwell in times where it's the norm for people to live in multigenerational households, we can choose to pitch our tents beside our neighbors and settle in for the long haul.

Dwelling with one's neighbors requires laying down the need to control what happens. It is not a brief encounter on the calendar. Dwelling involves embracing a way of life that will stop us doing things that have been important to us. Alan realized he could only dwell in his neighborhood if he got rid of his car. The car was continually taking him away from the neighborhood. It was not that taking this simple act changed everything. It didn't. It remained difficult to connect with people, but at least he had put himself in the place where dwelling could start. Alan is now figuring out how to become a guest rather than the host. The challenge is that almost all the relationships of church people are with church people. Further, church folk have been schooled to believe that forming relationships with people is mostly to have them join the church and become part

21. A sign of this came a few days later when a bottle of wine turned up at Al's front door from Phil. He didn't know what else to do except turn gift into reciprocity.

of a church's social life. Defaults and habits are hard to break. A wise leader gently invites people into this dwelling.[22]

Roy tells the story how, during his first pastorate, the church engaged in a week of mission, deploying a team of Bible college students. Every home was visited during the week, using a tried and tested evangelical survey method with ten questions, with the answer to the last one hopefully leading people to say they wanted to give their lives to Christ. Nobody did so through such a fabricated, artificial methodology. The day after the students returned to their college, Roy found himself in the local post office queue when one of the local residents asked him, "Is the silly season over and is it safe to come out again?" Outsiders, well-intentioned, but totally disconnected from the neighborhood, had little if any fruit for their labors. Asked about the survey's findings, Roy shared with the church that the greatest needs identified by the estates' residents were for a chemist and a butcher. The congregation took this response seriously, listened to the residents, and, following negotiations with the local medical practice, arranged for prescriptions to be delivered and distributed from the church building. This saved residents the challenge of walking over a mile for medications.

Two other incidents were to prove decisive to the congregation's relationship with its neighborhood. There was an arson attack on the church buildings. It was an area of high unemployment. Roy worked with a job creation agency to employ six local young men, under the supervision of a joiner and a decorator, to work for three months in refurbishing the premises. On another occasion, the neighborhood's under-fourteens football team manager collapsed and died on the touchline during a game. He was forty-two. The tragedy was felt deeply throughout the community. The grieving family turned to Roy and the church to conduct the funeral and make a presentation to the British Heart Foundation. There were over four hundred people present, mostly men, members of the local working men's club. Making the presentation, Roy knew what it was to dwell in the neighborhood. It was in the streets, not in strategies, in the building of relationships with neighbors, that the Spirit was at work.

The monastic phrase "a cloistered life" suggests a withdrawal from people. However, George Lings, in his book *Seven Sacred Spaces*,[23] points

22. For helpful resources in inviting our people into this dwelling, see https://www.themissionalnetwork.com/stepping-out/ and https://www.themissionalnetwork.com/neighbourhood-project/.

23. Lings, *Sacred Spaces*, and Williams, *Way of St. Benedict*, 57.

out that the cloister, far from being a place of withdrawing, is a place of connection. The architecture of the cloister is a sheltered walkway between other spaces. It is connected rather than separated. As Lings writes:

> Joining is a function that deserves noticing. To be disjointed is a significant handicap . . . Joining places matter. Cloister was where people met informally and sometimes by choice. Here is where friendships are nurtured and conversely where enemies could be made. The parallel would be the school playground. It is not part of the curriculum, but crucial in school social life.[24]

Joining God in the neighborhood, discovering God's agency in the world, takes the church out into places of connection and community. Fast disappearing are the days when the church was host, putting on services and events to which people were invited in. Attractional church usually meant inviting people into what the church had organized. In this new era, the Spirit of God is turfing us out of our buildings into our neighborhoods, into the bumping places, the cloistered and connecting places.

A Little Experiment in Beginning Neighborhood Dwelling

Here is a simple way to begin this journey by choosing times you'll be present in your neighborhood each week. It might mean some of these activities:

- Walking around and being alive to what's happening at different times of day.
- Joining a community organization as a volunteer.
- Getting involved at a local gym or sports club.
- Offering a few hours each week or month at one of the many charity shops in the area.
- Going with others to pick up litter from the streets and places where people hang out.
- Reading up on the founding and development of your community (a local library has this material readily available).

24. Lings, *Sacred Spaces*, 86.

- Choosing a neighborhood coffee shop, pub, or park and hanging out at regular times.

The list of ways to practice can go on. You just need to try on a few as a start. What you're wanting to do is develop a habit of being in your neighborhood. This being present, which can only happen over time, is how we learn to see people and places beyond the cursory glances when driving by in our cars. Developing such a rhythm is a way to slowly start this practice of dwelling. You may like to make notes around what you're seeing. Here are some questions you might find helpful:

- Am I in a place where I can be present in my neighborhood outside of roles or positions?
- What's my agenda here? Am I seeking ways of being with these people and hearing their story or do I feel the need to do something for them?
- What kinds of questions help me invite people to talk about their experiences (examples: How long have you lived in the neighborhood? What brought you here? What do you find life-giving about this community? What concerns or fears do you have for the neighborhood?).

Find someone in your church community to talk with about what you're doing. Share what you're seeing; name the questions that are beginning to come to mind. Don't be present in the neighborhood with the intention of solving people's problems or doing something for them. There is a time and place for that, but it can close down our ability to hear and see what is happening among people. Find a few people you want to get to know. Without an agenda, listen to the stories of who they are and why they're in the neighborhood. These are often people one wouldn't meet in church. They can be very different from you, but in them you are stretched out of your comfort zones. It's a way we hear God. In Acts 16, Paul and his companions were trying to figure out why the Spirit had brought them to Philippi. They were confused about what the Spirit was saying to them. Only as they risked moving outside their normal patterns and relationships did they meet Lydia. In that relationship they discerned a whole new direction for the church.

Dwelling and Patterns of Leadership

These four dwelling practices invite leaders to reimagine their own identity and roles. Clergy careers involve moving from place to place in response to search committees or bishop placements. The pattern of ministry is to move from the place of calling to a theological school, then to another location for training placement and then, following ordination, to yet another context, often removed geographically and culturally from the neighborhoods from which they had come. The neighborhoods where they formed and experienced the call of God are abandoned. In this pattern, there is little importance put on place. It is the opposite of dwelling.

Established practices of training turns one into a moveable, replaceable professional holding a contractual relationship with a congregation for a period of time before moving on to the next contract. At this moment we need leaders who dwell with people over the long haul. They need to be those who pitch their tent and stay (stability). Like Ruth and Naomi, they need to grasp the covenantal life to which God calls them. This will mean stepping out of contractual professionalism to be rooted, covenantally, in the communities where they dwell. Like Ruth, they are leaders who say "your people are my people" not just for a few years as a professional, but for the duration as "one of us."

We are all aware of the fractured state of our communities and the parlous state of Christian communities. The need for healed communities is palpable. There is no journey of hope without the commons, without one another. Furthermore, the healing we need in this darkening moment requires time. There are no quick fixes or formulas that come from the outside. There is so much we have to let go of in our fearful, tightly clenched firsts. We can make a start with a humble willingness to take on these practices of dwelling that have been hollowed out of our living.

The Spirit is calling Christians to form ways of life together that can reweave our social, economic, political, and environmental ecologies. Forming such communities of hope will be difficult. Our instinctual responses to the impending crises are to make something happen, take on one of the multiple issues clamoring for attention and make that the focus of our leadership. If we can just address the latest hot issue, hatch a bold plan, set goals, announce a revival, measure outcomes, and set strategies, then we might stave off the unraveling. Like the multiple global climate conferences held over the past decade or more, conferences led by experts, politicians, economists, and scientists, if we can get the right plan with the right signatures, then we can change all this. If we can do the analysis to see what needs to be done, then we can act, and that acting will, at least for a time, reduce the anxiety and make it feel like we can make a difference. These responses keep defaulting to the elite, the professionals, the politicians, the experts, rather than understanding that the reweaving comes from this dwelling.

Dwelling is the beginning point to transforming our societies and reweaving the torn threads of our planet. The story of center-out strategies, of the power of the expert and the control of elites goes all the way down in the modern narrative. Therefore, our primary response is to look to experts and elites. These dwelling practices can seem off the mark. They can feel like a waste of time. People ask: What's the point of dwelling? It sounds like the naive inaction religious people talk about. What's it going to achieve? What leader wants to risk talking like this? Congregations will lose patience and ride one out of town on the back of an ass. But our story tells us that such dwelling forms communities of hope that can discern where God is working in our world.

In Late Modernity

These dwelling practices are counterintuitive to how life is lived in late modernity. One leader invited some in her congregation to join her in dwelling in the Word. Out of that, she hoped they would explore what was involved in dwelling with neighbors. Initially, the group was enthusiastic, even though they weren't sure what this was all about. She introduced them to the process of dwelling in Scripture. Learning to listen to God through one another was energizing. They loved the process.

After several months, she invited them to take a small step in dwelling with neighbors. The language was strange to them. They weren't sure what it meant or what to do. The pastor pointed out that dwelling was about discovering how to pay attention, how to listen to the other, how to hear God. Dwelling with a neighbor involved things like paying attention, listening to a neighbor's stories. She introduced them to some simple questions for inviting their neighbor to share a story about themselves. Pushback came quickly. This was too big a stretch for people. Several members visited the pastor, expressing their support and appreciation for her, but, at the same time, raised doubts about the whole dwelling process, especially dwelling with neighbors. At the heart of the pushback were two things. First, they were confused. There were no outcomes to this dwelling with neighbors. What was the point of it? Where was it going? What, they asked, were the deliverables? Would this kind of activity result in growing the church? Second, having these conversations with their neighbors was not a normal part of their lives. They didn't feel safe taking this step. Their outcome/deliverables questions were ways of deflecting their fears. Dwelling with a neighbor wasn't a comfortable thing to do for these church people. They needed to know the purpose, the results their efforts would bring. This dwelling with is a counterintuitive practice for congregations that believe they need outreach strategies for bringing people to church.

There are other forms of pushback. For example, it's argued that in a networked world we don't dwell by being with people in a place, a geography. In the new metaverse, we're beyond place. Relationships, the argument goes, are through online, virtual communities. We can be in a place as an addition to the lives we construct online, but it's not essential to the construction of the self. Therefore, this practice of dwelling is nostalgia for a bygone era.

Neighborhood as a way of life has diminished greatly over the past fifty years. We see it in the disappearance of local newspapers, the closing of movie theaters, the erosion of organizations such as the Lions or Rotary in North America or the sports and Working Men's clubs in the UK. The undermining of the local is a result of globalized capitalism. As Maurice Glasman writes: "[A] sense of belonging, of place, of mutuality and responsibility is undermined through a lack of power."[25] In urban centers, one can watch this loss of common power among ordinary members of a community. It is present in the long withdrawal of the small, mom-and-pop stores, operated over several generations by immigrant families in rented premises. They contributed immensely to the street life of the neighborhood and cultivated a sense of place that rooted people in a community. Alan has become familiar with the local barber shop where a family from Iraq had built a business that was now in the neighborhood's ethos. But many of these local mom-and-pop businesses are being squeezed out. Land becomes ever more expensive. As the new high rises get built, rents keep going up. Many can no longer

25. Glasman, *Blue Labour*, 20.

afford to live in the neighborhood. As people leave, part of the glue of the community goes with them.

Land and rental prices everywhere have been exploding upward, not just with the pressures of population growth, but with the financialization of land and buildings. As land value inflated, a series of domino effects kicked in. City governments raise property taxes to cover the costs of infrastructure development. Rentiers[26] keep increasing their rents to ordinary people. Low-end apartments get torn down or gentrified so that working-class people can no longer afford the rents on their shops and markets, or homes. On balance, the concern is not how to keep the small, mom-and-pop corner store open because of the ways they contribute to the common good. It has become more lucrative in a market economy to create a real estate model that empties older buildings of the people and businesses in order to build new, high-rise flats, condos, and rentals at far higher costs. Those moving in are higher income (generally white-collar professionals) with few expectations of staying long.

We confront a powerful market economy that, along with a virtual world where one works from anywhere, treats place as an economic exchange, a profit mechanism. This is a massive assault on our capacities to form sustainable communities. Working people are left vulnerable. Neighborhoods are a way we reweave the social ecology of our broken world. We need institutions and structures for people to dwell with one another if we're to create the hope of a better world. But we support an economic structure that undermines the systems (place, geography) essential for forming a different world. The call to the churches is to dwell in the local. It's not a tactic, but a gospel imperative. As Christians we only know God in the One who came all the way down to a particular place and dwelt among a specific people without power.[27] The only way our humanity thrives is in place. The ethereal claim to some kind of hyperreality where we remake ourselves over and over again is about our loss of hope in what it means to be human. It's a retreat into an anti-human digital no-space (u-topos: "place that cannot be") with a few winners and an expanding number falling through the cracks into a

26. See Christophers, *Rentier Capitalism.*

27. When the Enlightenment philosopher Gotthold Ephraim Lessing (1729–1781) said about history that the accidental truths of history (contingency in all its unpredictable materiality) can never become proof of necessary truths he was pointing to the stubborn, immovable problem of Christianity—it's all unavoidably about contingency, the utter messiness and uncontrollability of unmanageable place, as if God in Jesus has said "this is the only place where you'll find me."

precarious world.[28] Of the few benefits that came out of lockdown, one was the rediscovery of relationships with one's immediate neighbors, of connectivity with people in the local. For some churches, the required constraints led to the realization of the Spirit at work in the local. This is leading to the emergence of pioneering communities dwelling in their neighborhoods. A consumer church is giving way to local, indigenous communities sharing life and faith together.

From Dwelling to Discerning

This chapter introduced practices of dwelling as critical ways to form communities of hope. This multifaceted practice reorients God's people to ways of being a sign, witness, and foretaste of the kingdom. Dwelling practices are an essential precursor to the practice of discernment. Discernment comes out of a community that dwells with one another, with God and their neighbors. Within these practices, one can ask the discernment questions: What is God doing among us and in our community? How then do we join with God?

28. The experience of lockdown during the global COVID pandemic gave back to some communities that sense of dwelling together with their neighbors. It was in enforced circumstances where, ironically, people began to discover their neighbors and neighborhoods in ways they never imagined or experienced before.

CHAPTER NINE

Discerning

How to be placed in the world where the act of God can come alive . . .—Rowan Williams

The Slow, Imperceptible Loss of Our Language World

DISCERNING IS THE SECOND of the three practices. This chapter explores both its meaning and practice. Ours is a time that craves certainty.[1] In the words of William Bouwsma, the search for certainty is the "inevitable response to the growing inability of an inherited culture to invest experience with meaning."[2] The seventy-five-year story promised that certainty. Through analysis, predictability, control, and management we would construct our preferred futures.[3] As this story collapses, its practices no longer produce expected outcomes. Today, we are searching for new forms of certainty. Accentuating our crisis as churches is the loss of a practical sense of God being an Agent in the world. The conviction that the Spirit of Jesus is acting ahead of us in the reweaving of all things has ceased to be the operative story in which we live. In this unraveling,

1. See Schreiner, *Are You Alone Wise?*

2. Bouwsma, *A Usable Past: Essays in European Cultural History,* quoted in Schreiner, *Are You Alone Wise?*, xi.

3. It is obviously much longer than seventy-five years but for the sake of presenting a limited framework we choose to talk about transformations in modern Western societies since the end of World War II. The literature around this question of disruption and discernment takes us back into the early beginnings of the modern era and the search for certainty. Susan Schreiner's wonderful essay is one example. A popular framing of the conversation can be found in Toulmin's important book *Cosmopolis.*

the churches are not asking what God is doing among them or in their communities. They keep returning to what they know from within the seventy-five-year story, namely, data, analysis, visioning, expert advice, and technocratic methods.

The Euro-tribal church's understanding of discernment is akin to collecting data, asking experts, setting vision, then determining what actions to take. All this is baptized with prayer. Discernment and methods of analysis aren't exclusive to one another. Rather, we are arguing, the latter approach is the primary language world within which church leaders operate. The language world of God's Agency is mostly lost. How, therefore, do we practice discernment in our time?

Discernment is rooted in a theocentric question: *What is the Spirit of God doing amongst us and ahead of us in our communities?* That God is acting and calling us to join with Jesus is not how a majority of leaders and congregations operate. There are historical reasons why the language world of God as Agent among us has been lost.

Discernment in the *Saeculum*

One of Augustine's overarching themes in *City of God*[4] is that of the *saeculum*. He takes the term from the Latin in which it means "of the age." This is the source of our word *secular*. The distinction between sacred and secular history starts to develop around this time. Augustine confronted formidable critics who blamed Christianity for the fall of Rome and loss of faith in the traditional gods. These gods had been central to Rome's identity, protection, and success.[5] In his response to this critique, Augustine proposed there are two histories working themselves out simultaneously. One is the worldly city of man, epitomized by Rome. The other is the heavenly city of God.

Up to that point all history had been seen as more or less sacred. Now another distinction enters the nascent Western imagination. It will, by the time of the European Enlightenments, turn into a full-blown dichotomy where the secular/sacred are distinct and separate language worlds. The secular became the controlling imagination of an emerging

4. Augustine, *City of God*.

5. This is not an attempt to present a commentary on Augustine's understanding of time or the bifurcation of time and space and the emergence of the idea of sacred/profane history. It is a very brief attempt at a contextualization of our wrestling with the notion and practice of discernment.

modernity. God's Agency was pushed to the edges until, in movements like deism, God is, at best, the originator of a creation that functions by its own inner laws and, at worst, sees no need for such extraneous beliefs as a Creator.

God is relocated from being active and present in the whole of creation into the inner life of the individual and limited to moral/ethical engagements with the world. There is no longer a need for God as Agent in a world explained by causality and made available through rationality and method. This bifurcation of the secular became embedded in the imagination and practices of the churches.

Augustine's intention in the use of *saeculum* was to frame a universal history in which God was the guiding Agent. But the development of this secular narrative had profound, unintentional consequences on the Christian understanding of discernment. A particular framework gradually gets set into place in Western Christianity. It can be described in terms of three movements that interpret the relationship of God with us and Creation.

1. At the first movement (the incarnation), the Creator God, at a particular place and point in time, enters fully into history. "The Word became flesh and pitched his tent beside ours." In the incarnation, God is seen fully as Agent in the life, death, and resurrection of Jesus. Christians, therefore, confess that at a time and place in history, God was unambiguously present and acting as Agent. This acknowledgment of God's agency was built into our liturgies and confessions. Christians have little difficulty confessing that in Jesus Christ, God was acting in the world.
2. The second movement (the *saeculum*) follows the ascension. The clarity of God's Agency, so evident in the first movement, is gone. The Spirit is given to the church and, preveniently, to the world. This is the in-between time from the ascension to the coming again of Christ. This interim period is Augustine's *saeculum*. It is sometimes described as the era of the church. In this era, the question of God's Agency goes through a long series of transformations resulting, in the modern period, in the abandonment of God as Agent and the triumph of human agency.
3. The third movement is eschatological (the *parousia*). It will come with the end of history (time), when Christ returns. It is at that point that the era of the *saeculum* is ended by Christ. In the words

of Revelation, the dwelling of God will then be with/among us. This is the future time when God is fully present. There, in the language of Revelation, the dwelling of God is with us. The primary symbol of this dwelling is a great table filled with an abundance of food. All the nations are brought together in a healed creation. The primary sign of that reweaving of Creation is that God dwells with us.

The time between the second two moments (one in history, the other at the end of history) is, for Augustine, the time between when God works through God's people who anticipate the return to Christ to make all things new. This is the time when the Spirit is moving all things[6] toward God's making all things new, which was inaugurated by the resurrection of Christ. This in-between time, Augustine described as the *saeculum*. This framing of a Christian understanding of the *saeculum* involves the question of agency and, therefore, the nature of discernment. With the removal of God's acting in our world, discernment is transferred from questions of how God is acting in our neighborhoods and communities to be about the actions we as agents need to take in the context of our observations and assessments.

There are, therefore, these two moments in the Christian narrative around discernment. In the one, it's clear that God is acting and is the primary agent—this is in time and space in the incarnation. The other is at the conclusion of the *saeculum*. In between, the question of agency and what God is doing in the world is not clear. The tension of that situation is resolved in the Enlightenment when human, individual agency is elevated as the primary form of agency in the world. In this time, we see the atrophy of our capacities to discern where God is acting or to hear the Spirit in some form. The church understands this in-between time as the time wherein its own agency is primary. It is the time when we look to human method, technique, and skill as our primary forms of discerning what to do as Christians in a world separated from what comes to be called the sacred. Discernment became common sense, the capacity to adopt the best planning methods or use of the latest methods of organizational change. God is, functionally, absented from our practice of discernment.

This is where we've arrived. The question of discernment is not: *What is God (primary Agent) doing among us and ahead of us so we can discern how to join with God?* Rather, it is: *What does the data and*

6. See Ephesians 1:1–12.

research tell us about what is happening and what methods can we best use to engage what we are seeing? The latter is the dominant understanding of discernment in the Euro-tribal churches. The prior question now sounds strange and disorienting.

The Search for Certainty and Modern Skepticism

The modern era was born out of a crisis of knowing. It was formed from within a deep anxiety around the question of how we know as human beings. The fifteenth to seventeenth centuries was a period that experienced its own profound unraveling of the story that had dominated the West for almost a thousand years. During this time there emerged a period of disorientation like the one we've entered. On the agenda of many thinkers was the question of how to provide a method of knowing that would restore certainty to life.[7] This desire for certainty (a core agenda of Descartes) got embedded in the modern imagination. The methods that came to characterize the modern era were those that could promise some modicum of certainty. This is also an overarching characteristic of the seventy-five-year story. Therefore, when the question: *How do you know?* is asked, the question behind it is: *What's the method for providing certainty?* This is, in part, why we're driven by a desire for methods and a search for techniques that make the world clear, legible,[8] and certain.

In an era continually searching for methods of certainty, when the question *How do I discern?* is raised, it is almost always a question about methods that will produce certainty. Driving this is a whole class of educated, knowledge professionals whose identities are rooted in the conviction that they are supposed to have a method of knowing. Part of the anxiety of leaders is a new kind of awareness that we've entered this place where it is increasingly clear that we don't have the methods to give us certainty. These defaults became embedded in the seventy-five-year story, creating feedback loops that misdirect our practices of

7. See Roxburgh and Robinson, *Practices for the Refounding of God's People*, chapters 1–3.

8. This drive to make the world legible and, therefore, certain, is brilliantly expressed in Scott's *Seeing Like a State.* In his Introduction he directly states what is at issue: "The more I examined these efforts . . . the more I came to see . . . a state's attempts to make society legible, to arrange the population in ways that simplified the classic state functions of taxation, conscription, and prevention of rebellion . . . I began to see legibility as a central problem in statecraft" (Scott, *Seeing Like a State*, 2).

discernment. Discernment has become the search for legibility and the certainty of a method.

Our struggle with the question of discernment goes deeper. While we live in a story that purports to offer methods of certainty and control, we also live in a time that is skeptical of all claims of knowing. We are just as deeply awash in narratives of skepticism as we are in those of certainty. We are caught between a rock and a hard place that makes the question of discernment confusing and disorienting. In a world shaped by the desire for certainty and riddled with skepticism about claims of knowing, we fear being deceived. It makes us powerless to act. This is the confusing space of churches called to discern God's agency.

Discernment: Not as Simple as We Might Imagine

Discernment is not as simple as we have imagined. Functionally, most congregations work with methods that don't assume God is the Agent amongst us. As a result, we usually don't attend to what God is doing beyond the baptism of our own plans. Notions of God as an Agent seem wrongheaded in a universe made clear and accessible through scientifically informed, rational individuals.[9] God is not needed for our interpreting or acting in the world.

As a result, practices that have shaped Christian tradition are lost. Discernment is one. Varieties of empirical social analysis and strategic planning became the primary methods of discernment. Discernment came to be seen as proficiency in the skills of assessment: *How do we identify the needs of people in our community and develop programs and resources to meet these needs? What kinds of programs can we develop to assist and help people when they need it? What are the skill sets that make us effective participants in our community? What does the data tell us about the trends and how do we align our church's ministries and programs with them?* These questions and approaches have a place. The problem, from a Christian perspective, is that they operate inside a framework in which God is not the Agent. We are the agents. These methods promise us a discernment process that can get us close to certainty. Within these frameworks there's little need to ask *what is God doing here and how is the*

9. These were common themes in this seventy-five-year story. In North America, for example, the work of sociologists Peter Berger and Thomas Luckmann, in books like *Social Construction of Reality* and *Sacred Canopy*, explored this radical loss of God as Agent in the world.

Spirit calling us to act? It's all up to us. God has given us the tools to figure things out and is not a part of how we make decisions. Functionally, we are like all other citizens of modernity: we do not need this strange practice of discernment to assess what needs to be done. It's a matter of deciding what will best serve our goals and desired outcomes. We are in control until Christ returns.

How do we cultivate communities in which discernment becomes a normative Christian practice? The Canadian First Nations activist Glen Coulthard[10] writes about what might be involved. He uses the phrase "grounded normativity" to describe the capacity of a people to live out of practices that are at the center of their tradition. For First Nations people, this question has become central to the recovery of their identity in a colonizing story that has all but erased it. Could First Nations peoples be our guides in this journey? Euro-tribal emigrants to Turtle Island took away the traditions and stories of First Nations peoples. This was done by demanding they give up their languages and their identities. In this long colonizing process, First Nations peoples lost the grounded normativity of their stories; their identity became tenuous and frail.

Coultard writes, like Leanne Betasamosake Simpson,[11] about the need to recover this grounded normativity. By "grounded," he means ways of living, speaking, and practicing that which has been passed down among a people for centuries—it is the deep traditions that make a people a people. When people are grounded in their stories and practices, they know who they are. When people are removed from these practices of identity, they are lost to themselves. They are without a way of orienting their common life.[12] First Nations peoples' stories and rituals were intentionally taken from them. The colonizers refused to allow them their own language, thus taking away their identities. First Nations are finding ways of reclaiming their languages and traditions. It is part of their fundamental resistance to colonizations.

What is the meaning of these observations for Euro-tribal Christians and discernment? It means we need to reconnect with our grounded

10. Coulthard, *Red Skin, White Masks.*

11. Simpson, *As We Have Always Done.*

12. One fears that much of what is called contemporary worship has done exactly this to Christian identity. Gatherings shaped around an extended period of a certain kind of music followed by a Bible "teaching" event remove those regular times when the gathered church "confesses" together its story so that it is regularly rooted back into its grounded normativity.

normativity. A first step in reclaiming our tradition is in realizing that the loss of a language world and its traditions is what has happened to the Euro-tribal churches. Essential to the resurgence of Christian identity is the capacity to embrace the grounded normativity of our story through the recovery of its practices and traditions. This is why we have put so much emphasis on the traditional practices of dwelling and discerning.

This desire for certainty and control has been present throughout history. The story of the burning bush (Exod 3) is illustrative of such desire. Moses had to escape Egypt after taking to himself the agency for righting the wrongs of Israel's long captivity. He was dwelling in the desert, married and watching the flocks of his father-in-law in the land of Midian. One imagines Moses, in those long hours with flocks, thinking often about the cries of his people as they were systematically destroyed by Pharaoh. In this state, he wandered beyond the normal grazing areas and came upon a bush that burned but wasn't consumed. As he turned aside to see this bush, he was unexpectedly encountered by God. He had inadvertently stumbled into a thin space where God was present. Moses was told to take off his shoes because he was standing on holy ground, a God-space.

God told Moses that he had heard the cries of Israel and would deliver them. Moses heard that he, the murderer of Egyptian soldiers and the adopted son within the royal household, was being sent back to tell Pharaoh, his adoptive brother, to let the people go. Moses demurred. There was too much uncertainty. A verbal fencing match between Moses and God ensued. Moses retorted with the fact that he was a lousy public speaker and, therefore, couldn't adequately represent God to Pharaoh or his own people. God countered by giving him Aaron as his mouthpiece. Moses countered back with the realistic fact that he couldn't do the magic of the Egyptian sorcerers so he would make God look powerless and foolish. God countered once more by giving Moses the means of reproducing the magic.

Then came a final, most significant play. Moses told God he needed to know God's name, otherwise Israel would not know the source of who sent him and, therefore, not follow him. This was a power play on Moses' part. He was after something very particular. In such a society, to have someone's name (especially a god's) was to have their power. What Moses was asking for was the ability to have certainty, the power to manage outcomes at the front door. God gave Moses the ambiguous response: My name is YHWH—I am who I am. While there are many ways of interpreting this enigmatic naming, one reading of this expression is that God was, in effect, saying: "Moses, you will not have control of me. I am who I am and will do what I do and you won't control the outcomes. Go!" Built into the core of the biblical narrative, into God's very name, the grounded normativity of our story, is a remonstrance—you will never have certainty, you will not be able to predict, measure, or control outcomes. The Christian life lies in a different kind of normativity. This is what we have forgotten and lost in terms of discernment when we ask the question of *How*? There is no technique, no certainty, no control.

Discernment has a different path. God will never be pliable to our techniques because God is wholly other. As the YHWH-naming makes clear, the mystery of who God is cannot be made pliable to our methods. It is in the risk of relationality and trust that we discern the movements of God. That discernment always involves risk and uncertainty.[13]

Recovering Discernment as a Central Practice of Christian Communities

The recovery of discernment as a central practice of Christian communities is a critical act of Christian resistance. It is a primary means of living into the grounded normativity of our story. Discernment is shaped by the conviction that God is active in our communities in remaking the world. This is why we use the language of God "being ahead of us" and of "joining with God" in our communities. The former Archbishop of Canterbury, Rowan Williams, expresses this sense of discernment when he asks: "How do we learn to be placed in the world where the acts of God can become alive?"[14] Placing ourselves in our neighborhoods to see where God is acting and then joining God there is at the heart of discernment. This is why dwelling is such a central practice in the recovery of our grounded normativity.

The work of leadership is forming a people who are asking: *What is God doing amongst us, in our collective and larger communities? How is the Spirit calling us into this community?* These are discernment questions. They're not worked out by a leader, then delivered to people. They're the work of God's people dwelling in their neighborhoods.

13. For a more thorough engagement with this question of knowing as the risk of relationality rather than methods of certainty and control, see Roxburgh, *Joining God in the Great Unraveling*.

14. Williams, *Being Disciples*, 18.

Discernment isn't a strategy based on trends. It is a community asking together: *As we dwell in this place, with these people, what is God doing here in our lives and in this neighborhood? How might we join with what the Spirit is saying to us through one another?* Discernment is a "long obedience in the same direction"[15] that, in the language of Benedict's Rule, is achieved from within the practice of stability (a commitment to these people and this place). Discernment is how a local community of Christians dwelling in a place, listen to the Spirit with and through one another. It's about trust in relationships as the way we hear God among us and our neighbors. Discernment takes us out of certainty into the risk of hearing God in the other.

Practicing Discernment

In Scripture discernment happens in many ways. The world within which Paul lived was comfortable with this practice. Acts 16 is an example. Paul and his companions planned to revisit young house churches across Asia. Their plans kept being thwarted. Luke's interpretation is that the Spirit of Jesus was preventing them. Paul and his companions did not interpret this as primarily a matter of external circumstances (weather, illness, angry business leaders, war, missed connections, etc.). They understood the preventing as the actions of the Spirit. As a result, they stopped to attend to what the Spirit was saying in this preventing. In this posture of waiting, there came to them, via a dream, a new sense of direction. Together, they concluded that the vision of a man of Macedonia was the Spirit redirecting them to the Roman colony of Philippi in Europe. This conviction didn't come from smart planning, data analysis, or some group innovation process that suggested the future trend was Europe. The movement of Acts 16 suggests that these disciples would never have come to the conclusion that God was calling them to Philippi by themselves. It does, however, suggest that discernment was a normative part of their life together.

At Troas, God called them out of certainty and control (they knew where they needed to go and had a plan that had worked on the first journey). Their method had been to follow the Jewish-Christian synagogue routes across Asia, preach in a synagogue and seek converts. If the response was positive, they transformed the synagogue into a

15. Peterson, *Long Obedience in the Same Direction.*

synagogue of Jesus. If there was resistance (as there often was), they moved down the street and started a synagogue of Jesus. This innovation had been successful. There was no point changing anything. Then the method stopped working. Acts 16 suggests they became increasingly frustrated and disoriented. Rather than asking what new innovation they needed, they asked a discernment question: *What is the Spirit saying to us?* This involved waiting, praying, and listening to God through one another. It also suggests that they had become the kind of community in which there was a deep trust of one another. All of this led to Paul's vision in the night of the man of Macedonia. The result was a complete change of direction from anything they'd imagined. In their disorientation and readiness to stop and listen, they became open to a world none of them could have imagined.

Discernment is about risk. Sara Arthur and Erin Wasinger, in their little book *The Year of Small Things*, reflect on the question of what's involved in practicing discernment. For them, it

> isn't about receiving a sudden vision, or decided clarity about what you're supposed to do. Discernment is more like standing on a foggy mountain trail, peering into the gray mass that is your best guess at the trail. You take a few steps at a time, check your compass and crumpled trail map in your pocket. Sometimes there's a surprise vista when the fog clears; occasionally you miss your turn. Most of the way you're plodding along without a clear sense of what's next. But you don't go it alone. You hike with a team. And together you listen for the voice of the One calling in the fog.[16]

Discernment is a practice we learn as we risk going on a journey of listening to God with one another. It requires the Abram-like readiness to go to a place he hadn't seen. There's a lot of back and forth, trying and stumbling, imagining and testing, running ahead and needing to sit down to see. Like novices, we learn to walk with one another along foggy mountain trails. There is no certainty or method that guarantees outcomes. Discernment is a whole other order of being. It isn't a Lone Ranger activity, nor the prerogative of the ordained or an elite team of leaders. It is the work of the people as they dwell with one another and take risks in exploring what the Spirit is saying to them. It is a practice we learn together through trial and error.

16. Arthur and Erin Wasinger, in their book, *year of small things*, 13.

John Inge connects discernment with life as a sacramental community.[17] Being a community that gathers around the table to celebrate Christ's body and blood given for us is where a community of discernment is formed. The table reminds us that life together is about mystery, not method. It is about the One who has come to us whom we cannot control. Like the bush that wasn't consumed and the wind that blows where it will, the table keeps reminding us that God in Christ, YHWH, can never be controlled or managed. Discernment, then, comes from a table-shaped community that dwells with God together in order to ask the question of what God is doing. The answer to that question is this risky willingness to travel with companions into places we've never been before. This is why our third practice, exploring, is so important. The practice of discernment will seem far outside the ethos of most congregational life. But there are concrete ways we can use to initiate this journey of learning together to cultivate a discerning people.

Creating Spaces for Hearing the Spirit

Discernment is about listening to God; it is perceiving and responding to God in our ordinary, everyday experiences, not just in those rare, significant moments in time. Mark's Gospel presents Jesus' days as full of activity—traveling and teaching, healings and deliverance, crowds within and beyond the synagogue. In the midst of this we read: "The following morning, Jesus got up and went to a solitary place where he prayed . . ." Eventually, the disciples found him. No doubt they were eagerly awaiting another day of frenetic activity, responding to the needs and expectations of the crowds. But what they heard from Jesus was different. He said to them: "we're going on to other places." In accounts of constant action, we see withdrawal from frenetic activity into a quiet place. In the midst of many engagements with people comes solitude and contemplation, a withdrawing in order to discern. Jesus is not going to be driven by needs, obligations, or expectations, but by the Spirit, and this can only happen by times of stopping and withdrawing. There is nothing new, radical, or spectacular about this but it points to practices we will need for discernment to become a core part of our life together. Where and how are we inviting ourselves and our people back into this

17. Inge, *Christian Theology of Place.*

simple practice of stepping aside into stillness and prayer where the possibility of hearing a word becomes possible?

Discernment is the gateway to another way of seeing and acting. This is why traditional practices such as Examen, dwelling in the Word, and the Daily Office are activities we cultivate with our people. Without changing structure, programs, or roles, we gently invite people (such as leadership teams, boards, small groups) to take on practices that open us to discerning together.

Shaping Meetings for Discernment

A practical way to introduce the practice of discernment is to begin with a church's board or leadership team. They're usually run with taken-for-granted methods of any business organization. They have agendas, plans, and measurable outcomes. These agendas look much the same from meeting to meeting. A board will, normally, pray at the beginning and the end of meetings to ensure God is brought into their deliberations. These meetings are shaped by unconscious habits designed to get things done in a good business manner. With some simple steps it's possible to introduce the practice of discernment. Begin by creating a brief time (fifteen to twenty minutes) to practice dwelling in the Word. If this might be too much, invite board members to engage with a simple Examen question, such as, *Where are you seeing God at work in our congregation just now?* Introducing such simple activities into the rhythms of our established meetings, we can, without a lot of fanfare, start the practice of discernment.

Part of what we want to be doing as leaders is paying attention to the unconscious assumptions shaping how we go about decision-making as a church. In Acts 16, the team of apostles found themselves in a place where their strategies weren't working. Confused and feeling stuck, they didn't know how to proceed. Paul and his companions needed to find a way forward that was outside their existing assumptions. Their capacity to pause[18] was a key act. In a posture of waiting, their assumptions about

18. It seems that they were regrouping in Troas. It was a place where they stopped to ask the question of what was going on. One of the important things that happened in Troas is that others joined the team. In Acts 16 there is a subtle shift in pronouns suggesting that Luke, the writer of the Gospel and Acts, joined them at this point, perhaps with others. What we can see here is a team of leaders, albeit confused and disoriented, but they had been dwelling with one another on this confusing journey. The relationships were deep; the trust was high. One can see a shifting of imagination beginning to

how God was directing them were changed. Unconscious decision-making frameworks had kept them pressing forward with their plan to go into Asia with an established strategy. When they stopped to listen, their perspectives changed. The vision of a man of Macedonia was a partial, limited picture of what the Spirit was doing, but it created the space for them to risk steps into the unknown. Discernment involved a readiness to see where the Spirit was calling them. In Philippi, however, they didn't find a man of Macedonia or a synagogue. They were still operating according to pre-established strategies. Responding to the Spirit's nudging, they found themselves outside their comfort zones.[19]

As you begin some small explorations with your boards around discernment, find small ways to invite them into times of waiting and listening before making decisions. In the story of the healing of the man

---

take shape that wasn't about another round of planning. They (collectively) had, somehow, come to believe that in all the mess, the Spirit was at work (Luke reports that it was "the Spirit" who was preventing them). They recognized, therefore, that they needed to stop and find ways of listening to the Spirit. We don't get any more information than this so we don't get clues on the "how" of their discernment, just that they were now listening attentively to the Spirit.

19. Another example is in Acts 15. The young church in Jerusalem was confronted with decisions that would no longer fit inside its understanding of what God was doing after Pentecost. What were they to do with non-Jewish believers (Greek and Roman God-fearers, Greek widows of Jewish men who'd travelled to Jerusalem for the festival)? Should they be let into the community of Jesus (which would, without doubt, quickly overwhelm the Jewish character and majority in this new movement)? If so, what about the Law, the covenant, the dietary commitments, circumcision? Each, by itself, was a massive issue that went to the heart of this new community's identity. The conscious and unconscious assumptions of the Jerusalem leadership would have been sorely stretched. All their formation, tradition, and habits told them that this Jesus movement was about Israel and the Jewish people. This was, in part, why they had firmly set everything up in Jerusalem and around the temple. The Jesus movement was to be a renewed Judaism set in its historical center. There was no need to give this a second thought, all their decisions were set in these conclusions. With Pentecost and the mass conversion of diaspora pilgrims came a new set of challenges. Some of these new converts (Jews, God-fearers, and gentiles) left Jerusalem and headed up the coast speaking of Jesus. Before leaders in Jerusalem could figure out what was happening, we're told that the Spirit was bringing gentiles into the new community. What was to be done? Assumptions about what God was doing in the world through Jesus were being torn apart right in front of them. Decisions had to be made. Doctrine and practice had to be addressed. The leaders in Jerusalem entered a process of painful discernment, which must have stretched their relationships and felt like they were putting the whole movement at risk. We aren't told about the actual processes of discernment in which they engaged, but we can surmise that it was communal ("it seems good to us and to the Spirit"), requiring a readiness to dwell deeply with one another and in Scripture. Their discernment resulted in a remaking of their conscious and unconscious assumptions around how God was working and how they were to behave with one another and the outsider.

born blind (John 9), the religious leaders couldn't fit what Jesus was doing into their assumptions around who gets healed and who doesn't. For that reason, they were unable to discern what was happening. Jesus' actions didn't fit their assumptions of how God worked. They missed the opportunity to discern because their assumptions led them to the wrong conclusions.[20] This happens to us all the time. All kinds of cultural assumptions continually shape our beliefs around what is to be done and who is to be doing what. One pastor described how she introduced her board to the practice of dwelling with their neighbors. This program-driven congregation was unconsciously formed around the assumption that their role was to get more bums in pews and cash in the plate. Furthermore, the notion of dwelling with the neighbor was very unfamiliar to them. It was a scary strategy that did not make sense to them in terms of their roles in getting the church to grow. By building into board meetings listening spaces, like Examen and dwelling in the word, she could slowly create listening spaces where the possibility of doing discernment could begin.

Seeing Our Defaults

Ruth Haley Barton's *Pursuing God's Will Together*[21] describes how established habits can lead to structural blindness. Like the John 9 encounter, this can lead to built in blindness to what is happening around us. We might believe, for example, that making decisions requires a process built around data, good strategy, and well-defined outcomes. Such a process of decision-making requires little to no listening to God through one another. Barton argues that this structural blindness limits our capacity to practice discernment. The questions the disciples and religious leaders were asking Jesus about the correct ways of going about

20. In the case of this event in John 9, cultural assumptions about the meaning of blindness (rooted in "sin") rendered them incapable of discerning the presence of God in Jesus.

21. Barton, *Pursuing God's Will Together.* Barton talks of five foundational building blocks that help good discernment practices. First, spiritual discernment recognizes it is a work of the Holy Spirit by which we are able to discover what God is doing within our neighborhoods. Second, recognizing a dependency on God is the willingness to lay down our own desires, thinking, and planning in a willing surrender and openness to God, whose ways are often different from our ways. Third, a deep belief in the goodness and loving purposes of God for the world leads on to a conviction that our calling is ultimately to love God, neighbor, and self. And finally, there is a commitment to not only pray the words but implement, "Your will be done."

things were governed by their structured beliefs. Jesus wanted them to see that they were asking the wrong questions and, therefore, failing to see what was actually going on. Barton quotes Richard Rohr: "most people do not see things as they are; rather, they see things as they [i.e., the people seeing] are."[22] We read the world in front of us through preset, structured interpretations. This is why collecting data, running innovation seminars, or developing vision statements that define outcomes is a more comfortable way of leading than taking the risk of forming communities of discernment.[23]

Practicing discernment involves building a relational trust with one another. This trust enables us to name our assumptions and how they're influencing how we're seeing things. This goes a long way to explaining why we can't be in a hurry to get others to see what we are seeing in order to change them. Our capacities to discern are a function of the relational trust we're developing as leaders. If your leadership team makes decisions within established patterns, invite them to join you in an experiment that tests a process of discernment together. Such an experiment would be done over several months. People need time to dwell with (chew on) something they're trying on and not feel rushed. A way to start with your board is to invite them into activities such as these:

- Select an issue around which a decision needs to be made. Avoid big or divisive issues at the start. For example, start with a communication issue. Bring to the board a short list of communication issues that could be engaged, asking board members for input. Out of this, name a communication question around which they might practice discernment.
- Develop a summary for how to introduce the process to the leadership.
    - What would you like to propose?
    - Why?
    - How long will it take?

22. Rohr is citing Anaïs Nin. See Barton, *Pursuing God's Will Together*, 19.

23. Critical to any discerning process is self, group, ecclesial, and cultural awareness. The biases of our different backgrounds, outlooks, and experiences all come into play in discerning. Awareness of our passions and prejudices, our collective biases and blind spots are all part of the conscious and unconscious ways we see the world together. Good leadership knows this and forms communities that are cultivating the practices we've discussed.

  - How does this little experiment fit with the work of the board?
  - Signal that they will get to evaluate the experience when it is over.

- After the group has processed the summary, develop a more detailed description of the steps. When people are doing something new, they need more detail than we might imagine.

When the sessions begin:

- Start each session with a fifteen-minute dwelling in the Word to practice listening to God through one another.
- Present the issue in a simple, nontechnical sentence or two.
- Invite team members to take some time to personally "dwell" in the challenge with the question: "What's important for us here as a church?"
- After about five minutes create breakout groups where members share their responses.
- Groups come back together, people share the response they heard from another group member.
- Write the responses on a newsprint where they can all be seen.
- Invite the group to look over the responses on the newsprint with the questions:
  - As we look at our responses, what are we hearing together?
  - Are there common themes and questions we should attend to?
- On the basis of this, ask: Where might we be hearing the Spirit in this process?
  - List these.
  - Ask: What small experiment might the Spirit be calling us to risk in starting to address this challenge?
  - Design and carry out the experiment.
- Reflection questions:
  - What do you sense we are doing?
  - Where is this assisting you to see another way of leading?

- What questions is it raising for you?
- What is working for you?
- What isn't working and why?
- How is this way of leading different from how we normally operate?

Waiting, Listening, Stopping

The listening habits we develop in such simple experiments are the precondition for discerning. Mark 1 describes a time of great activity for Jesus, where lots of demands were on him. As he taught and healed, growing crowds followed. Any leader would be thrilled by the potential this growth represented. Today, leaders would be figuring out how to build momentum for a movement. Mark, however, stated: "The following morning, Jesus got up and went to a solitary place where he prayed."[24] The disciples, eagerly awaiting another day of teaching, healing, and growing crowds, were confused. They went to find him. When they found Jesus, what they heard from him was: "we're going on to other places . . ."[25] Amidst growth, movement, and constant action, Jesus gave counterintuitive words. To make sense of what the crowds meant and what was needed to shape his engagement with them, Jesus needed solitude, prayer, and withdrawal to discern. He was not going to be driven by need, obligation, the vision of a movement, or the expectations of disciples. To discern what to do Jesus listened to the Spirit. This listening is critical to discerning.

Listening, waiting, and dwelling with one another and God are practices for discerning. We respond to God out of our ordinary, everyday experiences as we wait and listen to what the Spirit might be saying to us. Discernment, therefore, isn't a "Hail Mary." It is one of the rhythms we need to reestablish our grounded normativity. A leader looks for places where he/she invites people to listen to people's stories, dwell in Scripture, and gently ask where we might be hearing the Spirit. In such small actions, over time, we gently invite people into the processes of discernment. After people have tried the practices for a while, a leader gently invites them to reflect on what they are learning and

24. Mark 1:35.

25. Mark 1:37–38.

experiencing about the practice of discernment. This reflective engagement opens up space for people to talk together about the next steps in building discernment into the rhythms of their lives.

Discernment is a gateway into a wisdom that comes from God. This communal dwelling and listening opens space to hear God. Growing together in practicing discernment replants the grounded normativity of Christian life. Discernment points us back to ancient ways of listening to the Spirit. We are in need of a way of wisdom, not the latest research trends or innovation principles. As Paul urged the church in Rome, "Don't conform . . . but let God transform you . . . by changing the way you think. Then you'll learn to know the will of God, which is good and pleasing and perfect."[26] Discernment is a radical stand against the machine and an anticipation of the One who makes all things new.

Discernment Practices

As we have noted, Barton talks of four building blocks for good discernment practices.

1. First, discernment recognizes this as a work of the Holy Spirit by which we discover what God is doing in our neighborhoods.
2. Second, in doing the practice of listening to God we're slowly being weaned away from our own desires and agency to become more open to the One whose ways are often different from ours.
3. Third, living into the regular rhythms of these practices there gradually emerges a deepening conviction of the goodness and loving purposes of God for ourselves and our world. This is the sign that a Christian grounded normativity is being built back into the frail ways of Euro-tribal Christianity.
4. Finally, building is the capacity to pray and act on the words, "Your will be done."

The practices are the pathways guiding our steps and sustaining us on this journey. Because these practices are largely lost in the modern era, a leaders' focus is on weaving them back into the ways of being God's people. As these practices develop, trust is built. People get a different sense of being

26. Rom 12:2 (NIV).

part of a community where they are heard and share life together. Here is the grounded normativity we're called to develop.

We were working with pastors in a country that highly values a strong work ethic. These pastors had one day off a week, working the other days from early hours of the morning until late at night. The church consumed their time. There wasn't a lot of discernment going on among them. We gently invited them to carve out time each week to dwell at home and in their neighborhood. Initially, the pastors were terrified of this prospect of meeting people in their community. And staying home for an evening with their family felt like they were failing their church responsibilities. Over time things shifted. In tears, one pastor confessed that he had slowly fallen out of love with his wife. Their relationship had come to feel like a contract with to-do boxes for each. The flame of their relationship was being rekindled in this simple act of dwelling and being present to one another. As the tender bonds of love were being rewoven, they could hear one another again. This risk of relationship is a doorway into discernment. Another person, the wife of a pastor, turned to Alan as they were driving him to the airport and with tears in her eyes said: "Thank you for giving us back a husband and father. He has rediscovered me and his sons again." What he had rediscovered was the discerning of the Spirit.

One leader was figuring out how to make connections in his community. It felt too threatening at first. It was because this kind of connection was outside his role and identity as a pastor. He didn't know who he was or how to behave in those contexts. Reluctantly, the pastor started dropping in to a local coffee shop everyday. Conversations slowly began with the owners in those early mornings, and a world that could never have been planned or imagined opened up before him. This pastor was being introduced to people who lived around him whom he had no idea existed. Soon they were sitting together over coffee and the stories of who they were and what they were experiencing in the neighborhood started to change his image of the community. Discernment was beginning through listening well to the stories of others. Simple activities such as these are the seedbed for discernment. They drive us to ask the question: *What is God's Spirit doing in this place among these people?*

Discernment, Listening and, Awareness

Awareness is seeing, hearing, feeling, smelling, and touching what is all around us that we often miss or take for granted. We enter the ways of God's Spirit as we redirect our senses past the obvious, the need to assess or categorize others (we're hardly aware of how quickly we pigeonhole people). An illustration is helpful.

Peter Wohlleben's 2015 best-selling book, *The Hidden Life of Trees,* tells the story of his own awakening to this gift of awareness of the incredible world that had been right before his eyes all the time. Our training as professionals and experts shapes how we engage our world in ways that turn practically everything into manageable objects and commodities (think, for example, of the taken-for-granted way people in church talk about others as "seekers" as if they were data points on a scale, or objects to be managed with certain kinds of strategies). Wohlleben was a highly trained arborist with years of experience, a professional and expert when it came to trees. If asked, he would claim that out of all the people around him he knew trees. He was a forester working for lumber companies. He had an eye for seeing trees; an expert in identifying trees that would yield the most planks and boards for his company. Despite all this, his awareness of trees was circumscribed; but he, the professional, didn't know it. Let's allow him to speak.

> When I began my professional life as a forester, I knew about as much about the hidden life of trees as a butcher knows about the emotional life of animals. The modern forestry industry produces lumber. That is to say, it fells trees and then plants new seedlings. If you read the professional literature, you quickly get the impression that the well-being of the forests is the only interest insofar as it is necessary for optimizing the lumber industry . . . Eventually it distorts the way they look at trees . . . Because it was my job to look at hundreds of trees everyday—spruce, beeches, oaks and pines—to assess their suitability for the lumber mill and their market value, my appreciation of trees was also restricted to this narrow point of view.[27]

His training had prepared him to miss the forest for the trees. As a degreed professional "forester" he had failed to grasp how they lived together. All he saw were potential planks—the economic stripping of forests. He missed the wonder and strangeness, the beauty and amazing life right

27. Peter Wohlleben, *Hidden Life of Trees,* xiii.

in front of him. He knew nothing, for example, of a whole other world of trees that were burgeoning under his feet. In our language, discernment is the way of seeing in a whole other way, with an expectation that God is at work in our world, in the places where we dwell. We are invited to join with God in the reweaving of all things.

Cultivating Expectancy

We're invited to expect God in the midst of the stories and the people in our neighborhood. The Spirit is continually bubbling up and breaking out in our everyday encounters. Expectancy assumes that this place where I dwell with others is "the kind of place where something extraordinary suddenly bursts into view."[28] This sense of God's presence has been sucked out of our Christian story. The anxious question people ask is: *How will I know if I see God?* The answer at the beginning is that you won't, you need to risk and trust.

Alan offers an illustration of expectancy from his learning to develop the physical ability to balance on a board. It is no easy task. Deep inside there was always a lingering inner voice—*this is impossible! It's a waste of time because it's never going to happen.* The board is no more than a foot in circumference with a small ball at the center of its base. Alan's assignment was to balance on it for a minute each day. At first it all seemed defeating. But then, slowly, he started to find himself standing and balancing on the board. He now came to the board not as a daunting task but with the expectancy of a new adventure.

Tensions

We're in regular conversations with church leaders about the challenges of leadership in this disruptive time. Though each describes their experiences in somewhat different ways, their underlying issues are the same. A common tension discourages them. While they agree with the practices we've outlined, they experience themselves as on a treadmill of bureaucratic management and firefighting they can't get off. The management systems set in place when denominations were thriving

28. Williams, *Being Disciples*, 5.

hardly make sense in this disruptive place. They're sucking up time and spending down hope.[29]

One leader, when asked what had surprised him about starting a new executive role, said he wasn't prepared for the amount of management and paperwork he had to deal with all the time, along with the constant crisis management the job required. The message we hear is that at the end of each month there's no time left to be a different kind of leader. The result is discouragement, a feeling there's no way out. Leaders agree with what we've written. They want to form communities of hope in a place we've never been before, but they feel there's no time left after they've expended themselves in management, meetings, metrics, and firefighting.

This is no easy tension to fix. We were never trained for this disruptive space. None of this will suddenly disappear. The disruptions will accelerate. The pressure to manage and fix will grow. There is no big system redesign that will fix this. Every attempt to restructure or reinvent will only exacerbate the tension. But there are ways forward. It will involve such things as:

- Embracing the practices of dwelling, discerning, and exploring.
- Starting in small ways with small numbers of people.
- Becoming co-learners in a community of companions.
- Seeing that this is going to be a long journey with few, if any, maps to guide us. In the words of Antonio Machado, we will make the road as we walk.

In this journey of making another road, the practices of dwelling are how we reweave a Christian grounded normativity. At the center of that normativity is the practice of discernment. It means becoming a community of explorers who are ready to risk and test together what we're discerning the Spirit saying amongst us. This is the subject of our next chapter.

29. Often, pastors express the sense to us that they have no time left to do anything more. This is one of the great anxieties they wrestle with that leads to feelings of failure and inadequacy. But this framing of the time question is misleading. We are able to show how, in simple ways, they can free up the time to begin the leading we're describing. We are also able to show them how they can communicate to their church leaders what they are wanting to develop and do this in ways that create a shared energy. But, more than anything else, it's when we connect a leader with a group of *companions* that they find the support to take this journey.

CHAPTER TEN

Exploring

Introduction

CHAPTER NINE OFFERED SEVERAL scriptural examples of discernment. Acts 16 was one such text. The seaport of Troas, a "colonia" (a place for retired Roman soldiers), was nestled on the Aegean Sea across from modern-day Greece. There, Paul and his companions stopped. They would take time to discern why this second journey was going so wrong. Part of that discernment involved the vision of a man of Macedonia calling them to come over to what would have been the world of Roman Europe. One suspects that they gathered in Troas to figure out why the Spirit was preventing them from carrying out the planned work in Asia. Europe wasn't in their plans.

Troas was linked in people's imagination to ancient Troy, where Greeks (Europeans) had invaded Asia. While Greek and Asian cultures had interacted with each other for a long time, especially since Roman colonization, a journey from Troas to Macedonia would have still carried with it the sense of a boundary crossing. For Paul and his companions this journey meant more than a logistical, or geographic, move from one place to another. It was more than a strategic adjustment to a plan. Literally, they were at the boundaries of this Jesus movement as they had understood it. They were at the far end of the journey of exploration as they had conceived it.

Their discernment began as a dream that was an invitation to exploration beyond the boundaries of their imaginations. Discernment in Troas gave them a renewed sense of direction. They set in place a strategy that took them by the most direct route to Macedonia and, specifically, Philippi. The reason for the choice of Philippi would have been that it was the strategic center of Macedonia. But, beyond that plan, their discernment in Troas didn't yield any clearly defined strategies or plans with well-marked outcomes. The Troas companions received a vision but had to figure out what it was the Spirit was doing. The only way they could do that was to become explorers. In a place we've never been before, our assumptions about how things work are turned upside down. We have to reimagine what God is doing ahead of us. More often than not, discernment starts with little more than clues and hints that need to be tested. For a culture controlled by the tools of certainty and a need for clarity that is a disorienting call.

In a similar way, Celtic Christians saw themselves being guided by the Holy Spirit. They understood themselves as being called by the unpredictable Spirit onto journeys of discovery they couldn't control. "The wind blows where it wills, and you hear the sound it makes, but you do not know where it comes from or where it goes; so it is with everyone who is born of the Spirit" (John 3:8). With these as our givens, along with our discerning, we will also become explorers together in time and place where we only see the picture as we explore the road we make.

Exploring, Discovering, Pioneering, Pilgrimage

We're encountering a plethora of new language that's attempting to convey the conviction that Jesus is ahead of us in our communities and we're being called to join with what the Spirit is doing there. This is why we have argued for a reorienting of imagination toward the question: *How do we discern what God is doing ahead of us in our communities in order to join with God there?*[1] Our proposals are set in the context of this question. We're encouraged by the increased attention this question is receiving. In recent years, language has emerged to express this turn. A word like *pioneering* describes the openness to take the Acts 16 way of stepping beyond established defaults to join with God.[2] The language of pioneering

1. See Roxburgh, *Joining God in the Great Unraveling*.

2. The Church of England has defined pioneering as follows: "Pioneering is about firsts. Being the first to lead ministry into new places for and with others. Pioneers must be able to see a new future, and have the skills and gifts needed to make it a reality now. Pioneers connect with people outside of Church, creating new ways of

expresses this willingness to risk discovering the forms of Christian life needed in any particular context. *Pioneer* avoids the language of *church planting*, which, too often, can smack of ecclesiocentrism. The language of *new* suggests that what we're doing is like a regular congregation except with some novel or cool differences (like deciding for a yellow rather than a gray car, a menthol rather than a mint toothpaste). Some propose the word *pilgrim* to express the sense of going with God while not getting caught in the defaults of power and control. Others are using the modifiers before nouns such as *communities*, *wineskins*, or *places*.

We commend these initiatives and the experimenting. Some of it will be little more than attempts to revivify forms of church we've known (different lipstick or cool haircuts with cut jeans and loud music). But that is the nature of going on an exploration in a place we've never been before. It is about many little misses and failures. It is also about discovering along the way the amazing work of the Spirit among people we would never have expected. Pilgrims and pioneers are helpful and important modes of this journeying, but they can also signal something not intended, namely, that this is work for a special class of people. This temptation has to be avoided because this is not how the Spirit works.

We're adding to this language the word *exploring*. For us, it expresses the conviction that we discern what the Spirit is doing by risking small explorations without too quickly foreclosing on what needs to happen or too quickly setting structures in cement. *While we don't believe the structures and leadership forms that have colonized the Euro-tribal churches over the past seventy-five years can carry us forward, nor do we believe the Spirit has given up on this part of the church.* Therefore, we shy away from

doing Church together in their community." (Church of England, "Faith and Life / Vocations / Pioneer Ministry," https://www.churchofengland.org/faith-life/vocations/pioneer-ministry.) We're not convinced that the language of "firsts" is really what this is about and that the language of "a new future" can sneak vision and outcomes back in to the equation (which suits funders because it brings in through the backdoor the kinds of dashboards they can use to count success), but it hints at the flavor of pioneering in terms of following God out into unknown and unpredictable spaces. The challenge, of course, is that we don't always know what the "skills and gifts" need to be. In this area pioneers need to be able to stay open to discovering and testing in this area of skills and capacities—they have to discern this from grounded presence and deep practice. The practices we have been outlining seem to us to provide the minimum base of capacities pioneers will need. They are not trying to squeeze such explorers into preset categories (pastor/teacher/evangelist/apostle/prophet) largely because if we start with these skill categories then we are already front-loading the pioneer with the definitions and expectations we already have set into these categories. This is probably why so much pioneering keeps looking a lot like what we already have in existing church life.

the language of *new* and fear that language like *pioneers* can unintentionally limit our openness to the Spirit to certain personality types. We believe that within the torn, fading wineskins of our existing systems are memory, hope, and tradition that, when invited into a space of dwelling and discerning, can call forth a ferment of risking and exploring that can reweave communities of hope. To not believe this is to fail to embrace the story of the One who came all the way down and dwelt among us in the shadows of ordinary life, *offstage from the press given to the next and the new.* This conviction shapes our understanding of exploring. It's too easy right now to applaud one more band of modernity's elites who, by their actions, discount the ordinary and the amazing plodder. Defaulting to elites and personalities dissociates us from the Spirit's off-stage movements among ordinary people.

Stories of Exploring

a. Playgrounds, Cafes and Places of Welcome

In the late 1970s Martin and Lynda, along with some friends, planted a church (Trinity) in a neighborhood of Birmingham, UK. Several years later (1987), the Trinity community moved to a rental hall in Rowheath Pavilion in Bournville. Bournville, the home of Cadbury chocolate, has an amazing history of Christian presence shaped by its founder, George Cadbury (1839–1922). Cadbury, a Quaker, saw the appalling social conditions created by the Industrial Revolution. Along with his brother, he sought ways of addressing the social evils industrialization had brought. Practically and concretely, the brothers built a model village for Birmingham workers, along with schools, churches, and community buildings. Their conviction that the gospel called them to reweave social life is now deeply embedded in the story of this part of Birmingham.

George Cadbury founded Bournville Village Trust to protect this vision. Nearly ninety years later, Trinity Church rented a hall in one of the most iconic community buildings of the trust, Rowheath Pavilion. At that point, in 1987, Mary and her husband, Steve, turned up at Rowheath to be a part of a church that was a few hundred yards from their home. They did, indeed, dwell as God's people where they lived as a family. Over thirty-six years, Mary has seen the church shaped in this dwelling by many adventures. Alongside this Rowheath journey, Mary and Lynda have been at-large companions of the Northumbria

Community.[3] Northumbria has a dispersed network of companions united in their desire to explore a "monastic" way of living in their local communities through a Rule of Life.[4] The Daily Office and a life of stability are two practices of this Rule. These practices shaped Mary and Lynda's participation in the Rowheath congregation.

Rowheath Pavilion not only had a large hall for the church to meet in, but also had changing rooms for football players, smaller meeting rooms, and a pub-like gathering space. It was managed by a group called the Rowheath Centre Trust. In early days, those directing the trust and those using the Pavilion's playing fields were somewhat resentful of the little congregation, ambivalent about its presence. A lot of hard, patient relational work had to be put in by the church community to build the relational connections that would shape their coming years. In the midst of this, the Rowheath Centre Trust went bankrupt. Because the church had been working at its relational capital, Bournville Village Trust asked them to take on the management of the building and its surrounding grounds. This turned out to be far more than simply an extended rental agreement. The church eventually became responsible for the oversight and management of the pavilion and its parkland and sports fields. They'd been handed something others had failed to achieve but saw this as a sacred trust from God, an incredible opportunity for shaping a community of hope in that place. Unexpectedly, they had gone from being renters to lease holders in a way that enabled them to incarnate Christ's life. They were now dwelling deeply in their local context.

Out of this new relationship, the church embarked on many adventures shaped by an exploratory imagination. As Mary described it, they "fiddled about," trying lots of explorations on a small scale—a mothers and toddlers group, a chaplaincy drop-in, and fairs and festivals. Many of these explorations lasted only for a brief period; most were carried out on a shoestring. They set up a tea room that consisted of a hot water urn, tea pot, and not much more. It was a little step that didn't last long and never got established. But they were testing and exploring ways of being God's people where they dwelt. Lots of mistakes were made; they didn't always count the cost and some suffered burnout. However, something was happening in the midst of all this. Rowheath was emerging not just

3. https://www.northumbriacommunity.org/.

4. For those in the Northumbria Community this Rule of Life can be summarized simply as availability and vulnerability (https://www.northumbriacommunity.org/who-we-are/our-rule-of-life/).

as a church meeting place, but a local community center. All of this was happening through members like Martin and Lynda, Mary and Steve, embedded in their church, in their own local community.

Around 2008 things began to accelerate for the church. Circumstances brought a group of students to the pavilion who were able to undertake a community survey. Their survey asked the community what they would like to see at Rowheath. The answer that came back was "a cafe and a playground." The church was expanding and deepening its relationships with the community. On the basis of the survey, they brought together people from the church and the neighborhood to raise funds and build a playground. In this creative partnership, everyone was working together for a common good. There was a sense everyone was in, carrying the load and doing the work. It was really physical stuff—digging foundations and post holes, hauling dirt, and building structures. This was a good time for the men of the church and of the neighborhood as they labored side by side. Boundaries were set aside by the rigors of the task.

Shortly after finishing the playground, the cafe was launched. Again, fixing up the rooms was very physical work that bound people together. Decorating was to be done, resources (kit for the cafe) to be found, and people to be trained. By listening to the community and doing this work together another exploration was underway between the church and its neighborhood. Initially, the cafe was run by volunteers but as it grew, something more than volunteers would be needed.

In the midst of all this creative connection with the community, the congregation continued to experience resistance. There were difficult times for the church as they felt their life was continually being lived in a battleground even as these other stories continued. Mary remembers how she, with others, wrestled with this tension of call and resistance, remembering a sermon from Nehemiah with its call to "move in" and "lay brick." Here was encouragement to keep on the journey. In it all, despite exhaustion and struggling to "see" what was happening, there was also excitement about being part of an emerging community of Christians, a belonging that meant something. The church changed its name to Pavilion Christian Community, then Rowheath Pavilion Church, more closely identifying with their physical context, their home.

What was also affecting the life of Rowheath Church was the way in which some members were also part of the Northumbria Community, with their commitment to place, rhythms of life, and the presence of

God in the local. Lynda and Mary were both members of Northumbria's geographically dispersed network. This was an important element of how they were present at the church. Lynda was appointed the community development coordinator for Rowheath. She was, in effect, an abbess in the midst of Rowheath. Her strong community vision and tireless relational work helped to bring down the us/them barriers. Lots of groups began to rent space in the pavilion and the language began to shift from *users* and *renters* to *community groups*, a sign of the changing ways people were seeing and experiencing one another. A midweek Communion service was begun and Northumbria Daily Office was shared at midday. All of this was shaping a new set of relationships for the church with the community.

The structures of these rhythms, the framework of prayer, helped the gathered community recognize that each day was a gift from God. People would sense being held together corporately by something bigger than the everyday demands on their lives. For a time, these practices were sustaining, but it was hard to hold the business and church together under one vision. Leaders were overstretched and divided by the complexity of the operation. The challenge of the business was overwhelming. Eventually, in the midst of conflict and hurt, the rhythm of prayer faltered and the team fragmented.

In the midst of this disappointment, the church community went on. Dwelling was a continued reality. Listening and discerning continued. New festivals under the banner "Love Bournville" were held at the pavilion, celebrating events in the year and lifting up the story of Bournville and its roots in faith and grace. The cafe and community center thrived, attracting thousands to some events, but eventually at the cost of a more commercial and business-driven culture. However, there was still room to explore and experiment.

There was talk of creating a Men's Shed at Rowheath, an Australian idea, a way of gathering men in a non-churchy, nonthreatening environment.[5] It was a casual proposal but the story awakened a desire in Mary and Lynda to, again, offer radical hospitality in their busy community center. This desire converged with a new movement, *Places of Welcome*, which was growing rapidly in their city.[6] The network was initiated by

5. See Menzie and Phelan, *Kingdom Communities*. Men's Sheds are informal places where men can connect and talk. They have caught on as a way of connecting with men alienated from what they experienced in the church.

6. https://www.placesofwelcome.org.uk/. There are now more that six hundred

Thrive Together Birmingham[7] as a response to a Birmingham Social Inclusion report published in 2012, called *Giving Hope, Changing Lives.* It sought to respond to the isolation often experienced in the city, particularly for newcomers and those suffering some trauma. Since 2018, Mary and Lynda have hosted at Rowheath a Place of Welcome every Friday morning (bar a few COVID weeks). It was simple but profoundly relational, a powerful way of welcoming and being with the other. There was nothing fancy about either the place or the resources (bread, cheese, coffee, flowers, and cake). Indeed resources, energy, and creative contributions often came from participants. This was a key aspect of any Place of Welcome, which was structured around basic practices of Christian life: hospitality of place, people, provision and attention, and also the opportunity to contribute.[8] There was no agenda to this gathering beyond relationships. On these Fridays, Mary and Lynda have seen relationships flourish across boundaries of church/unchurched, capacity (some participants have learning disabilities, some have dementia), and class. Other types of communities of welcome have sprung up at Rowheath (e.g., Rowheath Creative, Rowheath Active) among the many popular, more commercial, community events. City agencies have welcomed all of this and civic relationships have deepened too. Rowheath Pavilion continues to be an iconic building suggesting an alternative way of living in a culture of individualism and isolation. The Spirit continues to gestate kingdom life in the explorations of this community.

b. Forests and Church

The hamlet of Cranshaws sits in the valley of the River Whiteadder in the Lammermuir hills in the Scottish Borders. Rural and isolated, the settlement dates back centuries and its Kirk, which is first mentioned in 1275, was probably dedicated to the Celtic saint Ninian. Rebuilt in the late 1800s, it has been a place of worship in the parish for over eight hundred years. While the building remains open, its congregation is small and meets just once a month. Like many churches across the

---

Places of Welcome across England.

7. https://thrivetogetherbham.org/.

8. These are summarized as Place, People, Provision, Presence, and Participation by the Place of Welcome coordinators.

length and breadth of Britain, as a worshipping Sunday service community its days are numbered.

Over recent decades the denomination has undergone a whole host of reviews, strategies, and reorganizations in an attempt to arrest the decline throughout its many churches. What was once a local presbytery with many full-time clergy is now but a small remnant in a geographically huge, reconfigured presbytery that stretches across Lothian and the Borders. It represents yet another attempt to manage and reshape an aging, declining church in a changing world. An oft-repeated story, echoed throughout all the denominations and independent church streams, it is further proof that existing methods and metrics simply don't work anymore. It's a depressing tale.

In contrast, there are stories of hope emerging within this geographically isolated area. These stories recognize that the church finds itself in a place it's never been before. The past has mostly gone, the present confronts us with a myriad of questions, challenges, and opportunities. What the future might hold is simply unknown, but through the practices we're advocating, it is possible to see some of the ways God's Spirit is reweaving Christian life in unexpected ways. Cranshaws Forest Church is one such story.

Bill was brought up near Cranshaws, his parents moving there just after World War II. After a period away from the area, Bill married Alison, returned, and settled back among the farming community. His early career in the film industry took them to the States; but it was as a forester that Bill returned to Scotland, managing the estate at Cranshaws. In the early 2000s, he became a lay reader within the Church of Scotland and after further training and nearing retirement age, he was only allowed to be ordained as an auxiliary minister, a locum minister within the local presbytery.

He, like so many other clergy, full, part-time, or auxiliary, found himself ministering within an institutional framework that was broken and patently not working. What was emerging at Cranshaws hadn't come from any central directive, strategy, or aims and objectives programs, but from a place of dwelling, discerning, and exploring.

In the place of dwelling, living and working the land, putting roots down, literally and metaphorically, Bill, his wife and family (now three generations under the same roof) have settled in that place of stability. With the love of God and neighbor they have "presenced" themselves in the valley for many years. They have appreciated looking at the natural world and seeing it as a signpost to the transcendent. With a small group of locals, they're pioneering an adventure of planting a tiny, "wee" forest alongside the church building. It's an environment that causes people to stop and look. A fellow famous Scot, born not far from Cranshaws, John Muir, said: "I'd rather be in the mountains thinking of God, than in church thinking about the mountains."[9] Muir was a naturalist, environmental philosopher, botanist, and zoologist. He was an early advocate for the preservation of wildernesses in the States and encouraged the preservation of many of the country's national parks. The Cranshaws Forest Church ethos would concur with Muir's statement and reflect a societal movement of people embracing a spirituality that looks for the transcendent outside of the structures of Sunday services. The forest church demonstrated people's engagement from that of *something they go to* to *something we do* in their lives together. It birthed a way of being church that was not based on doing something *for* people, but doing something *with* people. It was not *us and them* but *we*. The outmoded attractional model of church (where control was too often in the hands of clergy, where the church was host inviting others to join with them) was being replaced by the folk of this unusual church. They became guests and fellow participants with others in the community, as they discerned God's loving purposes for this forest. They were discovering together how to trust one another in a creative partnering with God's Spirit.

A creative imaginer, Bill was never short of ideas. Even during his period of being treated for cancer, from his hospital bed his iPad was full of ideas and potential explorations! Yet it was from a place of dwelling and discerning that the idea of a forest church was born. This was something that has, literally, emerged from under their feet. It was an initiative that had the fingerprints of God's Spirit about it. Their awareness of global warming, the exploitation of the land, and their desire to conserve and respect the natural world, were all woven into the shaping of this initiative. It engaged people of all ages and backgrounds, believers, unbelievers, and seekers. People near and far experienced the natural world, with its invitation to see in physical matter the transcendent God. As the psalmist declares, "The heavens proclaim the glory of God. The skies display his craftsmanship."[10]As the poet Elizabeth Barrett Browning wrote in *Aurora Leigh*, "Earth's crammed with heaven, and

9. Muir, *John of the Mountains*.

10. Ps 19:1.

every common bush afire with God; but only those who see take off their shoes."[11] As the story of Cranshaws Forest Church relates:

> Come and explore the small plantation of trees and shrubs, planted in March 2022. Here is the beginning of a story in which a new ecosystem is developing. A neglected piece of ground is coming to life and you are seeing it as its very early stages. No fertilisers or other chemicals have been used. In time some trees will do well while others fail and a variety of wildlife will make their home in the wee forest.
>
> Enjoy a stroll along the path that leads up to the little pond and down to the gathering table, where you can sit and enjoy the view towards and beyond the river and the local community orchard. This is a place where it's good to pause and breathe slowly. A place to gratefully rest and refresh our senses.
>
> From the earth beneath our feet, teeming with creatures, to the sky and space beyond—from "cosmos to compost," we are part of and depend upon an extraordinary web of life. Our bodies, like all living things, can be traced back to the soil, where our story begins. But we also have a spirit within us, so that we are not just "dust." We are "animated earth"[12] and perhaps this is what makes human beings capable of great things.
>
> Follow the path round the far end of the church building and you'll find a gate in the wall that takes you into the wee forest. This is the designated meeting place of Cranshaws forest church. A place to meet, and greet, to share and serve, to gaze and wonder, to reflect, respect, play and pray.[13]

The church building still stands; as a listed building, it will stay. Its future, however, will look very different from its past. Outside of any rites of passage, services have decreased, and Sunday congregational services may become a thing of the past. The kirk could stand as a museum to a past age, but, instead, it has the potential to be a gathering place again. Any worship in the building will be very different because those who will gather are themselves in a different place in a changing world. It is quite possible that the building will be a place of hospitality and, no doubt, a shelter when the weather outside is inhospitable. It will be a storytelling place, relating its history, not constricting its present

11. Browning, *Aurora Lee*, seventh book.

12. "Animated earth" is an expression coined by Saint Augustine in describing the human being.

13. Cranshaws Briefing Paper, April 2023 (unpublished).

or holding back its future. Coming into view is an imaginative future. Its emerging stories are giving language to the experiences of people remaking church as they recreate a forest.

Bill's long dwelling in the community has given him the capacity to discern the movements of the Spirit in his listening with others. The result is a journey into unknown futures as they join together in an exploration of God's purposes in their neighborhood. By no stretch of the imagination could Bill be described as young. He fits into the category described by the prophet Joel: "Your sons and daughters will prophesy; your old men will dream dreams, and your young men see visions."[14] What Bill was exploring with companions has been birthed in dwelling, discerning, and joining God in a rural community. A tiny, out-of-the-way place, of little seeming significance to the outside world, has sprung up as a sign of the kingdom coming here on earth as it is in heaven. In biblical tradition, it is often from the margins and among ordinary people that new movements of hope are born.

c. Neighborhood listening, learning, and not returning to normal

In the northeast of England, a small but radically engaging fellowship of Christians on an urban housing estate has, through the ebb and flow common to any church, reached out to its neighborhood. Formerly a mission hall and daughter of a larger mother church in the town's center that drew its congregation from the suburbs, Portrack's demographics are very different, reflecting the social diversity of most urban estate cultures.

Prior to the pandemic and lockdown, Portrack modeled itself on the familiar lines of Sunday services, midweek meetings, pastoral care, and serving the community in numerous ways by meeting needs. It had also begun to engage its neighborhood more incarnationally. This included both its pastors and youth leader deciding to live on the estate among the people. Another young family chose to move from the suburbs onto the estate. A greater engagement of presence was beginning to have a shaping influence on the church.

Lockdown deepened that experience. People discovered new ways of being church and, in the process, came to a liberating awareness that things they'd once seen as essential to being church were no longer relevant. Relinquishing some of their once-normal activities gave time to

14. Joel 2:28.

rethink what it might mean to be a church on the estate. The constraints imposed by lockdown were creating a new sense of neighborliness. Dwelling with neighbors, even when socially distanced, created opportunities to quietly listen to what the Spirit was doing right there in the community. Levels of poverty and deprivation were high. Some individuals and families faced greater risks and hardship as a consequence of lockdown. Working collaboratively with the local authority and estate school kitchen staff, members of the church distributed meals to homes on the estate. This contact with neighbors brought an awareness of the need for friendship and support to young families, particularly to mothers giving birth to their babies without the usual support mechanisms of families, friends, and statutory services. They were all limited in their ability to help because of lockdown measures. Church members, as neighbors, became the supporting presence among such people. A baby bank had been established prior to lockdown, and now it became an even more significant center of support. Along with providing essential baby care, it was a bridge into the hearts and lives of providers and recipients alike.

Through social media, particularly WhatsApp groups, church members whose contributions were rarely heard in congregational or church meetings found a voice. In the safe space of a small group, in the comfort of not having to contend with real or perceived expectations of congregational behavior, a deeper sharing of life and faith was discovered between them. Challenges in relating to one another became adventures, relationships became explorations. Paradoxically, fewer church meetings created the time and space for a more authentic meeting of lives.

With the relaxation of lockdown measures came the opportunity for people to gather together in common spaces. The spaces opened to explore what God was calling the church to be in a changing world. The temptation to return to the prior normal was great. Such are the powers of our defaults and the beguiling influence of the seventy-five-year story. However, with courage and a considerable amount of uncertainty, the church hasn't returned to normal. They still gather on Sundays, but gone is the usual format of a congregational service (singing a collection of hymns and songs with traditional form of preaching and teaching). Instead, people joining on a Sunday find a place of welcome, drinks are present, chairs are around tables and the space is about people sharing and praying together. Creative worship takes place round the tables, issues of life and faith are explored, but it's rarely about someone standing at a pulpit preaching for any length of time. The pastors, along with others, facilitate, enable, encourage, and empower those at the table gatherings. People are encouraged to dwell in the Word as a way of seeking God and embracing his loving purposes.

A renunciation of the need to control and determine outcomes is setting people free to be more real with God and one another. It can be quite chaotic at times, as well as messy and unpredictable overwhelming, but it is becoming a community of deepening welcome, inclusivity, and diversity. As a church it connects and shares life and faith with so many people who would struggle in conventional church structures. And there is something deeply authentic about what is emerging. The church has become less of a congregation and more a community exploring its place and vocation. As people are searching for a place to be at home, Portrack is becoming a community held together by covenant relationships more than vision; relationships matter more than reputation; and there is a unity amidst diversity. By not going back to some perceived normal, Portrack is discovering ways of being a community of hope.

Such stories illustrate how communities of Jesus are being formed out of the practices of dwelling, discerning, and exploring. These stories are told from the perspective of looking back and reflecting on what God had been fermenting in local congregations. They do not come out of well-developed strategies or vision statements. These are stories of ordinary people who did not know the outcomes before they began their explorations. They're really not stories about outcomes. They are about explorations on the trail of the Spirit. They're about ordinary people being nudged to try out something the Spirit was stirring inside them. They had no idea where any of it would lead. Only as they looked back could they tell a story that brought the pieces together and started to show something of what the Spirit was forming. It was in these practices and explorations that there unfolded some sense of where God was at work. What we hear from people when they connect with these stories is excitement, but also, questions of *how?* Here we offer a simple outline of how to dwell, discern, and explore where you live.[15]

15. This is offered as an illustration of where, perhaps, you might want to make a start. Behind these basic steps lies a supporting process of how to reflect on actions we're taking in these steps and asking what we are learning along the way. This action-reflection cycle is the critically important companion piece to these activities.

An Experiment—Into the Neighborhood

This is a little experiment around dwelling, discerning, and exploring in your neighborhood. A leader might do this by him/herself but, equally, you can invite others to join with you. As you try on this exploration, build in time for reflection on the actions you take. To start off, begin a journal of your activities in the neighborhood through this exploration. Write notes about your observations and experiences. A journal helps us reflect on what we're doing and what we are learning from these experiences.

Before you begin, decide on times in your week you'll be present in your neighborhood. Setting specific times gives you a way of comparing the times you connect with your neighborhood. A journal is a great aid in reflecting on what is happening.

1. Setting Rhythms

Select different times in a day you'll walk around your community. The composition of neighborhoods changes throughout the day, with different groups of people present at different times. Select, for example, to walk the community on two weekdays and one weekend day at different times of the day. Note what's happening and who's there at different points. You'll be surprised who your neighbors are.

2. Having Conversations

Look for opportunities for conversation. Connect with people who've been around a long time, whom you know. Look for others who might be new to the neighborhood. Here are some questions to use in your conversations:

- How long have you lived in the neighborhood?
- What brought you here?
- What do you find life-giving about this community?
- What concerns or fears do you have for the neighborhood?

As you begin this exploration here are reflection questions you can use:

- How am I being present in my neighborhood outside roles or positions?
- What is that like?
- What's my agenda with people? Am I with them to hear their story or do I need to tell them something or do something for them?
- What might it mean to be friends with people in the neighborhood?
- As you listen with people over a period of time, are there themes, images, or words turning up?
- In these conversations are there ways the Spirit is speaking to me?

Build into your Morning Office a time to pray for people in the community.

3. Begin to Explore *Joining With*

Write down what you're discovering in your neighborhood explorations.

Are there ways you can join with what is already happening in the neighborhood?

Here are some suggestions:

- Identify a community organization that interests you and check out its meetings.
- Volunteer for a local community service agency.
- Join a local gym.
- Choose a coffee shop or local pub in the neighborhood and hang out at regular times several times a week.

4. Exploring Learning

In these explorations, how can I learn about the founding stories of this community? Here are some illustrative questions to ask people (and remember that a local library has so much information and librarians love to help):

- How has the community developed over the last twenty years?
- What has changed in this time?

- Who makes up the community?
- Can people name the issues the community faces?
- How are they being addressed?
- What is its future going to look like?

Developing the habit of becoming an explorer in our neighborhoods will be a new practice for most. Initially, it will seem awkward. Learning a new practice takes time. In these small explorations you're developing habits that can slowly reshape your old habits and challenge your defaults. Be attentive to your intentions and posture when in the neighborhood. In this little exercise you're not solving problems or helping people. There are times and places for those activities, but focusing on them outside of relationships blocks the ability to hear and see what is happening among people. Find a few people you want to get to know without any agenda except being with them and listening to their stories. Your neighbors can be different from you in so many ways, and because of this they will stretch you out of your comfort zones. This is where we encounter God.

Several leaders were trying to figure out how to make connections in their communities. The posture of *being with* rather than *doing for* felt a bit threatening at first. It called them outside their roles and identities as pastors who help others and have answers. When asked to spend time in their community just being present as a regular person without a role, they didn't know how to behave. One pastor, however, took a risk. He started dropping into a local pastry-coffee shop early each morning. Slowly, conversations started with the owners. In those early mornings a world that could never have been planned or imagined opened up before him. The Spirit was introducing him to people who lived around him whom he had no idea existed. Before long he was sitting with them over coffee and the stories were being shared of who they were and what they were experiencing in the neighborhood. His image of the community was transformed. These simple explorations are the seedbed for the question: *What is God's Spirit doing in this place among these people?*

Like an apprentice, start this journey with small steps. If you want to involve others, start small. With others, you become co-learners, a community of companions rather than experts who ought to know.[16]

16. Often, pastors express the sense to us that they have no time left to do anything more. This is one of the great anxieties they wrestle with that leads to feelings of failure and inadequacy. But this framing of the time question is misleading. We are able to show how, in simple ways, they can free up the time to begin the leading we're describing.

Exploring calls us into the risk of relationship with the other. Discernment happens as we risk testing what we're hearing through one another. We've discussed the Acts 16 passage when Paul and his companions' carefully worked out strategies were no longer working ("the Spirit of Jesus prevented us . . .").

Jon's been a pastor for many years. He was dwelling in the Word with others in his congregation. The text was the sending of the seventy in Luke 10. He'd used the passage many times in his preaching, but this time something happened to him in this dwelling. He found himself stopping at the place where the seventy were sent out into the towns and villages, places where many of them had likely grown up. Jon got stuck at these instructions. What hit him like a thunderbolt was the recognition that he had no real relationships with people in his neighborhood. He honestly shared this with the group. Over several meetings, others shared a similar story about themselves. Some were members of volunteer groups serving the needs of refugees or helping to feed and house the poor. It came to them that these good works, as important as they were, involved no relational connections with people beyond *doing for others*. This *seeing* began new explorations.

The group sensed the Spirit saying something to them. They weren't sure what it was or what steps to take. They were sure, however, that the Spirit was pressing them about their role in the community. Discerning what the Spirit might be saying felt like searching in a fog more than having a clear direction and manageable outcomes. They started suggesting some *what ifs* (possible explorations) to each other. At first, it all felt awkward. Based on the *what ifs*, they decided each would try something in terms of connecting with neighbors and report back what they discovered.

Jon decided his exploration would be a simple one. A senior couple lived several houses down the street. They'd waved at each other going by and talked about the weather, but not much else. Jon wanted to begin a conversation with them. It was a Friday near noon when John saw an older woman struggling with a heavy bag of groceries as she limped toward her front door. *This is my chance*, Jon thought. He ran across a couple of lawns and asked if he could help. After he'd deposited the bags

---

We are also able to show them how they can communicate to their church leaders what they are wanting to develop and do this in ways that create a shared energy. But, more than anything else, it's when we connect a leader with a group of companions that they find the support to take this journey.

inside the front door, the woman thanked him for his kindness. Then Jon asked, "Where's your husband? I haven't seen him in a while." Looking at Jon with tired eyes, she responded with a sad whisper, "Mike died six months ago. I've been alone since." Jon was stunned! He stood there in silence. After expressing condolences he walked back to this house with his head spinning in a deluge of questions: *How could I not know that a neighbor had died? How could I miss that this elderly lady was struggling with grief and the demands of keeping up an old house? How did I get to the place of preaching the gospel every week to my congregation but miss it in my own community?* Jon brought his exploration experience back to the dwelling group. He'd begun to recognize how much of his life was taken up running, managing, and leading this congregation. Unexpectedly, the Spirit had invited him to get stuck in a part of Luke 10 that started Jon on further explorations in reshaping his habits so he could dwell in his neighborhood. In retrospect Jon would say that in the dwelling group he was being challenged by the Spirit to explore steps he couldn't have known at the front end. Discerning invites us to explore how and where the Spirit is taking us in the unraveling.

Dwelling, discerning, and exploring are the practices for forming a community of hope in a place we've never been before. Celtic spirituality offers us direction on this journey that cuts across traditions, differences, or secular-holy divides. Its spirituality is about breaking boundaries and building bridges to an alternative, hopeful way of living in a world falling apart. Exploring was at the heart of the Celtic Christian imagination. The Celtic church wasn't a uniform, well-organized ecclesiastical body. It was more like a loose federation of virtually autonomous communities bound by a common ethos and value system. Their organizational life was creative and chaotic, shifting often as they sought to be a movement responsive to the heart of God and the Spirit's leading. In the seeming chaos, patterns and structures could be found, much like the threads and interlacing ribbons of the Celtic knot.

This ethos of provisionality (a culture of exploring) is a core ethos for this interrelationship between dwelling, discerning, and exploring. This Celtic impulse toward a loose federation and a provisionality of structures is how we can shape our approaches to this time.

CHAPTER ELEVEN

Taking the Journey

Introduction

> Ours is clearly an age of upheaval. As war rages in Europe and the world counts the cost of the deadliest pandemic in living memory, an ominous mood reigns over the earth. After years of economic turmoil, social unrest and political instability, there is a widespread sense that the world has been cast adrift—like a rudderless ship in a terrible storm.—Jerome Roos

> [I]n this world of oligarchs, you know, Bezos, Zuckerberg, and all these people, economic and political power are held by them. This is very Pharaonic. And it seems to me essential that the church stresses the dignity of the human person, the sacredness of our natural inheritance, the importance of love and relationship; it shouldn't back off from these fundamental notions of human existence that it has protected for two millennia. You know, the church does not need to contort itself to modern management theory and markets. In fact, its salvation is to resist those by building relationships with people around what is sacred.—Lord Maurice Glasman

THIS BOOK HAS ENGAGED the question of how we lead God's people in the great unraveling. It has asked how we should interpret this moment, what attitudes and actions we should take as God's people. There seem to be three primary responses to the unraveling of our societies and the churches:

- First, there is a growing apocalyptic resignation shaped by increasing levels of fear about loss. There is wearied resignation and little sense of hope about what lies ahead. This can be seen in so many different ways, from the specter of climate collapse to a coming apart of the Western story. The numbers seem to tell us there's no way out. Climate disaster, declining birth rates, collapsing institutions, and declining church affiliation are deemed unstoppable. The experience is that everything is on a slippery slope. There's little that can be done in the face of multiple cascading crises. As one British leader shared with us, we're confronted with VUCA (Volatility, Uncertainty, Complexity, and Ambiguity). These voices see little hope for any real change. All strategies are too little, too late.
- Second, there are the techno-optimists who see our crises through the lens of technological progressivism. Advances in technology will overcome our crises, making things better. Through technological advances in battery development, wind power, solar energy, artificial intelligence, and human communications, real change is already happening. Global death rates are in decline, birth rates are stabilizing, and with new innovations we're addressing problems and improving our capacities.[1]
- Third, for some there is the longing for revival. The anticipation is that dire happenings are the prelude to a religious revival, an outpouring that will reverse the decline of the church.

It can feel like we're pressed into choosing one of these narratives to make sense of our unraveling world. Are apocalypse, progressivism, or revivalism the only options before us? There is another way. It involves forming communities of hope. It means coming to see that this is God's creation all the way down. Right in the midst of these multiple crises, God is present down on the ground, in the holiness of the mundane and the ordinariness of the everyday. As Christians we are being summoned to reorient our attention around the conviction that a different story is at work in the world. Therefore, we embrace a story that has nothing to do with these other options. It doesn't have anything to do with fixing the church or opting for some form of personal spirituality. Our vocation is to discern and join with God in the reweaving of the mundane, the

1. See for example Pinker, *Enlightenment Now*, and Robinson, *Ministry of the Future*.

everyday, for this is where God dwells, making the places we live holy places of God's transformative grace.

Leaders are not being called to save the church as we know it. It's not the time or place for our energies and attention to be focused on renewing, fixing, or even reforming the church. These are misdirecting engagements. Even at this moment in the unraveling, so many church systems remain honed in on ecclesiocentric directions. This does not mean the church is irrelevant in this unraveling (though at this moment this seems to be the trajectory). There is this other vocation for leaders. It is forming local communities of God's people who, in the mundane ordinariness of the everyday, are discerning and joining with God in the redemption of the holy mundane right where they dwell. This is neither apocalyptic fear, progressive optimism, or fanciful revivalism, but the forming of a common life around the practices of dwelling, discerning, and exploring right where we live.

It is in forming a people around these practices that we cultivate communities of anticipatory hope. Such communities do not need tools to predict, manage, or innovate some bold new future. On the contrary, in learning to discern God at work among them, they are able to lay down the anxious need to control outcomes or predict futures. They settle into seeing God's active presence in the mundane. This way of life is practiced in the confident hope that it is this One, who comes all the way down and pitches his tent right beside ours, who is remaking and reweaving our world. Right in the center of our disruptive moment, God's Spirit is "making all things new," the kingdom of God is coming here "on earth as in heaven." Through the practices of dwelling, discerning, and exploring these little, local communities discover how and where they join with God in this work that is God's to do. The question this book has been pressing is *what kind of leaders form and serve these kinds of communities?*

So many of the stories (progress, the state, the autonomous self, the power of technology) shaping our societies and the churches are being swept aside. No technological utopia will emerge to save us, but neither will there be an apocalypse. We, God's fallible, fearful, redeemed people are being called to become a people of anticipatory hope. What an amazing invitation! It is an antidote to fatalism, fear, false optimism, and religious delusion. Could there be anything better than that in which to invest our lives?

- To dwell, discern, and discover what the Spirit of God is doing in the world.
- To join in with God.
- To be partners with God and others in forming communities of hope.
- To be part of a movement that brings transformation and hope to the world. These communities of hope will emerge out of the practices of dwelling, discerning, and exploring.

We do not need to succumb to the false option of retreating into ourselves or accepting the lie that the right method will make us future-proof. The illusions of escaping or predicting are different versions of the "it's up to us" mantra, not the way of Jesus.[2]

How, then, do leaders participate in the formation of anticipatory communities of God's people? We won't achieve this by focusing on the church. Nor is such leadership focused on casting visions and strategizing. It is a leadership that awakens God's people to the holiness of the ordinary and mundane. Seeing that God, the Holy One, is present in the everyday, is working out the forms of the new creation right here in our neighborhoods and communities. Therefore, Christian life is formed out of the rhythms of worship and the practices we have named. We form relationships in the mundane believing this is where we hear and see the ways God is calling forth a new creation. This is the task of leadership.

It is often difficult to imagine this kind of leadership because pastors and clergy (the ordained) have been formed around a certain type of congregational life, consisting of paid clergy staff in each congregation, looking after the life and needs of those in the congregation. As these congregations become ever fewer in the unraveling there seems to be little imagination about alternatives. The kinds of communities we're describing don't have to be in this form. In most cases they are going to be small, local bands of Christians (perhaps twenty to thirty people) located in neighborhoods. Instead of the current congregational ministers or pastors (trained with an MDiv for leadership in current congregations), the leaders of these communities (they'll be both lay and ordained) will be more like abbots or abbesses providing nurture and oversight for two,

2. "In its manifold forms, the modern narrative myth is constant in this: it marginalizes God as an actor in human history . . . Most commonly, the modern vision does not say: 'God does not exist,' but rather, 'God does not matter . . .'" See Shea, *From Christendom to Apostolic Mission*, 85.

three, or five such local gatherings. A real mindshift will be needed here where our attention has to shift from meeting the demands of existing congregations to these smaller bands of Christians in the local. Some get concerned that these bands might be too small and become insular. But the work of the abbot/abbess is to shape them around the practices of life that involve discerning what God is doing among and ahead of them in their neighborhoods. The beauty of these little bands, communities, is that on a regular basis (monthly or bimonthly) they can come together to worship, share stories, and resource one another.

The following proposals suggest some of the postures of a leader taking this journey of forming communities of hope.

Ways of Leading

a. Shaped by the Wild Goose Chase, Not Strategically Planned Outcomes

The question we introduced in chapter 3 was: *When God's people have found themselves in places of great disruption, how has God turned up among them?* This is about discernment, not strategic visioning. Furthermore, the question *How has God been present in other times of unraveling?* is designed to turn our attention from strategies toward God, away from abstract vision statements to the holy in the mundane. What we saw, in Scripture as well as in Benedict and the Celts, was that in places of disruption and unraveling, strategies for fixing were no longer options. Those roads had been closed off. Rather than coming up with some vision for a preferred future, or some innovation that would overcome their situation, these diverse communities of God's people took on specific rhythms and practices that would form them into hopeful signs of God's kingdom. We've named those practices as dwelling, discerning, and exploring.

When introducing these practices, leaders often ask about outcomes: *What's the end game? What are the measurable results? What's the return on investment?* Such questions come from the default out of which so many leaders continue to operate. This default is about the conviction that we can and need to manage outcomes because that is what we can do and are expected to do as leaders. Here, the drive is to know what the future is going to look like. It seems that if one can get a picture of the outcomes entailed in a set of actions, then it will be easier to get others on board. For a long period these assumptions and methods seemed to work. Our challenge, however, is that we're now in a place we haven't been before. The journey ahead is unpredictable; it can't be managed in the normal ways. What lies before us is the journey of Abram and Sara, not that of modern explorers with their GPS and voice-directed Google maps. What we are now embarked on as leaders is more like what the ancients called a wild goose chase. It is generally believed that one of the names for the Holy Spirit was *An Geadh-Glas* or "Wild Goose." While the image may seem strange to us, it was one of the ways in which Christians expressed their experience of the Spirit—like a goose, the Spirit was wild, uncontrollable, going where it chose, moving in unfamiliar and unexpected ways. This is why Jesus spoke of the Spirit as the wind that blows where it wants.

To some degree, this is how Celts understood their vocation. Like our ancient parents Abram and Sarai, the Spirit is calling us into an unpredictable, wild goose-like journey on which we can't name the outcomes while we're on the road. With neither map nor compass, our ancient parents let the wind and road direct them. "The wind blows where it wills, and you can hear the sound it makes, but you do not know where it comes from or where it goes; so it is with everyone who is born of the Spirit." These words of Jesus express this journey.[3] With its loud, siren-like warnings, the wild goose was how the Spirit called them. Pulled out of their status quo, they were on a journey without maps. The Wild Goose would guide them.

It's a struggle to find language that captures what all this means for leading at this moment. This way of leading will involve coming to a place where one can lay down control over outcomes. Initially, this is a bewildering, disorienting way of thinking for leaders who are already disoriented and bewildered. All of our defaults and attention have been exercised toward being in control and managing outcomes. These are deeply set patterns that this culture keeps feeding back to us. Because of them, leaders can struggle to know where to begin. This takes us back to the fundamental need for companions and, wherever possible, an abbot/abbess to walk with us. This is a journey where the source of our security and confidence has to shift from our own capacities to know, manage, and control to trusting the Spirit in the midst of a company of companions and the wisdom of an elder abbot/abbess. Beginning in the safety of companions is how we discern and test out some of the

3. John 3:8 (NIV).

initiating steps to take where we are. It is with companions and abbot/abbess that we find the guardrails to keep us safe as we launch out. The greatest fear many of us have as leaders is expressed in the unspoken question: *If I fall, will I be caught?* As companions we discover that, yes, we will be caught and held out there on the road.

It is with a company of companions that you start to figure out those small, initiating steps that you can take to invite your people onto this journey. Only as you discover others on the road, companions, do you find the trust to go on this Wild Goose chase. You gradually find, together, ways of resisting the demands for a plan or strategy to future-proof the church. It is with companions that we will learn how to practice dwelling, discerning, and exploring.

b. Forming Monasteries in the Everyday

Benedict's way of following the Spirit was not the Wild Goose but a monastery. He chose to form a local community of Christians right in the midst of a crumbling society. At that moment in time, this was a bold, counterintuitive move. What had been happening over a long period of time was that Christians who were serious about seeking God gave up the fleshpots of Egypt (in this case Roman society) to retreat into the desert. Following a tradition that emulated Jesus' travail in the desert, these monastics believed that God was to be encountered in the austerity of the desert. Spirituality was located in withdrawal. The desert was viewed as a purifying place. A spiritual life with God was, therefore, achieved through withdrawal into the desert.

Benedict had been a part of this movement and so knew desert spirituality well; but, amidst the dissolution of Roman society, this is not the option he took. He founded a lay order and formed a simple monastery on the site of a former pagan temple at Monte Casino. The original monastery was some eighty miles from Rome. It was, therefore, deliberately situated in the midst of a crumbling society. Situated amidst fertile terraces, the new order developed agricultural life among the people of the area. Benedict didn't let the tides carry him to a distant, remote place, he built a community of hope in the midst of a collapsing society. He did this through a small band of ordinary people who became novices in a new order. Practices such as the Daily Office, prayer, and attending to the sick made it a movement of hope in a dying time. Benedict's Rule was formed from a blending of his experiences with both desert and urban monasticism. It would be in the everyday life of crumbling communities that he explored what it might look like to form a community of hope.

This, too, is the work of leaders in our moment. A leader's posture is no longer to manage and provide pastoral oversight of existing congregations shaped by affinity, but to discern how to form these congregations into a lay order, built around stability and rooted in their local community. This will require what Benedict called the vow of stability, the readiness to stay in one place over a long time. It will also call for an imagination in which we are doing this with companions—leaders who are learners and novices in this new place.

c. Leading Through Practices Rather than Vision, Strategy, or Outcomes

Neither Benedict nor the Celts had any sense of how their explorations in forming communities of hope would turn out. Each, in their own ways, explored practices and rhythms for life in dark times. The practices gradually became the pathways along which Christian communities sustained a common life of anticipatory hope. In the words of Alasdair MacIntyre:

> A crucial point in that earlier history occurred when men and women . . . turned aside from the task of shoring up the *imperium* and ceased to identify a continuation of civility and moral community with the maintenance of that *imperium*. What they set themselves to achieve instead . . . was the construction of local forms of community . . . through the new dark ages . . .[4]

In such communities, we discern a response to the question of how we live in a dark time.

These communities did not turn Christian life into a private, personal spirituality. God was not excluded from relationships with their neighbor or participation in the common life of a community. Jesus dwelt and poured himself into the ordinariness of the everyday. This was the place of divine encounter. The reweaving of a broken world is only possible through a radical commitment to people and place. For both Benedict and the Celts, this involved reorienting their lives around two things, place and common rhythms of life. Monastic communities

4. MacIntrye, *After Virtue*, 263.

were not religious versions of social aid societies helping people in need (they did do this work). They were communities of prayer and common practice rooted in Christ and committed to a place and people. These communities, in sixth-century Italy and seventh-century Ireland, Scotland, and Northern England, understood that remaking a precarious world called for communities rooted in place with the One who dwelt among them. Our vocation as leaders, with few exceptions, is, as Tyler Kleeberger and Michael Beck encourage, "to put the telescope down and allow our feet to take root."[5]

Contemporary communities of hope may not come in the form of ancient monasteries, but they can't be the congregations currently shaping Protestant Christianity. They may not be guided by abbots or abbesses, but they can't be led well or served by current clergy guilds. In the dark days of Nazi power, Bonhoeffer, reflecting on another descending darkness, saw that the renewal of Christian life could only come from some new form of monasticism, which, in common with Benedict and the Celts, would be shaped by an uncompromising allegiance to the Sermon on the Mount. He wrote:

> The expansion of Christianity and the increasing secularization of the church caused the awareness of costly grace to be gradually lost . . . It was decisive that monasticism did not separate from the church and that the church had the good sense to tolerate monasticism. Here, on the boundary of the church, was the place where the awareness that grace is costly and that grace includes discipleship . . . Monastic life thus became the living protest against the secularization of Christianity, against the cheapening of grace.[6]

This is a challenging call. For a leader to lay down the need for control, determining outcomes, and prescribing futures are incredible risks in terms of status, role, salary, and position. Letting go of these ways of leading are revolutionary acts in the face of how our societies regard authority.[7] Contrary to so much of our contemporary drive to predict and control, Benedict's leadership in the formation of his monasteries was radically different from these contemporary ways of being God's people.

5. Kleeberger and Beck, *Fresh Expressions of the Rural Church*.

6. Bonhoeffer, *Cost of Discipleship*, 46.

7. See Neiman, *Left is Not Woke*, especially chapters 3 and 4 where she discusses the influence of Michel Foucault's theories of power and how these have come to pervade our understanding of relationships among people.

Abbots and abbesses were not autocrats, chiefs, or authoritarian leaders. They were to be Christ figures in their communities, leading by example, living simply, immersed in seeking and loving God, welcoming friend and stranger and guarding the ethos of their communities.

The conclusion of Alasdair MacIntyre's *After Virtue* describes the moral situation of modern societies and their political institutions as "a new dark age," where "civility and the intellectual and moral life" will find no support, except in "local forms of community," which MacIntyre compares to the Benedictine communities of the Roman Empire at the time of its decline. In the final paragraph of the book, MacIntyre writes that, "we are waiting not for a Godot, but for another—doubtless very different—St. Benedict."[8]

d. Making the Character of a Community the Priority

Stanley Hauerwas, in his *Community of Character,* frames the issue of leading in disruptive times in terms of this concern:

> [We must] reassert the social significance of the church as a distinct society with an integrity peculiar to itself . . . Christians rediscover that their most important social task is nothing less than to be a community capable of hearing the story of God they find in scripture and living in a manner that is faithful to that story . . . I contend that the only reason for being Christian . . . is because Christian convictions are true; and the only reason for participation in the church is that it is the community that pledges to form its life by that truth.[9]

He goes on to argue that any consideration of the truth of Christian convictions cannot be divorced from the kind of community the church is and should be. This is all about forming God's people in the primary practices we have identified in this book. Here, at its most basic level, is the work of leadership. It has been and will always be these practices, in one form or another, that form communities of hope. Such a community can never be simply a gathering of people who feel good about each other or who share common memories of times together over generations. As wonderful as these things are, they are not the

8. MacIntyre, *After Virtue*, 263.

9. Hauerwas, *Community of Character,* 9.

primary characteristics of transformative communities calling forth a healed world in the name of Jesus.

The character of a leader and of the community is more important than anything else a church does. The great wrestling for any leader at this disruptive moment of disintegration is calling Christians into lives that are oriented around these practices. All else is parlous. The glaring absence of these practices leave the churches malformed, dysfunctional, and out of touch with the unraveling that is breaking our societies apart—it means that we labor to nurture shallow roots that cannot last. Congregations built on the strength of their enjoyment of one another and doing things for, or worse, to others, will wither and fail in the dark times ahead. Those beginning to grasp the integral connection between character (a life formed around these basic practices of Christian life) and conduct will offer hope. When this happens, authenticity is evidenced and communities of integrity are formed. In such communities, leaders focus on dwelling with God and the other.

Leadership is, therefore, about being a signpost of how to live in these practices, guiding and imparting by example, how others can go on this journey and being a support to those who are already on the way. Through his Rule of Life, Benedict formed the character of his communities as lovers of God and people. Such leaders renounce empire building. They possess humility, courage, and a confident trust in God.

e. Shaping Spaces of Anticipatory Hope

A leader wanting to form a community of anticipatory hope begins with the personal decision to dwell with people of both the congregation and the neighborhood. This is hard work. You might begin by inviting people to explore with you some of the forms of dwelling outlined in this book. As dwelling takes root, invite people into further explorations around listening and naming where they might be seeing the presence of God among their neighbors. A leader is like a midwife, calling forth what God is gestating in the people; helping people see where God is already at work in their communities.

Awakening each other to discern the Spirit of God at work among us requires much patience and deep love. It involves continually reminding ourselves that our people aren't our projects, the objects of our innovations and strategies. Only in a context of love for the other can we awaken to God's life in each other. At first, we shouldn't be surprised when the invitation to dwell or discern sounds strange, awkward, and mysterious for people. These are new practices that will take time to take root. Old securities, new fears, conscious and unconscious biases, preferences and prejudices, often masked as convictions, will surface. The constraints of traditionalism, not tradition, will be resistant to change. The journey of dwelling, discerning, and exploring is a vulnerable one. It will expose hearts and stretch minds, challenge as much as inspire. The habits and practices have to be embraced in the formation of the embryonic and emerging communities of hope. They cannot be formed on enthusiasm. They have to have intentionality, discipline, and depth to sustain them on the unfamiliar journey into an unknown but hope-filled future.

To intentionally spend time dwelling with our people and in our communities, leaders will need to change some priorities and rhythms of life. Too many of us spend too much of our time managing programs and preparing sermons. Consequently and unintentionally, we've lost connection with our communities. Intentionally dwelling will gradually open our eyes to see where God is present in the unraveling. Through dwelling we'll avoid any tendency to see people as statistics and opportunities.[10]

Dwelling, discerning, and exploring call for leaders to reorder their time toward their neighborhood. Neighborhoods are the sacramental places where one discerns the agency of the Spirit. This relocation of energy and focus enables a leader to see that we're dwelling in "the kind of place where something extraordinary suddenly bursts into view."[11] These sacramental places are where we encounter God's presence.[12] Worship and liturgical life are formed within and out of a sacramental rhythm of life in our neighborhoods not separate from them. When this happens, our worship gathering becomes a place where we tell stories of God at work in our neighborhoods. An important part of our liturgy, our ways of worshipping, will involve our telling where we've seen God's presence that week. These are the stories and encounters that tell us how our imagination is being changed, how our focus is awakening to what the Spirit is doing in the neighborhood. A community of hope and expectation is being formed.[13]

10. Mark 8:23.

11. Williams, *Being Disciples*, 5.

12. See Casey, *Fate of Place;* McClay and McAllister, *Why Place Matters;* Rumsey, *Parish;* and Tjorhom, *Embodied Faith.*

13. To explore more of this sort of leadership, check out https://www.themissional

5. Reorienting our attention

Leadership involves reorienting our own and our people's attention to the presence of God in the mundane elements of our common life.[14] A way to begin this reorientation is with a simple Examen question: *Since we last met, where have you seen God at work in your neighborhood or community?* When this question is first introduced, there's often a lot of silence. It's not the kind of question leaders are used to being asked of themselves or of asking their people. It's not a question people are used to hearing in church gatherings. It doesn't seem normal to share and listen like this. If you ask a different question, such as *What do you see people in your church doing just now?* leaders quickly respond with stories. But, *Where are you seeing God at work?*—not so much. Talking about where we're attentive to God at work among us and in our communities is largely absent from a congregation's narrative life. Most of the responses that are given around seeing God at work are about what's happening inside the church. This tells us a lot about what we've been formed to notice and what we filter out. It tells us a lot about where we locate God's presence in our lives and where we don't. Our default attention, as leaders and people, is toward what is happening *inside* the church. This is part of the reorientation that is needed. We want our people to begin attending to what God is doing in the ordinary, in the mundane life of their neighborhoods and communities. To look for the signs of God's kingdom on the streets. How might this reorientation begin?

It can begin with the introduction of simple, everyday practices designed to invite people to awaken to God's presence in their everyday life. This might involve, for example, inviting a few people to join you in keeping Morning Office. It might involve people agreeing to keep the Office several mornings a week.[15] What is important about this regular practice is that the Office directs our attention toward God. In these prayers we begin our day reminding ourselves of God's presence. This is not about quick change. The Daily Office is about entering a *rhythm* of life that becomes a *pattern* of life. As we live into that pattern, the words of the Office begin to affect how we see our world. By inviting some others to

---

network.com/stepping-out/.

14. The Leaders Table: https://www.themissionalnetwork.com/leaders-table/.

15. There are many resources available around the Daily Office. We use the excellent online resource provided by the Northumbria Community (https://www.northumbria-community.org/offices/morning-prayer/).

keep Office with you (you don't need to be in the same space) you can reflect with one another around what is happening to us in terms of how our attention is being reoriented toward God present in our everyday lives. Beginning with a small number of people allows us to create a space where others can tell stories of what is happening to them, of how their attention is being attuned to God's presence.

Another way to begin this is by inviting some people into a brief exploration. You might agree among yourselves to deliberately pause in a day to quietly ask: *Where am I seeing God present in the rhythms of my life on this day?* Each week you could gather to share your responses to this pausing. These practices are simple ways of beginning to reorient our attention toward God's presence in the everyday. A leader supports this listening, blessing, and encouraging people as they tentatively take these beginning steps.

Forming communities of hope is about how we reorient our attention as a community. What we attend to shapes what we see and that determines how we act. For example, if practically all our formation has been shaped by certain practices for leading a congregation (preaching, teaching, liturgy, pastoral care, etc.), then these are the things we pay attention to and *see* over everything else. Our attention has been schooled to see in certain ways.

There is a story about an Aboriginal visiting New York. It's the first time he has been out of his homeland and he is taken around the busy streets with the noise of traffic, shopping malls, people, and background hum of a city that never sleeps. He stops, stands still, and asks if his host hears the cricket. His bemused host can't comprehend how he could hear the sound of a tiny insect in such a noisy environment. Walking a few paces, his Aboriginal guest stoops down and picks up the small insect and says to his host, "It depends on what you're listening for." What we pay attention to can mute our ability to listen to the sound of the Spirit in our neighborhoods. Seeing and sensing the Spirit at work is often drowned out by the noise of our activism.

Reorienting our attention is a matter of practice. Initially, it takes a lot of energy to refocus:

- from the things we attend to as leaders: preparing sermons, managing meetings, our own and people's expectations, ensuring economic sustainability, planning for growth through outreach, etc.

- to something else: forming ourselves and our people to be able to dwell in our neighborhoods and, therefore, listen to what God's Spirit is doing ahead of us in these places.

Over time, however, this attending can become a new habit; it can become a *normal* way we attend. Examples in everyday life abound. It's now so common, for example, for people to be *on* their iPhones that we hardly notice it anymore. Once, if we had seen someone crossing the street with their face glued to their phone and their fingers banging out a message, we'd have been horrified. Now it's normal—we no longer pay attention to how this device has claimed all our attention. The activity has become automatic. In a different example, everyday Al's granddaughter attends to the piano by doing scales and practicing classical pieces. That attending now shapes her life. Roy is one of the founders of the Northumbria Community. The community has a Rule of Life (Availability and Vulnerability) and encourages a Rhythm of Life. For over thirty years, Roy, along with a whole dispersed community, have attended to this Rule and its rhythms. Roy is who he is today because of what he attends to each day.

The question we're addressing is how to form communities that orient their attention toward God's agency among them and in their neighborhoods. The seventy-five-year story directs our attention to our own agency and capacities. We're not accustomed to seeing God in everyday life. The philosopher and psychiatrist Iain McGilchrist addresses the power of this modern story in forming what we attend to. He argues that it determines what we think about and what we see through the lens of technique, control, counting, and outcomes. Ordinarily, this is our way of seeing. McGilchrist proposes that rather than more quick fixes, "We need a shift in the paradigm."[16] To form communities of hope, we need a radically different way of seeing ourselves and our world. We need to change our attention from techniques to seeing God as the active Agent among us. In Christian language, it is the need for a *conversion*, for a changing of the mind, a remaking of our imagination that transforms what we are paying attention to, of attending to God where we dwell.

As McGilchrist states, to be shaped by the modern story is to live inside a "self-reflexive hall of mirrors, where the logic seems to lead back to a solution within the system itself, rather than a need to break out of it."[17] The seventy-five-year story has trained us to be focally attentive to

16. McGilchrist, *Master and His Emissary*, xxi.

17. McGilchrist, *Master and His Emissary*, xxiv.

technique and method, to power and program, to our own agency. This is the "hall of mirrors" in which we're caught. It keeps eroding the possibility of our awakening to other ways of seeing and hearing. The crisis of the churches is their colonization by a story that closes us off to seeing God at work in the midst of the unraveling.

An executive leader of a major, historic denomination described the responses of its clergy and national leaders to their unraveling. They are, he said, in a state of crisis. They feel abandoned because nothing seems to be working and precipitous decline can no longer be denied. These leaders speak of "God abandoning us" with little sense that all their working at making things work is, itself, a barrier to their seeing God's presence in their unraveling. How do we respond to this situation? Writing with insight and brilliance, McGilchrist states:

> In fact, I believe there *is* something that exists apart from ourselves, but that we play a vital part in bringing it into being. A central theme of this book is the importance of our disposition towards the world and one another, as being fundamental in grounding *what it is that we come to have a relationship with*, rather than the other way round. The kind of attention we pay actually alters the world: we are, literally, partners in creation.[18]

It's hard for those of us raised in the modern story to imagine that what we attend to alters the world. But that is what we've done in the seventy-five-year story. All of our training, practicing, imagining, and modeling has determined that our attention has been directed toward technique, control, management, programs, and outcomes. We've created societies and congregations that mirror this, where the default is that of control, measurement, and method. It has precipitated a world on the brink of catastrophe. What we attend to matters! It alters the world. It creates a way of being in the world that becomes the inevitable norm. What if our attention was toward what God is fermenting and reweaving among us? Then we might begin to see the healing of our societies and of our planet.

In the context of McGilchrist's observations, we argue that the seventy-five-year story has closed us off to the central reality of all creation—God as Creator, Redeemer, and Agent in the world. It is not that we don't believe these things as an orthodox confession—we do. However, for all the practical, material aspects of our lives (including how we run our

18. McGilchrist, *Master and His Emissary*, 5.

churches and form our leaders), our attention is not on God as Agent, it's toward technique, method, control, and outcomes. Our confessions about God's Agency have little practical involvement in our everyday lives. We do not see, nor do we expect to see, God as the active Agent in our everyday lives. This is well illustrated in the responses of leaders to the Examen question. What we pay attention to (plans, strategies, data, methods) determines how we participate in the world. What we attend to determines the world we're creating.

Reorienting our communal attention toward God as Agent is a first-order task. Many leaders want to embrace this way (dwelling, discerning, exploring), but wonder how to practically implement it when their people still push for some return to the normal that seemed to exist before the pandemic. Leaders fear that if they undertake this journey their people will push back and they may well lose their ministries and income. When you have families to care for in a fragile economy, such fear is real. Church systems struggle to know how to address this tension. As leaders want off the program/projects/techniques treadmill, they often feel alone and unsupported. What is needed, in this space we've never been before, are companions.

Leading: Hope Through Practices

> Nothing that is worth doing can be achieved in a lifetime; therefore we must be saved by hope.—Reinhold Niebuhr

Hope is not optimism or good intentions. Its source is in God (Ps 121). Hope characterizes a community that is being shaped by the rhythms of dwelling, discerning, and exploring. As we have said this is no easy journey. The desire to be formed in these practices is often followed by the admission that it is difficult to be shaped by them over time. Acknowledging this can contribute to a community becoming discouraged. Forming a people in this rhythm of life is hard work. In formation we are called to turn our everyday attention toward seeing God where we dwell. Hope is birthed where we hesitantly learn to name our Christian experience in terms of God at work among us and in our communities. This transformation in what we attend to is the way we become like detectives of divinity, discovering how to follow the Spirit ahead of us.

This hope is called forth as a leader steps into these practices. In Jesus, as with the monastics, a central act of formation involved coming apart from the demands, expectations, and times with people. Jesus had huge crowds wanting to see him, yet he took time to come apart to be alone with God. The disciples were unsettled seeing Jesus stepping away from what appeared to be great opportunities and engagement with people at the start of a powerful movement. When the Celts found a place where they would dwell among a people, the first thing they built was a prayer cell; they knew that in dwelling in a place among people they had to first be alone with God. Their prayer in solitude, alone with God, was the foundation and informing practice that governed their lives. Where might we build into our liturgies and rhythms of life, moments of coming apart, of solitude and silence? Where can we introduce the practices of Examen or Dwelling in the Word?

This is a time for leaders to engage in the slow work of coming apart in a busy, frenetic, anxious world, in order to stop and listen to God's presence among them. This won't be something that is achieved through special events. It will involve bringing these practices into everything we do with our people. Examen, Dwelling, Daily Office, discerning are part of our normal, everyday lives. It is slow, gentle, intentional work. We're not the makers of the future. In this unraveling, we're not the managers of outcomes. Instead of being the controllers of outcomes or the curators of the past, we are called to be co-creators and collaborators with God of a new hope-filled, Spirit-inspired future. The outcomes are God's work. We are called to dwell and listen, to discern what God is doing, and to explore how we join with God. We can do this through the practices we've introduced in this book.

Undergirding these practices is the foundational practice of worship formed around the table (Communion, Eucharist). The eruption of hope does not lie in painting visions, proposing futures, or reading the tea leaves of data; rather, it is in the inglorious repetitiveness of these practices and focus on worship around the table, that our attention is, like sunflowers following the sun, turned toward a proper hope. In the unraveling, God will not let our foot slip if we dwell with one another in these practices.

Leading: Prayer That Invites Awareness

Reorienting our attention back to the reality of God's agency in the ordinary places where we dwell will take quite some time. Replacing busy activism with attentive prayer is no easy task. Learning to listen to the heartbeat of God for the world is a contemplative discipline that requires cultivation. Prayer is how we awaken to our situation, it is how we turn our attention toward God's actions and how we are sustained on the journey. If we only become aware of the multiple, cascading crises confronting us we will be overwhelmed with demands, expectations, discouragement, and fear. Prayer opens windows to hope by reorienting our attention toward God's presence in Christ, through the Spirit. Prayer, in recognizing our dependence upon God, removes our need of being in control, lifts the burden we and others place upon us for desired outcomes. Prayer helps us to let go and let God, by the Spirit, determine happenings and realize hope. Awakening to this hope comes from a combination of being aware of what confronts us and becoming attentive to God's presence.

The seventy-five-year story became what Charles Taylor describes as the immanent frame, that is, our normative way of seeing the world.[19] We are entering a time in which more and more people are searching for ways to get out of this purely immanent frame. We will be beguiled into a less than helpful understanding of our time if we limit our reading of this moment as just secularity. Even in modern, Western societies this secularity is wearing thin. A certain subtractive story that continually removes God from all conversations about our lives or how the world works has dominated the twentieth century and right into the present. It is now losing its hold on people as they search for alternatives. Part of the crisis of our moment is that we have, functionally, removed all notions of God's Agency. Our world has sought to expunge the reality of God in the everyday. The alternatives of secularity, individualism, and the market no longer satisfy. It will be among local communities whose rhythms of life are framed in prayer that we will create spaces for hope and this awakening to God among us.

It's hard to see the water in which we swim or the air we breathe. When leaders awaken to the damage done by the seventy-five-year story they ask: *What do we do?* As we've said, this question is about strategy (doing) and method (what). The work of leadership is to assist people to embrace another *way of seeing*. Rather than jumping to the *what do we do?* question, they turn people toward the question: *How do we see what God is already doing among us?* A leader will do this, first, by taking on the three practices named in this book and, second, by finding companions with whom they can explore how to slowly shift their own gaze

19. See Taylor, *Secular Age*.

toward God in their everyday. This shifting of attention, imperceptibly, changes how they lead. Prayer shifts what we attend to. Listening to the other changes what we attend to. Prayerful listening changes the world in front of us. When we look at the world differently, we change not just ourselves and others, but our world. Prayer is about experiencing an alternative account of who we are and what the world is for—an alternative construction of society, history, of people, of our present malaise and the way of hope.

A choice lies before us: keep trying to make the church work by the canons of the modern story or join the resurrected Christ in a story where God, as the Agent, is reweaving the frayed threads of creation.[20] This choice echoes St. Paul's words in addressing Christians confronting the powers of Rome. Paul implored the believers to "not be conformed to the patterns of this world, but be transformed by the renewing of your mind. Then you will be able to test and approve what God's will is—his good and perfect will."[21] The work of leadership involves shaping forms of life that call forth this renewing our minds so that we attend to our world in a different way.

God has created a way that is radically different from the seventy-five-year story. Prayer invites us to see the new situation God has created in the death and resurrection of Jesus Christ. There now exists the possibility of living and acting in and with God. The word of hope is that in the unraveling, God has not abandoned us. This transformation of our mind Paul commends in Romans means God that has created a situation in which we can now see this other story. This is expressed in the Morning Prayer of the Northumbria Community's Daily Office. Its prayer deliberately turns our attention every morning to this renewing of our minds, to "the one thing necessary":

Opening sentences

One thing I have asked of the Lord,
this is what I seek:
that I may dwell in the house of the Lord
all the days of my life;
to behold the beauty of the Lord
and to seek Him in His temple.

20. See Harink, *Paul among the Postliberals*, 235–37.

21. Rom 12:2.

Call: Who is it that you seek?

Response: We seek the Lord our God.

Call: Do you seek Him with all your heart?

Response: Amen. Lord, have mercy.

Call: Do you seek Him with all your soul?

Response: Amen. Lord, have mercy.

Call: Do you seek Him with all your mind?

Response: Amen. Lord, have mercy.

Call: Do you seek Him with all your strength?

Response: Amen. Christ, have mercy.

Our calling in this great unraveling is to redirect our gaze to the One who is acting to shape a new creation.[1]

1. See also Doug Heidebrecht in https://directionjournal.org/25/2/renewal-of-perception-romans-12-2-and.html.

CONCLUSIONS

Exploring a Path Together

Starting a Journey Without Maps

WE HAVE DIFFERENT WAYS of taking a journey. Some of us need detailed, clear instructions before we're ready to travel. Others love to wander, letting the path be the journey. We have been proposing a journey that is more like wandering than following maps. Like Abram and Sarai, who wandered to a place they didn't know, so we are being called onto a road that is not mapped. J. R. R. Tolkien wrote to the effect that, *not all who wander are lost*. For most of us, the idea of taking a journey in this unraveling, without maps or clear outcomes, can be incredibly disorienting. We'll hardly be willing to embark on such a journey, though perhaps we might, if we trust the One proposing such a journey. That kind of trust (and the wisdom it entails) is in short supply in our time. What does it take to form a community that, even tentatively, will trust themselves to a journey that cannot promise expected return on investments or outcomes?

Tolkien explored this question in his trilogy. One suspects it's part of the reason The Lord of the Rings is such a powerfully evocative story. Its primary characters are such mundane creatures. They love their comforts and have no interest in exploring anything beyond the borders of their beloved Shire. They've known each other generationally through family and clan. They are deeply embedded in place and belonging. Alan remembers a time, as a nine-year-old boy in his Liverpool neighborhood, running away after he'd damaged something. Mrs. Hockey stepped out of her door shouting after him: "I know who you are, Alan Roxburgh; your mother will hear about this." On another occasion he was being chased by a policeman. When he was caught, the first words out of the policeman's mouth were: "You're Jessie Crosbie's son." Crosbie was Alan's mother's maiden name. In that policeman, Alan was encountering generational connections he knew nothing about. This is what it means to be rooted in a place generationally. Tolkien's story of hobbits assumes something which would have been ordinary for his time—people rooted in a place and story. This is why, as the four friends raced through the Shire, terrified of the dark horsemen chasing them, Sam stopped to fearfully confess that this was the farthest he'd ever been as he stood at the edge of the Shire. He would go farther, not because he wanted to, but because he knew and trusted these friends. While far more trust would be demanded of each on that journey, as a start this trust was enough.

Those times of rootedness and belonging are gone and with them that kind of trust.[2] Tolkien's narrative is no longer our reality. As Ben Peterson points out:

> The loss of shared norms has paralleled an increase in individual choice and personal freedom, and that's no accident. As the range of choices in terms of mobility, identity, and lifestyle expands, we diminish what is called "collective efficacy"; that is, it becomes harder for each of us to make binding commitments and hold each other accountable for adherence to shared norms. In turn, the quality of our shared social experiences deteriorates, with devastating consequences at the extremes.[3]

Over these past seventy-five years we've been torn from place and belonging to become individuals who tentatively associate with one another (think of the temporariness of marriage), as consumers determining what is and is not of value for us. This uprootedness is what makes us feel alone and vulnerable in the great unraveling. It is not a situation that evokes trust. We do not have Tolkien's world from which to start a journey into a disruptive, unpredictable time; yet, this is the journey the Spirit is calling us to take. For leaders, this will require turning our attention from the norms and practices of leadership that have shaped us through this seventy-five-year era. These are, most often, the norms

2. "Levels of trust in this country—in our institutions, in our politics, and in one another—are in precipitous decline. And when social trust collapses, nations fail. Can we get it back before it's too late?" Brooks, "America is Having a Moral Convulsion."

3. Peterson, "Governing the Social Commons."

like the heroic leader, the vision caster, the transformative agent, the effective manager, the change expert, the innovator of adaptive change, the namer of preferred outcomes, the designer of preferred futures, and the strategic planner.

This book has proposed a set of practices for forming communities of hope. Without a doubt, we confront an unraveling of our norms, an upturning of our lives, and, therefore, a very different vocation from that in which leaders have been trained. It is a journey that leaves us exposed and vulnerable, but this unraveling is not the final word. Hope is the final word because this is God's world and God is active in the world. The overpowering reality of modernity's wager, in the churches, demonstrated in their dependence on method, technique, and our own agency, has limited our capacities to see the presence of God in the places where we dwell. Hope comes when we open our eyes and turn our attention to another world that is right in front us, to which we have been blinded. The journey of hope is the journey of our awakening to this other story. This awakening is the key to setting out on this other journey.

In chapter 9 we introduced the story of Peter Wohlleben. His book *The Hidden Life of Trees* chronicled such an awakening. He experienced a disorienting conversion that awakened him to the life bubbling and fermenting in the earth and the trees he thought he knew. What prevented him from seeing this world was his very profession as an arborist. His book tells the story of his awakening that called him to step away from the story of forestry in which he'd achieved success. He'd been formed to see trees as products, economic units, and board feet. He was an expert with university degrees and status in knowing how to get the most product out of trees in the most efficient ways. Wohlleben had to experience that conversion of the mind (the whole self) described by St. Paul in Romans 12. This was no easy conversion. His identity was in being a professional, an expert in the harvesting of trees. Wohlleben awoke to see that his knowledge of trees was woefully limited. In that awakening, another world of trees and forests came into view.

Clergy trained within the profession of ministry confront a similar situation. Think of the taken for granted church language people use to describe what they do. It tells us a lot about how we are seeing others and how we connect with them. Churches often characterize people as "seekers." In effect, it means people are placed as a data point on a scale, objects to be reached and managed within a set of assumptions and strategies. Think of how pastoral leaders have been schooled and socialized to use the word *ministry*. It conveys being in a special class of doing special ordained things. On balance the lay people of congregations pick up on and are shaped by these absurd narratives.

One of us was sitting outside a seminary bookstore in the late summer. On the same patio sat two men in conversation. One, who identified himself as the senior pastor of a large, contemporary church, was talking about his Sunday service. The words that came out of his mouth were astonishing in the way they expressed how he saw people. "We worship about seven hundred people each week," he said. He was unaware of the story shaping him as a leader. A language world of professionalism and expertise shapes how we see ourselves, how we relate with others and how we behave. Think about how, somehow, congregations create in us a posture of seeing our communities and neighborhoods in terms of needs. In this narrative, therefore, we look at people in our neighborhoods in terms of the ministry (therefore, professional engagements) involving us helping and managing people. This is a distorted imagination that removes from the story of the One who dwelt right beside us.

The cultural narrative of the seventy-five-year story gave Wohlleben a narrow field of attention that missed the immense wonder and strangeness, the beauty and dazzling life all around him. He had been formed inside a utilitarian discourse that saw everything as a management resource rather than the holy mystery wrapped in the tangled interconnections of trees, fungus, light, and earth. He was unaware of this other world of trees burgeoning under his feet.[4] Wohlleben stumbled, unexpectedly, onto this other world while considering the ways mushrooms grew on trees. This innocent seeing changed his world, awakening him to things beyond his own field of vision. The practices outlined in this book are a way to this awakening. They're how we begin this journey of forming communities of hope. In this unraveling, the path can't be laid out ahead of time as if by following specific steps we'll arrive at a specific destination. Rather than being a map pointing to a destination, these practices invite us on a journey where we make the path as we walk. We are at a moment in our history as Western Christians where we can't name the outcomes, nor predict what the Spirit is unfolding in front of us fifty, one hundred, or two hundred years from now. This is what Benedict understood when forming his Rule of Life. He gathered small groups of Christians who

4. See Scott, *Seeing Like a State*, 11–22.

would dwell with one another amidst a crumbling Rome, adapting practices learned from the desert fathers.

The journey of Abram and Sarai was the same. In faith, they set out for a country they could not see, convinced that in a failing world, God was up to something amazing. There was the irony, a couple of shriveled-up, elderly, good-for-nothing human beings being the light bearers of the One who makes all things new. What an amazing response to a world coming apart! Instead of wringing our hands around how to fix our churches, we could choose to join with God in Christ in embodying this new creation in the ordinary, mundane, and human. This is a hope that cannot come from visionaries, gurus, innovators, strategic planners, or Pied Pipers. It emerges from among ordinary men and women in neighborhoods, in lives formed around practices of dwelling, discerning, and experimenting.

Traveling Together

One wishes we could conclude this book with a well-crafted story of whole movements of renewal across the churches shaped by dwelling, discerning, and exploring. That would be amazing, but it would also be an illusion. We have to take seriously that we're in a great, disorienting unraveling. We are at the beginning of the end of the forms of church we produced in the twentieth century. Our natural response is to ask what to do and where we can find the successful models. What we can do is share stories of those who have begun this journey and point to a way forward.

John[5] is part of a group of companions who've been traveling together for almost two years. They've started to live into the practices of dwelling, discerning, and exploring with one another and in their congregations. John is an experienced pastor in a congregation still trying to come to terms with the unraveling. The default forces compelling them to go back to their way of being church remain strong. John has to work everyday at figuring out how these practices connect with the realities of the congregation's desires, their conflicted desire to go back and their sense of needing to start this strange journey. He brings his own questions about it all and wrestles with how to lead in this place. His questions are:

5. Here and following, we employ pseudonyms.

- How do I lead in the *now*, within these conflicted desires of my people, with an understanding of the *not yet*?
- How do I sustain my own hope amidst this push and pull of people who are confused and disoriented?

His companions wondered what he was asking with these questions. They know John by now, and are fully aware that he's an experienced leader. John went on to elaborate on what he meant. What he's struggling with is that the way of leadership introduced in this book is so different from the models and postures of leadership in which he, and most clergy, were formed. Because of this, he doesn't always know what to do. There is this tension in which John and his companions know there is no going back to church as they knew and loved it; but, even in wanting to move forward, the people of the congregation want John to take them back to the impossible. What happens is that, initially, John's people go along with him as a leader as he introduces these practices. Sooner than later, however, they come to experience these practices as distractions from the forms of church that they've known. At some point, people push back, pressing for a return to their more established ways of being church. For John, this is a tough place to be in as a leader. He believes in and is committed to this journey, but it's hard to know how to invite one's people along for the long haul.

Similarly, Sue shared with her companions how, on a retreat with her board, she'd introduced the idea of dwelling with their neighbors. Her leaders expressed interest in embracing this way of being present to their neighborhood. As Sue quickly discovered, however, what they meant was very different from what she was trying to introduce, in terms of being with and listening with neighbors. They wanted to use denominational materials that would help them discover needs in the community so that the church could figure out ways it could minister to people through meeting needs. Sue was discouraged. Implicit in her telling this story to her companions was a troubling question: *Why is it so hard for my people to shift their attention from tactics (finding needs and filling them) and growing the church's membership to the practices of dwelling, discerning, and exploring?* She wondered when her church would see that their vocation is not meeting needs or being helpful, but dwelling with neighbors and seeing what God is doing. Sue's companions listened to her wrestling. They affirmed her question, but then they asked her other questions about herself and her frustrations. Over time, Sue saw that she needed to ask very different questions about her leading. With her companions, she began to see different actions she could take. That's another story.

This is a challenging journey. It is not one that births easy answers or quick victories. What we are proposing is leadership for the long haul when we can't name outcomes or predict how this unraveling will turn out. This is about a leadership that lives deeply into the expectation that it is God who is reweaving this broken world. At the same time, even in the beginnings of this long journey, the Spirit is gestating spaces and moments of hope, if we are able to turn our attention toward God's work in the mundane.

One of those places is in the prairies of North America. There, for generations, immigrants have farmed the land and made it into one of the breadbaskets of the world. These are not good times for farmers or their families. A way of life built upon over generations on family farms is unraveling. These farms are becoming increasingly difficult to sustain in our current economic systems. As farmers go into debt, they face the unimaginable choice of selling off their family's heritage to investors. Tim is one such farmer. He's also a pastor in his community with university and seminary training. In his companion group, Tim has shared about his congregation and about the ways the unraveling is affecting himself and all his neighbors as farmers. In the companion group there is conversation about the church and the call to form communities of hope where we dwell. He has wrestled with the question of what a community of hope might look like where he lives, amongst his neighbors and the perilous situation of the farms.

What these friends and neighbors face is nothing less than that they sell off their farms to investors. What is unfolding is a tragedy of massive proportions, not just for the farmers but for a whole way of contributing to the thriving of communities. One is reminded of James Rebanks' story we shared in chapter 1, about the unraveling of a way of life. For quite some time Tim has fretted, reflected, and prayed about what he sees unfolding on the farms around him, including his own. Through all this reflecting and wrestling with the question of what's to be done, Phil has been part of a band of companions. He and Tim have spent time dwelling in Scripture and with one another; they have dug deep into the meaning of the unraveling, and they've done a lot of theological reflection around the question of what God is doing in the midst of such perilous times. Tim is continually asking: *What does a community of hope look like on these prairies where I live?*

Slowly but powerfully, God began to give Tim a picture he decided to explore. It wasn't clear as Paul's "come over to Macedonia and help us," but through prayer and quiet reflection, the picture turned into a set of actions. At first, these actions seemed scary. The risk of being laughed at by his neighbors was high, but Tim persisted. Several things were happening for Tim. First, in what could only be called a revelation of the obvious, he started asking himself: *If bankers and investors who know nothing about farming could buy land and turn it for a profit, why couldn't farmers figure out how to "buy" their own land and own it in a new way?* That question led to his recognition that God was up to something that one single person could not achieve on their own. Other kinds of people would be needed. Once the question was formed (without lots of details that would be essential), however, Tim began to see that there were, already, in the community of farmers lots of people with the kinds of skills he would need to form a group of people who could take this journey.

The story is unfolding. This group is beginning conversations with other farmers roundabout and they are not being mocked or laughed out of court. Something is shifting, people are ready to listen to what once would have been seen as a crazy idea with no possibility of success. One pastor also happened to be:

- a farmer, who is immersed in a theology of God's presence and agency in the midst of the unraveling,
- a pastor/farmer who dwells with the people of the community,
- a person who is ready to risk his reputation by asking questions about what God's Spirit is doing among them in this unraveling.

This ordinary person is creating a community of hope and participating in the reweaving of society.

There are so many stories of leaders on this journey. Some stories involve risking simple steps and discovering that among their own people the Spirit is creating a hunger to dwell, discern, and explore. When we gather with leaders we use a simple series of steps that, collectively, invite us to turn our attention (what we're looking at and desiring) from the default narratives of tactics, programs, and techniques to asking how we listen to the Spirit amongst us. Gatherings begin with a simple Examen question: *Where have you seen God at work since we last met?* In listening and sharing responses, leaders discover that they are gradually turning their attention toward discerning what God is doing among them.

Second, we turn to Dwelling in the Word through a Scripture text. In this simple exercise leaders lay down the role of being expert exegetes of text to listening to and dwelling in the Word with and through one another. Our questions here are: *As you listened to the text, where did you stop? What was catching your attention?* We then take the time to listen to one another's responses, as we are learning how to turn our attention (desire, what we look at) from our technique and control toward God, as Agent. There are many other ways we go about this. But, as leaders step into such practices, some find the courage to risk doing Examen and dwelling within their own congregations. The reports they bring back cause tears of joy. People are ready for these practices. The Spirit is preparing the way, the ground is fertile, God is about the work of reweaving creation right where we live, right in the midst of the unraveling.

A Long Obedience in the Same Direction[6]

We began this book out of conversations with hundreds of leaders who, in the immediate aftermath of COVID, were asking: *Where are we?* Across denominations and on both sides of the Atlantic, leaders were wrestling with the recognition that there was no going back to normal after the lockdowns. Something had been shifting. It was as if the taken-for-granted solid ground beneath our feet had, somehow, shifted.

Along with the question of where we are, came another: *What do we do now?* Leaders are searching for ways to understand our situation and for methods that will fix whatever it is that has gone wrong since COVID. In asking this second question, leaders were increasingly struggling or unwilling to embrace programs of formation, discipleship, innovation, or adaptation that had once held out so much promise. There was emerging an incredulity toward all their promises of fixing the unraveling.

In conferences, Zoom conversations, and other encounters, these same questions kept being asked. Our overall response to the first question, *Where are we?* has been to describe the great unraveling. You have encountered this language throughout this book. People wanted us to say more, to explain what we meant by this unraveling, why it is taking place and what it means for the churches. The first chapters of this book addressed these questions, proposing we're living at the end of the only story

6. This is taken from the title of Eugene Peterson's book *A Long Obedience in the Same Direction.*

we have ever known, a seventy-five-year story about the central place of human agency, about modernity's wager, about our belief in our own powers as individuals to make the worlds we want. This is a story about powerful methods and techniques of control and management that came to dominate and determine the ways we've led and lived over this period. The unraveling is another way of saying that this world, so central to our identities as leaders, is coming apart. It is ending; it cannot be fixed or put back together. We've entered a time and place we've never been before. This is why we're finding that the methods and techniques that brought us some measure of success are no longer working. They were developed for a world that is coming apart and disappearing.

Our disorientation directs us to the next question leaders are asking: *What do we do now?* We believe this is the wrong question. It is one shaped with the seventy-five-year story. It will continually loop us back into the techniques and methods of the seventy-five-year story, keeping us on the treadmill of our own agency. In a place we've never been before, we have to ask very different questions. As those who confess that we're shaped by a Christian imagination, we have to start asking questions about what God is doing among God's people and in our communities. In other words, we need to turn our attention away from technique and methods of fixing to the questions: *When God's people have found themselves in disruptive spaces, places they've never been before, how has God shown up? What is God doing in such times?*

Churches in the West, guided by their leaders, have been functioning inside the wrong story for a long time. Their attention has been directed toward trying to fix and save the church with the methods of the seventy-five-year story. They are still asking the wrong questions and, therefore, continually failing to discern the shape of Christian life in this unraveling.

Section One proposed much more than our being in the wrong story. We are proposing something counterintuitive for most leaders, namely, there isn't going to be a short period of disorientation and then a new, stable normal will emerge. We are proposing:

1. There is no renewal or revival or reformation just around the corner.
2. The unraveling will go on for a long time.
3. We are entering a new, dark time in which there will be no solutions, answers, or fixes for a long time.

4. This period, therefore, calls for radically different leadership responses from strategic planning or visioning for outcomes.
5. It requires a readiness to trust that God is ahead of us, calling us onto a journey for which, right now, we have no maps.

These realities make the proposals of Section Two so critical and radical.

Section Two, therefore, turned toward a different question, one which directs us toward God's agency and the question of what God is doing when God's people find themselves in times of unraveling. This turning of our attention toward a radically different story is a difficult undertaking. It demands that we step outside the seventy-five-year story. When we begin to do this very different answers to the question of what the church does in this great unraveling appear before us. As we look at Scripture texts and some sample stories from the early church, we discern that God is calling us into a set of counterintuitive practices we've identified as dwelling, discerning, and exploring. These are necessary practices for Christian communities that are hopeful witnesses in a dark time.

Section Three picked up on the practices outlined in Section Two, exploring more deeply what they mean for forming Christian life in local communities.

Section Four examined what these practices might mean for leading in a dark time.

Another Journey

We end this book by returning to a text that has guided us through much of this journey: Acts 16:6–15. It is the story of how the Spirit was at work unraveling and reframing the imagination of Paul and his companions. At the start of their journey, they had a clear strategy and tried methods for moving forward the mission of the young church. We have followed the contours of this second missionary journey with its perplexing narrative of the Spirit, or the Spirit of Jesus, preventing them from accomplishing all they had planned to expand the kingdom and plant new congregations across Asia. The first missionary journey had been so successful, why was this one proving so challenging? What had gone wrong? Why weren't these tried and trusted plans working? In Troas, at the easternmost edge of Roman Asia, these companions gathered to collect themselves and fathom what had gone wrong. How could they discern what it was they were supposed to do? They were sure the Spirit of Jesus was guiding them but they were struggling to understand why their plans kept being thwarted. They could not make sense of what was happening. Troas was a place for regrouping, of trying to make sense of what was happening. In the context of these interactions, Paul had his famous missionary dream. It involved a vision of a man of Macedonia pleading with Paul to: "Come over and help us."

Whatever sense they could make of this turn of events, Luke reports that they became convinced that the Spirit was speaking to them out of the dream and calling them to cross over into Europe. Immediately, they set off by boat for Macedonia, with a renewed sense of energy and direction. At the same time, they remained stuck in their default methods and strategies with which they had started this journey. In Philippi they were most likely looking for a synagogue in which to talk about Jesus. Luke tells us that they wandered around Philippi for several days, perhaps looking for some Macedonian man, but, most likely, looking for a synagogue. The text suggests that they couldn't find one because on the Sabbath they went outside the gate to find a "place of prayer." That phrase describes what we would call a proto-synagogue where there weren't enough Jewish males to formally be a synagogue. Paul and his companions seemed caught in a world of half-steps, trying to be obedient to the Spirit out of their established patterns. Their attention, their "seeing," was still shaped by the imagination that had gotten them this far. But it was no longer working. The Spirit was preventing and they kept stumbling over their frameworks and language worlds.

It would be outside the city wall on a Sabbath without a synagogue, a man, a need, or an institutionalized place of prayer, that a radically different journey was revealed to them by the Spirit. It seemed that they had to be disrupted from all their preconceived plans and commitments before they could see what the Spirit was saying to them. This seeing came in the form of a woman and her pressing them with the reality of the gospel. Whereas the "man" of Macedonia asked them to come over and "help" (such a beguiling, siren-like call for modern, middle-class Christians in the West), this woman of Asia living in Macedonia invited them to dwell with her. Here is the radical call to the churches in this unraveling. The practices and ways of leading we are proposing are about taking a journey that embraces Lydia's invitation, moving us from being host to becoming guest, from helper to walking with. Only within such a posture is it possible to form communities of hope in this great unraveling. Let the journey begin.

Bibliography

Ahmari, Sohrab. "Apostolic Empire." *First Things*, March 2023. https://firstthings.com/apostolic-empire/.

Arendt, Hannah. *Without Roots*. New York: Penguin, 2023.

Augustine. *City of God*. Markham, ON: Penguin, 1972.

Barth, Markus. *Ephesians 1–3*. The Anchor Yale Bible Commentaries. New Haven: Yale University Press, 1974.

Bauman, Zygmunt. *The Individualized Society*. Malden, MA: Polity/Blackwell, 2001.

———. *In Search of Politics*. Oxford: Polity, 1999.

Beale, G. K., and Mitchell Kim. *God Dwells Among Us: A Biblical Theology of the Temple*. Downers Grove, IL: InterVarsity Academic, 2021.

Simpson, Leanne Betasamosake. *As We Have Always Done: Indigenous Freedom Through Radical Resistance*. Minneapolis: University of Minnesota Press, 2020.

Barton, Ruth Haley. *Pursuing God's Will Together*. Downers Grove, IL: InterVarsity, 2012.

Berger, Peter. *The Sacred Canopy*. New York: Anchor, 1990.

Berger, Peter, and Thomas Luckmann. *The Social Construction of Reality*. New York: Anchor, 1967.

Bonhoeffer, Dietrich. *The Cost of Discipleship*. Philadelphia: Touchstone, 1995.

Branson, Mark Lau, and Alan J. Roxburgh. *Leadership, God's Agency and Disruptions*. Eugene, OR: Cascade, 2020.

Brindle, James. *New Dark Age Technology and the End of the Future* New York: Verso, 2018.

Brooks, David. "America is Having a Moral Convulsion." *Atlantic Monthly*, October 5, 2020.

Brown, Peter. *The Rise of Western Christendom*. Hoboken, NJ: Wiley-Blackwell 2003.

Browning, Elizabeth Barrett. *Aurora Lee*. New York: Worthington, 1890.

Brueggemann, Walter. *A Commentary on Jeremiah*. Grand Rapids: Eerdmans, 1998.

———. *Hopeful Imagination*. Minneapolis: Fortress, 1986.

Burgis, Luke. *Wanting: The Power of Mimetic Desire in Everyday Life*. New York: St. Martin's, 2021.

Casey, Edward S. *The Fate of Place: A Philosophical History*. Berkeley: University of California Press, 1998.

Cavanaugh, William T. *The Migration of the Holy*. Grand Rapids: Eerdmans, 2011.

Cayley, David, ed. *The Ideas of René Girard*. Toronto: Independently published, 2019.

Christophers, Brett. *Rentier Capitalism: Who Owns and Who Pays for It?* London: Verso, 2022.

Coulthard, Glen. *Red Skin, White Masks: Rejecting Colonial Politics of Recognition*. Minneapolis: University of Minnesota Press, 2014.

Crawford, Matthew B. *The World Beyond Your Head*. Toronto: Penguin Random House, 2015.

Davies, Oliver, Paul D. Janz, and Clemens Sedmak. *Transformation Theology: Church and World*. London: T&T Clark, 2007.

Del Noce, Augusto. *The Crisis of Modernity*. Montreal: McGill-Queens University Press, 2015.

Dodds, E. R. *Pagan and Christian in an Age of Anxiety*. Cambridge: Cambridge University Press, 1991.

Du Mez, Kristin Kobes. *Jesus and John Wayne*. New York: Liveright, 2021.

Dunkelman, Marc J. *The Vanishing Neighbor: The Transformation of American Community*. New York: Norton, 2014.

Fletcher, Paul. *Disciplining the Divine*. Milton Park, Oxfordshire: Routledge, 2009.

Fisher, Mark. *Capitalist Realism: Is there No Alternative?* Winchester, UK: Zero, 2009.

Fukuyama, Francis. *The End of History and the Last Man*. Los Angeles: Free Press, 2006.

Hall, Douglas John. *The Future of the Church: Where Are We Headed?* Philadelphia: Westminster, 1989.

Gabriele, Matthew, and David M. Perry. *The Bright Ages: A New History of Medieval Europe*. New York: Harper Perennial, 2021.

Galbraith, John Kenneth. *The Affluent Society*. Cambridge, MA: Harvard University Press, 1958.

Girard, René. *When These Things Begin*. Lansing: Michigan State University Press, 2014.

Glasman, Maurice. *Blue Labour: The Politics of the Common Good*. Cambridge: Polity, 2022.

Grant Adam. *Think Again*. New York: Penguin Random House, 2021.

Gray, John. *The New Leviathans: Thoughts after Liberalism*. New York: Farrar, Straus and Giroux, 2023.

Guilluy, Christophe, and Malcolm DeBevoise. *Twilight of the Elites*. New Haven: Yale University Press, 2019.

Harink, Douglas. *Paul among the Postliberals*. Eugene, OR: Wipf & Stock, 2013.

Hauerwas, Stanley. *A Community of Character*. Kindle ed. Notre Dame: University of Notre Dame Press, 1991.

Henry, Patrick. *Benedict Options*. Collegeville, MN: Liturgical, 2021.

Holland, Tom. *Dominion*. New York: Basic Books, 2021.

Inge, John. *A Christian Theology of Place*. Farnham, UK: Ashgate, 2003.

Jacobs, Jane. *Dark Ages Ahead*. Visalia, CA: Vintage, 2005.

King, Martin Luther, Jr. *Letter from a Birmingham Jail*. New York: Penguin, 2018.

Kleeberger, Tyler, and Michael Beck. *Fresh Expressions of the Rural Church*. Nashville: Abingdon, 2020.

Kotan, Kay. *Being the Church in a Post-Pandemic World*. Charlotte, NC: Market Square, 2022.

Lasch, Christopher. *The Culture of Narcissism*. New York: Warner, 1979.

Lings, George. *Sacred Spaces*. Abingdon, UK: BRF, 2020.

Machado, Antonio. "Walker, Your Footsteps." In *Border of a Dream: Selected Poems.* Translated by Willis Barnstone. Port Townsend, WA: Copper Canyon, 2003.
MacIntrye, Alasdair. *After Virtue.* Notre Dame: University of Notre Dame Press, 2007.
McClay, Wilfred, and Ted V. McAllister. *Why Place Matters: Geography, Identity, and Civic Life in Modern America.* New York: New Atlantis, 2014.
McGilchrist, Iain. *The Master and His Emissary.* New Haven: Yale University Press, 2019.
Meek, Esther Lightcap. *A Little Manual of Knowing.* Eugene, OR: Cascade, 2014.
Menzies, Andrew, and Dean Phelan. *Kingdom Communities.* Kindle ed. Victoria, AU: Morning Star, 2019.
Merton, Thomas. *New Seeds of Contemplation.* New York: New Directions, 2007.
Molloy, Dara. *The Globalisation of God: Celtic Christianity's Nemesis.* Inis Mor, Ireland: Aisling Arann, 2009.
Moyles, Trina. *Lookout: Love, Solitude, and Searching for the Wildfire in the Boreal Forest.* Toronto: Vintage, 2022.
Muir, John. *John of the Mountains.* Boston: Houghton Mifflin, 1938.
Newbigin, Lesslie. *Foolishness to the Greeks.* Grand Rapids: Eerdmans, 1986.
———. *The Gospel in a Pluralist Society.* Grand Rapids: Eerdmans, 1989.
———. *The Open Secret.* Grand Rapids: Eerdmans, 1995.
———. *Proper Confidence.* Grand Rapids: Eerdmans, 1995.
Neiman, Susan. *The Left is Not Woke.* New York: Polity, 2023.
Nin, Anaïs. *Seduction of the Minotaur.* Athens, OH: Swallow, 1967.
Northumbria Community. *Celtic Daily Prayer.* New York: HarperCollins, 2015.
Pally, Marcia. *Commonwealth and Covenant: Economics, Politics and Theologies of Relationality.* Grand Rapids: Eerdmans, 2016.
Pelagius. *The Letters of Pelagius: Celtic Soul Friend.* Little Giddings Books. London: Arthur James, 1996.
Peterson, Ben. "Governing the Social Commons. *Comment,* August 2023.
Peterson, Eugene. *A Long Obedience in the Same Direction.* Downers Grove, IL: InterVarsity, 2021.
Pinker, Steven. *Enlightenment Now: The Case for Reason, Science, Humanism and Progress.* New York: Penguin, 2019.
Polanyi, Michael. *Personal Knowledge.* Chicago: University of Chicago Press, 2015.
Putnam, Robert. *Our Kids: The American Dream in Crisis.* New York: Simon & Schuster, 2016.
Rebanks, James. *Pastoral Song.* New York: Harper Collins, 2021.
Rieff, Philip. *The Triumph of the Therapeutic.* Chicago: University of Chicago Press, 1987.
Robinson, Kim Stanley. *The Ministry of the Future.* Chesham, UK: Orbit: 2021.
Root, Andrew. *When the Church Stops Working.* Grand Rapids: Baker Academic, 2023.
Rosa, Hartmut. *The Uncontrollability of the World.* New York: Polity, 2020.
Roxburgh, Alan J. *Joining God in the Great Unraveling: Where We Are and What I've Learned.* Eugene, OR: Cascade, 2021.
———. *Missional Map-Making: Skills for Leading in Times of Transition.* San Francisco: Jossey-Bass, 2010.
Roxburgh, Alan J., and Martin Robinson. *Practices for the Refounding of God's People.* New York: Church Publishing, 2018.
Rumsey, Andrew. *Parish: An Anglican Theology of Place.* London: SCM, 2017.

Scott, Drusilla. *Everyman Revived: The Common Sense of Michael Polanyi.* Grand Rapids: Eerdmans,1995.

Scott, James C. *Seeing Like a State.* New Haven: Yale University Press, 2020.

Schreiner, Susan. *Are You Alone Wise? The Search for Certainty in the Early Modern Era.* Oxford: Oxford University Press, 2012.

Sennett, Richard. The *Corrosion of Character.* New York: Norton, 1998.

———. *The Culture of the New Capitalism.* New Haven: Yale University Press, 2006.

———. *The Fall of Public Man: On the Social Psychology of Capitalism.* New York: Vintage, 1974.

Shea, James P. *From Christendom to Apostolic Mission.* Bismark, ND: University of Mary Press, 2020.

Tjorhom, Ola. *Embodied Faith: Reflections on a Materialist Spirituality.* Grand Rapids: Eerdmans, 2019.

Singh, Devin P., Randal J. Thompson, and Kathleen A. Curran, eds. *Reimagining Leadership on the Commons.* Leeds, UK: Emerald, 2021.

Taylor, Charles. *A Secular Age.* Cambridge: The Belknap Press of Harvard University Press, 2018.

Toulmin, Stephen. *Cosmopolis: The Hidden Agenda of Modernity.* Chicago: University of Chicago, 1992.

Tran, Jonathan. *Asian Americans and the Spirit of Racial Capitalism.* Oxford: Oxford University Press, 2021.

Van Den Heuvel, Albert H. *The Humiliation of the Church.* Philadelphia: Westminster, 1953.

Volf, Miroslav. "The Trinity Is Our Social Program." *Modern Theology* 14.3 (July 1998) 403–23.

Wasinger, Arthur, and Erin Wasinger. *the year of small thing.* Grand Rapids: Brazos, 2017.

Weston, Paul. *Humble Confidence: Lesslie Newbigin and the Logic of Mission.* Eugene, OR: Cascade, 2023.

Wheatly, Margaret. *Leadership and the New Science.* Oakland, CA: Berrett-Koehler, 1994.

Williams, Rowan. *Being Disciples.* Grand Rapids: Eerdmans, 2020.

———. *The Way of St. Benedict.* London: Bloomsbury, 2020.

Wohlleben, Peter. *The Hidden Life of Trees.* Vancouver: Greystone, 2016.

Wray, Britt. *Generation Dread.* Saanich, BC: Vintage Canada, 2023.

www.ingramcontent.com/pod-product-compliance
Lightning Source LLC
LaVergne TN
LVHW100526110826
845146LV00002B/792

* 9 7 9 8 3 8 5 2 2 0 8 9 2 *